THE RECRUITING GUIDE TO

# INVESTMENT BANKING

Other books by the authors

# THE PRACTITIONER'S GUIDE TO INVESTMENT BANKING, MERGERS AND ACQUISITIONS, CORPORATE FINANCE

**SCOOP**BOOKS
THE RECRUITING GUIDE TO

# INVESTMENT BANKING

Jerilyn J. Castillo and Peter J. McAniff

circinus business press

First edition printing 2006
Printed in the United States of America
Library of Congress Control Number: 2005936229

Castillo, Jerilyn J.

    The recruiting guide to investment banking / Jerilyn J. Castillo and
    Peter J. McAniff. -- 1st ed. -- Solana Beach, Cal. : Circinus Business
    Press, 2006.

        p. ; cm.
        (ScoopBooks)

        ISBN-13: 978-0-9761548-9-1
        ISBN-10: 0-9761548-9-7
        Includes glossary of technical M&A and corporate finance terms
    and concepts.
        Includes bibliographical references and index.

        1. Investment banking--Recruiting. 2. Investment bankers--
    Recruiting. 3. Financial services industry--Recruiting. 4. Financial
    planners--Recruiting. 5. Investment advisors--Recruiting. I. McAniff,
    Peter J. II. Title. III. Investment banking.

HG4534 .C37 2006            2005936229
332.66/023--               dc22 0606

Cover and interior designed by Alejandro Paul

CORPORATIONS, UNIVERSITIES, COLLEGES, AND PROFESSIONAL ORGANIZATIONS: Quantity discounts are available on bulk purchases of Circinus Business Press books for educational, corporate training, gift, and sales promotion purposes. Special books or book excerpts can also be created to fit special needs. For information, please contact Circinus Business Press.

circinus business press
www.scoopbooks.com

*The secret of success in life*
*is for a man to be ready*
*for his opportunity when it comes.*

**Benjamin Disraeli**

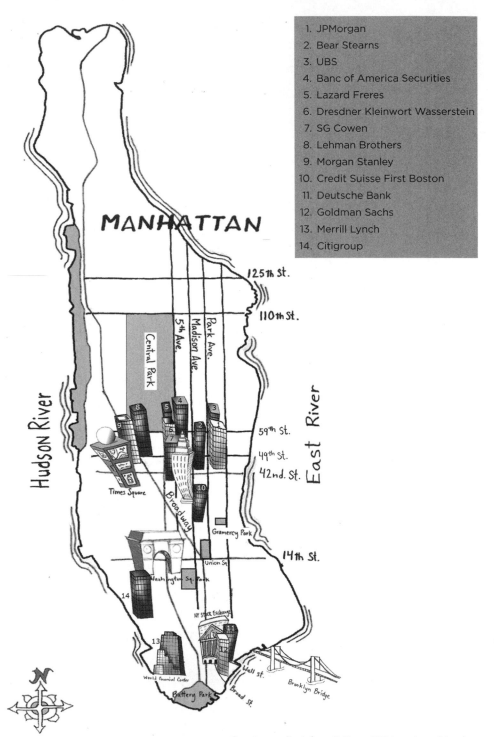

MANHATTAN

1. JPMorgan
2. Bear Stearns
3. UBS
4. Banc of America Securities
5. Lazard Freres
6. Dresdner Kleinwort Wasserstein
7. SG Cowen
8. Lehman Brothers
9. Morgan Stanley
10. Credit Suisse First Boston
11. Deutsche Bank
12. Goldman Sachs
13. Merrill Lynch
14. Citigroup

Hudson River

East River

Central Park

5th Ave.
Madison Ave.
Park Ave.
Broadway

125th St.
110th St.
59th St.
49th St.
42nd. St.
14th St.

Times Square
Gramercy Park
Union Sq.
Washington Sq. Park
NY Stock Exchange
Wall St.
Broad St.
Brooklyn Bridge
World Financial Center
Battery Park

N

See Appendix A for a listing of 50 investment banks

# CONTENTS

**FIGURES AND TABLES**

# Commonly Used Financial Acronyms

Definitions provided in Appendix B - Glossary of Terms

| Acronym | Meaning |
| --- | --- |
| ADR | American depositary receipt |
| AICPA | Association of Independent Certified Public Accountants |
| APB | Accounting Principles Board Opinion |
| AVP | Analysis at various prices |
| CA | Confidentiality Agreement |
| CAGR | Compound annual growth rate |
| CDS | Credit default swap |
| CF | Cash flow |
| CP | Commercial paper |
| DCF | Discounted cash flow |
| DD&A | Depreciation, depletion, amortization |
| DEV | Discounted equity value |
| DRD | Dividends-received deduction |
| EBIT | Earnings before interest, taxes |
| EBITDA | Earnings before interest, taxes, DD&A |
| EBT | Earnings before tax |
| EPS | Earnings per share |
| EV | Enterprise value |
| EV | Equity value (also called market value of equity) |
| FASB | Financial Accounting Standards Board |
| FCF | Free cash flow |
| FTC | Federal Trade Commission |
| FV | Firm value (also called enterprise value) |
| g | Growth rate |
| GAAP | Generally Accepted Accounting Principles |
| HSR | Hart-Scott-Rodino Act |
| IPO | Initial public offering |
| IRC | Internal Revenue Code |
| IRR | Internal rate of return |
| IRS | Internal Revenue Service |
| JV | Joint venture |
| LBO | Leveraged buyout |
| LIBOR | London interbank offer rate |
| LTD | Long term debt |
| M&A | Mergers and acquisitions |

Definitions provided in Appendix B - Glossary of Terms

| Acronym | Meaning |
|---------|---------|
| MAC | Material adverse change |
| MACRS | Modified accelerated cost recovery system |
| MBO | Management buyout |
| MD&A | Management's discussion and analysis |
| MOE | Merger of equals |
| MTN | Medium term note |
| MV | Market value of equity |
| NASD | National Association of Securities Dealers |
| NDA | Non-disclosure agreement |
| NI | Net income |
| NOL | Net operating loss |
| NRSRO | Nationally Recognized Statistical Rating Organization |
| NYSE | New York Stock Exchange |
| OCF | Operating cash flow |
| PCAOB | Public Company Accounting Oversight Board |
| P&L | Profit and loss statement or earnings statement |
| PP&E | Property, plant and equipment |
| P/E | Price to earnings multiple |
| r | Discount rate used in discounting or interest rate used in compounding |
| R&D | Research and development |
| ROE | Return on equity |
| ROI | Return on investment |
| ROIC | Return on invested capital |
| SEC | Securities and Exchange Commission |
| SG&A | Selling, general and administrative expenses |
| SIC | Standard Industrial Classification |
| SOX | Sarbanes-Oxley Act of 2002 |
| S&P | Standard and Poor's |
| STD | Short term debt |
| WACC | Weighted average cost of capital |

# INTRODUCTION

*Any idiot can face a crisis.*
*It's this day to day living that wears you out.*

### *Anton Chekhov*

Hollywood has done much to glamorize the life of an investment banker. In the movies, bankers are often portrayed as multimillionaires with beautiful offices and penthouses overlooking the Brooklyn Bridge or Central Park, with personal assistants attending to their every whim. They have limousines to transport them around town and private jets to fly to meetings; they stay in the most expensive hotels and eat in the best restaurants.

The reality is that investment banking is not very glamorous. It is more about hard work, long days, and working with interesting people than the lifestyle described above. If you are interested in a career in banking because of what you have seen in the movies, consider a career in entertainment, not on Wall Street. If, however, you are interested in banking because you are intellectually curious about finance and corporate strategy, have above-average critical thinking and analytical skills, enjoy working on teams, and are willing to work hard in an apprentice environment, then Wall Street can be one of the best places to begin a business career.

Many people begin investment banking careers without knowing much about the world they are signing up for or, worse yet, what will be expected of them once they begin working. Even today, an information asymmetry exists that provides a distinct advantage during the recruiting process to those candidates with a parent, sibling or close friend in banking. Some good candidates are overlooked not because they are incapable but because they are not as well prepared as others. Even after obtaining a job, the danger is not over. Some young bankers with potential are weeded out in the first few years because they did not find the proper guidance.

This book and its sister book *The Practitioner's Guide to Investment Banking, Mergers and Acquisitions, Corporate Finance* were written by two experienced bankers who believe strongly that success is a function of hard work and access to the proper tools. In the course of their 18 years of combined experience, the authors have screened thousands of resumes, interviewed hundreds of aspiring bankers, and trained and mentored numerous investment banking analysts and associates as well as strategic planning professionals and corporate executives. In addition, more than fifty professionals with investment banking, law, strategic consulting, and industry backgrounds shared their insights and experience in reviewing portions of the books related to their areas of expertise. These exceptional professionals, to whom the authors owe a great debt of gratitude, are cited in the Acknowledgements section. They and the authors hope that these books serve as useful tools to help guide you on your way. The hard work is up to you.

## On Recruiting

It is incorrect to assume that preparation for a career in banking begins with the recruiting season in the fall of an MBA's second year or in the fall of one's senior year in college. Given how competitive it is to obtain a banking position, interested candidates should try to begin gaining relevant experience a few years before the actual recruiting season.

To succeed in investment banking, or any competitive endeavor for that matter, you need a passion for it. The hours and expectations are simply too great to survive without a strong interest in finance, working with people, and winning. Passion is extremely difficult to fake. The seasoned recruiter and interviewer know how to spot those who are not genuinely interested.

Success in banking has a lot to do with being likeable in addition to being highly competent. This is the case externally with clients from whom you will try to win business as well as internally with senior bankers who will preside over promotion and compensation decisions. Despite stereotypes to the contrary, the most successful bankers are fun, well-rounded, and have interests outside of work. Cultivating outside interests and trying to maintain some semblance of balance is critical. A quant-jock who walks and talks only finance is not likely to go far (he or she might land an analyst position but promotion to higher levels will be difficult). Thus part of the "preparation" for banking is developing interests outside of finance.

## On Interviewing

A number of chapters in this book describe how to prepare for investment banking interviews. If the interviewing advice in the book had to be distilled to four main points, they would be:

- Be hungry (but not overly aggressive). Investment banking is a job for go-getters. This is not a job for people who sit back and let opportunity come to them but rather a job for people who go out and grab opportunities.

- Be knowledgeable about the position itself and about the firm with which you are interviewing, including its corporate history, recent major deals, areas of strength and areas of weakness. In short, be prepared.

- Be confident about what you bring to the table, and verbalize it. Confidence and a willingness to learn will take you far in any business, including investment banking.

- Do not oversell yourself, drink too much at a recruiting event, gossip or be arrogant. There are plenty of candidates who want a job in banking and if you provide people with a reason not to hire you, they may use it.

## On Apprenticeship

A career in finance begins with learning the trade in an apprenticeship environment. Learning any trade requires three important ingredients. First, the apprentice must be eager to learn. Second, the apprentice must have a master (or its modern day equivalent, a mentor). Third, the apprentice must be willing to study all aspects of the trade, from the lowly and mundane to those that require more technical expertise and creativity. If any of these three ingredients is missing, the young banker is not likely to last long.

In spite of its hierarchical structure, banking is a meritocracy; excellence is rewarded and incentives are transparent. In fact, after professional athletics and the performing arts, banking is among the most meritocratic industries. Essentially, you will rise as fast and as far as you are able. The logical corollary is that if you are not able, you will fall or, worse yet, be pushed out. In banking, there is no franchise on good ideas: from the first day you can make a meaningful impact, and the extent of your impact is largely dependent on the effort and capability you demonstrate.

For those who are competitive by nature and enjoy personal and group success, this "excel or be let go" mentality is quite refreshing since, unlike many other organizations, in an investment bank you usually know where you stand. If at the end of a year you still have a job, you know that you have performed well. How well you performed will also be transparent in the amount of your annual bonus. It is as clear as an incentive system can be. Teams are rewarded for good work, both financially and in terms of promotion. Those who do not pull their weight are generally let go.

When you begin in banking, you are labeled as part of a start class. At the end of every year, you are either promoted to the next class year (e.g., from second-year associate to third-year associate) or you are fired. Most investment banks let go of the bottom five to ten percent of their employee base after each annual performance review cycle. In challenging economic times, such as in the U.S. from 2001 to 2003, that percentage can reach forty percent or more.

A finance professional's tool chest must be built systematically – it cannot simply be cobbled together. Given the sheer amount of work an analyst or associate does in banking, one is forced to quickly develop a highly portable skill set in a relatively short period of time. This tool chest, if learned well and used properly, provides immense value to your employer right off the bat and will serve you well far into the future.

## How To Use This Book

*The Recruiting Guide to Investment Banking* is broken up into three distinct parts.

**Part I: *The Recruiting Season*** begins with an overview of the different functional areas within an investment bank and goes on to describe the recruiting process in detail. It includes advice on developing your own recruiting strategy, drafting your resume, preparing for interviews, and choosing among firms. Chapter 5, The Interviews, includes more than 60 sample interview questions.

**Part II: *Life for a Junior Banker*** describes day-to-day life for an analyst or associate in investment banking. This section provides straightforward, non-sensationalized information and advice about the lifestyle, the hours, compensation, performance reviews, corporate policies, mentoring and diversity.

**Part III: *Preparing for the Interviews*** includes three technical chapters intended to help prepare you for finance-related interview questions. These chapters are also included in their entirety in *The Practitioner's Guide to Investment Banking*. In Part III, you will find explanations of the basic financial terms and concepts most often used by bankers, a discussion of corporate strategy and how companies choose to undertake financing or strategic transactions, a discussion of synergies and how M&A can create value for a company, and an overview of the most commonly used valuation methodologies.

**The Glossary** from *The Practitioner's Guide to Investment Banking* is included here in *The Recruiting Guide to Investment Banking* as a resource. It provides M&A and corporate finance terms and concepts, all of which are described in detail in *The Practitioner's Guide*.

**The Appendix** provides a listing of investment banks, resources and recommended reading. In addition, Appendix D provides a review of basic corporate finance concepts.

If you are already well versed in the topics covered in Part III, you are well ahead of the competition. Instead of preparing for interviews by brushing up on more technical concepts, spend your time practicing oral delivery and effective communication.

Many guidebooks promise that if you follow a prescribed set of steps, you will achieve what you set out to do. The multi-billion dollar "how to" market survives on this fallacy. We would be remiss in our job as advisors if we told you that simply by reading this book you should land a job in banking. Nothing in life is that straight-forward. Books and mentors can help lead the way, open doors and clarify concepts. However, there are too few investment banking jobs and too many people who want them for it to be that easy. This book will help you navigate the recruiting process so that you are as prepared as you can be for what lies ahead, but the work --like all things in life-- is up to you.

The authors would like this recruiting guide to be as useful a resource as possible. If you have suggestions, ideas or comments about the book or if this book helped you earn a job, they would enjoy hearing from you via email at **jerilyn@scoopbooks. com** and **peter@scoopbooks.com**. If you are beginning a career in finance, be sure to read *The Practitioner's Guide to Investment Banking*, a desktop companion for anyone working in mergers and acquisitions or corporate finance. It can be ordered at **www. scoopbooks.com**.

THE RECRUITING GUIDE TO

# INVESTMENT BANKING

# PART 1
## THE RECRUITING SEASON

# Investment Banking

## CHAPTER 1

*I love the man that can smile in trouble,*
*that can gather strength from distress,*
*and grow brave by reflection.*

### *Thomas Paine*

An investment bank is an organization that helps clients raise and invest capital and advises clients on strategic matters, including mergers, acquisitions, financings, and restructuring transactions. Specifically, an investment bank serves as an intermediary between clients who need capital (e.g., corporations, governments, municipal agencies) and clients with capital to invest (e.g., institutional investors, funds, insurance companies, corporations, high net worth individuals). Within an investment bank, there are various groups, one of which is the Investment Banking Group (often called IB or IBD for Investment Banking Division). Bankers in the Investment Banking Group advise clients who need capital or are contemplating a strategic action (such as a merger) and execute transactions on behalf of their clients.

Figure 1.1 (opposite page 5) illustrates the organization of an investment bank. Every year, each of these groups hires new analysts and associates. However, the largest pool of entry-level analysts and associates is for the Investment Banking Group (shown in the left-most column). A brief description of each group is provided in Figure 1.1. Not every investment bank operates in all of the lines of business listed under the column "Other Businesses."

Companies provide bankers in the Investment Banking Group access to confidential information which is not generally available to the public, in the same way companies provide confidential information to other advisors such as attorneys and accountants. Bankers outside of the Investment Banking Group (such as bankers in Sales and Trading or Equity Research) do not have access to a company's confidential information. These bankers do their work using public information. Whereas a banker in the Investment Banking Group generally interfaces day-to-day with corporations, a banker in Sales and Trading or Equity Research generally interfaces day-to-day with investors.

# Figure 1.1 - Typical Functional Breakdown of an Investment Bank [1]

An Investment Bank serves as an intermediary between clients who need capital (e.g., corporations, governments, municipal agencies), and clients with capital to invest (e.g., institutional investors, funds, insurance companies, corporations, high net worth individuals).

## Investment Banking Group [2]

### Corporate Finance (Coverage Groups)
Advise clients in partnership with product groups

- Healthcare
- Energy & Power
- Chemicals
- Financial Sponsors
- Banks & Insurance
- Real Estate
- Middle Market
- Industrials
- Consumer
- Retail
- Technology
- Media
- Telecom
- Public Finance
- Governments

### Corporate Finance (Product Groups)
Execute transactions for clients

- Mergers & Acquisitions
- Leveraged Finance
- Restructurings and Workouts
- Credit Advisory
- Project Finance

### Capital Markets (Product Groups)
Execute capital raising transactions for clients

- Equities
- Equity Linked [3]
- High Yield
- Syndicated Finance
- Structured Finance
- Fixed Income
- Loans
- Private placements
- Municipals
- Derivatives

## Trading and Principal Investments [4]

### Sales & Trading
Sell and trade securities in the secondary market

- Equities
- Equity Linked [3]
- Treasuries
- Municipals
- Currencies
- Credit Derivatives
- Fixed Income
- Derivatives
- Commodities
- Asset Backed
- Mortgage Backed

### Investment Research
Further subdivided by industry and company

- Equity [5]
- Credit
- Commodities
- Currencies
- Fixed Income
- High Yield
- Economic
- Global Markets

### Proprietary Trading
Trade with bank's own capital

- Trading
- Risk Arbitrage

### Private Equity / Merchant Banking
Acquire companies using bank and investor capital

### Risk Management
Internal risk management

## Other Businesses

### Investment Management
Sell and manage mutual funds and other products

### Private Banking
Banking for high net worth individuals and estates

### Treasury and Securities Services
Clearing, trade, custody, and securities services

### Commercial Banking [6]
Accept deposits and provide loans to borrowers

### Credit Cards
Provide credit cards to clients

### Retail Brokerage
Sell mutual funds and products to retail investors

### Mortgage Banking
Provide mortgages to retail and commercial borrowers

### Insurance
Provide insurance services to clients

---

[1] Banks may organize and name their business units in different ways. For example, some Mergers and Acquisitions bankers work within client coverage groups.
[2] When working on a transaction on behalf of a client, bankers in the Investment Banking Group have access to confidential information.
[3] Equity Linked products include options, convertibles, and other specialized products the value of which is derived from underlying equity securities.
[4] Bankers in Trading and Principal Investments generally do not have access to confidential information; the dividing line between Investment Banking and Sales, Trading and Research is called the "Ethical Wall" or the "Chinese Wall".
[5] Some banks have separated equity research into its own independent group.
[6] Some "universal banks" fold their Corporate Banking function into the Investment Banking Group.

## Advisory vs. Capital Raising

The Investment Banking Group can generally be divided into two major functions: (1) Corporate Finance and (2) Capital Markets.

The Corporate Finance Group is principally responsible for winning new business from clients and executing strategic transactions, such as a merger, on behalf of clients. Many bankers in the Corporate Finance Group are industry specialists (who call on clients in a particular industry such as energy, healthcare or consumer products). The largest specialty group within the Corporate Finance Group is usually the Mergers and Acquisitions Group. Other specialties within Corporate Finance include the Financial Sponsors Group (whose clients are private equity and leveraged buyout firms), the Middle Market Group (whose clients are mid-sized companies, many of which are privately owned), and the Restructuring Group (which focuses on bankruptcy-related restructurings or workouts).

While bankers in the Corporate Finance Group advise clients on strategic transactions and/or cover clients in a specific industry, bankers in the Capital Markets Group raise capital for clients, usually across all industries. Equity and Fixed Income Capital Markets raise capital directly from investors by issuing securities such as stocks and bonds on behalf of clients. The Syndicated Finance Group provides large loans and lines of credit to clients and then sells portions of the loan to other banks. Other specialties within the Capital Markets Group include Equity Linked Capital Markets, which works with clients to issue specialty financial products the value of which is derived from underlying equity securities (e.g., convertible debt and preferred stock), Structured Finance, which works with clients on highly structured transactions (e.g., leveraged leases, sale leasebacks), and High Yield Capital Markets, which works with clients to issue high yield debt and preferred stock.

Bankers from the Corporate Finance Group and the Capital Markets Group often work together on a transaction on behalf of a client. For example, if a steel company wanted to acquire a competitor for cash, bankers from the M&A group might advise the company on valuation, deal structure, and deal negotiations, bankers from the Capital Markets Group and the Syndicated Finance Group might help the company raise capital to fund the acquisition, bankers from the Credit Advisory Group might help address potential rating agency and/or debt holder concerns, and bankers from the Industrials Corporate Finance Group might oversee the transaction and ensure that all of the product groups are sharing information and working together to best serve the client.

---

**ᐤOOᐤ Product bankers vs. coverage bankers**

Bankers who specialize in either advisory work or capital markets work are often referred to as **product bankers**. Product bankers are distinct from **coverage bankers** who, instead of focusing on a particular product such as M&A, focus on building relationships with clients. Product bankers execute transactions for clients whereas coverage bankers originate new business and maintain client relationships. Coverage bankers are also called "relationship bankers."

---

It is important to note that this is a general description of how an investment bank might be organized. Some banks may be organized differently from what is described here. Many banks, in fact, reorganize every few years if they believe a different organizational structure will allow them to serve their clients better. Instead of thinking of the various groups of an investment bank statically, think of them as a dynamic functional group of specialists. If a client has a problem, teams of specialists are formed to address the client's problem and then, when the client's issue has been solved, that specific team disbands and the specialists join other client teams, to solve other clients' needs.

## Strategic Planning vs. Financial Management

In order to better understand the distinction between a corporate finance and a capital markets banker, it may make sense to look at it from the perspective of a financial manager within a company. There are two major financial responsibilities within a company: (1) strategic and financial planning, which is generally forward looking, and (2) financial and liability management, which tends to focus on the financing needs of a business, including the management of financial risk. In smaller companies, these two roles might be undertaken by the same group of people (and in the smallest of companies these roles might be the responsibility of only one or two people). However, in larger companies these two roles tend to be handled by two separate groups.

1. The **Strategic Planning Group** or **Corporate Development Group** would likely handle the strategic and/or financial planning for the company, including preparing forward-looking financial statements and projections, identifying and analyzing potential strategic transactions, and executing mergers, acquisitions and divestitures on behalf of the company. This group is often headed by a Director of Strategic Planning, who usually reports to the company's Chief Financial Officer. In general, the Strategic Planning Group works on transactions that affect the asset side of the balance sheet. Corporate De-

velopment professionals usually interface with bankers from the Corporate Finance and M&A Groups.

2. The **Treasury Group** is likely to handle functions related to financial management, financings, liability management and risk management. Whereas the Strategic Planning Group tends to work on issues related to the asset side of the balance sheet, the Treasury Group tends to work on issues related to the liability and shareholders' equity side of the balance sheet in addition to cash and marketable securities. For example, the Treasury Group generally takes the lead when a company issues new bonds or refinances an existing loan that is coming due. The Treasury Group also handles all of the issues related to short term liquidity and financing. Because of its role in raising and managing financing for a company, the Treasury Group also tends to handle most of the responsibilities related to managing the company's credit rating. The Treasury Group is generally headed by the Treasurer, who typically reports directly to the company's Chief Financial Officer. Sometimes, the accounting and financial reporting responsibilities (headed by the company's Controller) are rolled into the Treasury Group. Many companies, large and small, have a Controller who doubles as a Treasurer. In smaller companies, the Chief Financial Officer also functions as a Treasurer. Professionals in the Treasury Group usually interface with bankers from the Capital Markets Group or Syndicated Finance Group.

## Confidential Information

When bankers, lawyers, consultants, accountants, and others ("advisors") are working for a company on a transaction, their work products are generally privileged (meaning confidential) and seldom made publicly available. One of an investment bank's few work products that is disclosed is a Fairness Opinion provided to public companies. Since these advisors have access to confidential or "inside" information, there are many SEC governed restrictions on their actions (from insider trading, for example) that are designed to protect shareholders. All inside participants in an M&A or capital raising process for a public company are subject to these SEC rules and regulations. These advisors also may be subject to additional rules and regulations set forth by their companies, industry oversight boards or other organizations.

Those without access to inside information include investors, traders, arbitrageurs, hedge fund managers, research analysts, the general public, and others who could potentially profit from a transaction. It is a breach of confidentiality if someone with access to inside information shares it with someone without access to inside information (including spouses, relatives and friends). It is illegal if someone with access to inside information makes, participates in, or facilitates investment decisions in public companies based on that confidential information.

## What is a CA or an NDA?

Advisors are required to sign a Confidentiality Agreement prior to gaining access to confidential information. A **Confidentiality Agreement** ("CA" for short) is synonymous with a **Non-Disclosure Agreement** ("NDA" for short). A CA or NDA is a legal agreement which prevents the recipient of confidential information from sharing that confidential information with anyone except under highly defined circumstances (for example, with members of the deal team). If confidential information is shared with an unauthorized person, the party that shared the information is considered to be in breach of the Confidentiality Agreement and could be legally liable to the other party for the consequences of the breach.

A few third-party participants, such as credit rating agencies and federal or state regulatory commissions, are sometimes provided confidential information before it is made publicly available. These participants are in a position of public trust and are not allowed to profit from that inside information. Outsiders who are provided confidential information are subject to the same insider trading restrictions that apply to other insiders.

The **Ethical Wall** or **Chinese Wall** is an imaginary line drawn between those with access and those without access to confidential information. Within an investment bank, for example, there is an Ethical Wall between bankers in the Investment Banking Group and other bankers (Sales & Trading, Equity Research, Private Banking). Bankers in the Investment Banking Group are provided confidential information whereas others bankers utilize public information to conduct their business. Because of the Ethical Wall, a banker in the M&A Group, for example, is not allowed to have a company-specific conversation with an equity research analyst.

## A Career in Banking

From lowest to highest level of seniority, the titles within an investment bank include analyst, associate, vice president and managing director. Some banks subdivide the vice president and managing director levels into two additional levels. College graduates are recruited for analyst positions. MBAs and JDs are recruited for associate positions. Analyst positions generally last two years, although if after the second year an analyst seems to be on track for direct promotion to associate, the analyst may be asked to stay for a third year. Typically, associates are promoted to vice president after four or five years as an associate. As shown in Table 1.2, from first-year associate to managing director can take anywhere from eight years for those on a particularly fast track up to fifteen years.

## Table 1.2 – Levels within Investment Banking

| Level | Sublevel | | Hiring Pool | Term |
|-------|----------|---|-------------|------|
| Analyst | - | • | College graduates | 2 to 3 years |
| Associate | Some banks have senior associate designations | • <br> • <br> • <br> • | Third year analysts <br> MBAs <br> JDs <br> Industry hires | 4 to 5 years |
| Vice President | Some banks have senior vice president designations | • <br> • | Senior associates <br> Senior level industry hires | 4 to 10 years |
| Managing Director | Some banks first promote to director, then subsequently to managing director | • <br> • <br><br> • | Vice presidents <br> Senior level industry hires <br> Senior level law hires | Indefinite |

Traditionally, transactions are staffed with four bankers, one of each level. Larger or more complex deals often require more than four bankers and smaller deals might function with only two or three bankers. In general, for each project, an analyst reports to an associate, vice president and managing director; an associate reports to a vice president and managing director and manages one analyst. Below are brief descriptions of the general responsibilities of analysts, associates, vice presidents and managing directors.

*Analysts*: On a typical project, the analyst runs the analytical models, gathers and analyzes information, writes sections of presentations, and coordinates activities on a transaction. Analysts usually begin interacting regularly with clients in their second or third year. Most analysts only have two or three projects at a time due to the in-depth nature of their involvement with each project. Internally, analysts participate in recruiting and help organize training sessions.

*Associates*: The associate manages the day-to-day aspects of the project, is primarily responsible for drafting presentations and writing memos, is ultimately responsible for the analyst's financial models, runs the more complex financial models and interfaces regularly with the client. On smaller transactions, the associate runs the deal and is usually the primary contact with the client. An associate might have two to five projects at a time. Internally, associates are expected to train and mentor analysts and actively participate in recruiting.

***Vice Presidents***: The vice president is ultimately responsible for running the deal. He or she reviews all of the analyst's and associate's work, communicates on major issues with the client, makes critical decisions, presents conclusions to the client, mobilizes any other groups within the bank and is actively involved in negotiations on behalf of the client. Vice presidents are also expected to cultivate relationships and win business. A vice president might have five to seven projects at a time. Internally, vice presidents participate actively in recruiting, development, training and mentoring.

***Managing Directors***: Managing directors are generally responsible for winning business, managing relationships, making critical decisions, presenting materials to the client, negotiating the transaction agreement, and ensuring that the firm's resources are used appropriately for each deal. Managing directors might have up to ten transactions at any given time. A managing director who is also a group head could have more than ten projects at any given time. Like vice presidents, managing directors are expected to lead recruiting and development efforts. In addition, managing directors drive internal strategy, allocate resources, determine compensation levels, and make decisions whenever the firm's capital is at risk.

# Getting in the Door

## CHAPTER 2

*Perseverance is a great element of success;*
*if you only knock long enough and loud enough at the gate*
*you are sure to wake up somebody.*

### Henry Wadsworth Longfellow

A bank's success, like that of any service business, is almost entirely dependent on its employees. Hiring smart, talented, driven, and committed people is the first step toward developing a strong service business. A bank has many professionals who can teach the motivated and dedicated candidate how to perform the responsibilities expected. No one, however, can teach the candidate desire, commitment, common sense, or enthusiasm. These are all innate qualities, and banks spend a significant amount of time, energy, and money seeking candidates who possess these characteristics.

Bankers at all levels are expected to participate actively in the recruiting process. This includes the most junior bankers (first and second year analysts) as well as the most senior bankers (group and department heads). Not doing so can have a negative impact on one's end of year review. Participation in recruiting is actively monitored, and some banks have minimum requirements with regard to the number of interview sessions or company presentations each banker must attend. Not only are bankers expected to participate in the recruiting process by conducting interviews and attending or speaking at presentations, but bankers are also expected to build relationships with target recruits and maintain an open dialogue with them during the recruiting process. Building relationships may include phone conversations, ongoing e-mail dialogue, and drinks or dinner if the recruit is in town.

While the recruiting process can be daunting and the stakes are high for potential candidates, they are equally high for the bank. Just as recruits try to convince a firm that it should hire them, the firm works diligently to convince qualified and sought-after recruits to come work for it. The **war for talent,** or competition among banks, other high-end service firms, and major corporations to hire and retain the most qualified candidates at all levels, is fierce. Each bank competes for the best candidates, which is why it is not surprising when some candidates receive multiple offers while others receive none.

## Determining Hiring Needs

Although recruiting is not a science, there is a fair amount of critical thinking employed by the banks with regard to how many first year analysts and associates they hire each year. The number of junior bankers a firm needs is primarily driven by transaction and client demand. First, transaction and client demand determines the number of senior bankers the firm needs. Each senior banker then needs to work with a certain number of junior bankers to maximize efficiency.

Each bank has an optimal senior banker-to-junior banker leverage ratio and this ratio determines the total number of junior bankers hired. Senior bankers are vice presidents and managing directors; junior bankers are analysts and associates. If a firm determines that the optimal leverage ratio is three junior bankers to one senior banker (and the firm currently has 300 senior bankers), then the firm will need a pool of 900 junior bankers. If it determines that it has 750 junior bankers committed for the next twelve months (after accounting for those expected to leave within the year), it will then hire 150 junior bankers during the coming year's analyst and associate recruiting season.

Depending on transaction and client demand, most major investment banks will hire between 75 and 300 college graduates for first year banking analyst positions, and between 75 and 200 business school graduates for first year associate positions annually. These first year analysts and associates would get placed in various corporate finance and capital markets groups throughout the firm. Most analysts and associates would work in the firm's New York office, but some might be hired to work in a regional office (e.g., San Francisco, Los Angeles, Houston, Chicago, etc.). Keep in mind that these numbers fluctuate based on market conditions, but during average years the figures are near the middle of the ranges.

> ### 🕐 Investment banking hiring is cyclical
>
> The investment banking business tracks the market in the sense that when the market is good, there is more business to be done. Due to the market environment during 2001 and 2002, major investment banks shed thousands of jobs. During those recruiting seasons, many banks dramatically reduced the number of offers they extended relative to the number of offers made during the previous years. However, with the IPO and M&A market recoveries that began in mid-2003, banks found themselves with too few professionals to handle the onslaught of new business. The result was a significant step-up in hiring numbers for the 2004 and 2005 recruiting seasons.

## The Recruiting Department

In order to fill these positions, every investment bank has a dedicated recruiting department that is responsible for finding college graduates, MBAs, JDs and others interested in becoming members of its upcoming **start class,** the analyst or associate class that will begin together as a group in a formal training program. A start class is like a number stamped on your forehead and, unless you are promoted early, this will be the class of people you will be compared to every year during annual performance and compensation reviews. For most of your banking career you will be referred to as a member of your respective class (analyst class of 2005 or associate class of 2000, for example).

At some banks, the dedicated recruiting departments are small (three to ten people) and rely largely on support from bankers to assist in the firm's recruiting efforts. At other banks, the recruiting departments are large and, although bankers actively participate in recruiting, the departments handle many of the logistical recruiting issues. Your first and main point of contact during the recruiting season will likely be someone from the recruiting department.

> ˆOO ̂ **Recruiting departments**
>
> Don't make the mistake of treating people in the recruiting department differently than bankers you meet. Recruiting coordinators can be important allies since they essentially oversee the campus level search process.

## The Recruiting Process

There are various phases to the recruiting season. For full-time hiring, planning for the upcoming **recruiting season** (generally August to February each year) typically begins in early summer so that the banks are prepared to visit schools as early as the end of August or beginning of September.

Although some firms have recruiting processes that vary somewhat from the structure laid out here, most firms follow the process described in Figure 2.1.

## Figure 2.1 – The Recruiting Season

**Step 1 – Company presentations:** generally take place at the beginning of the school year

**Step 2 – Resume drops:** your resume must be submitted electronically by a certain due date

**Step 3 – Resume reviews:** school teams review the resumes from each target school and select anywhere between thirty and ninety students to interview on campus

**Step 4 – First round interviews:** generally take place on campus or at a hotel near campus; usually last thirty minutes and involve meeting one or two people from the firm

**Step 5 – Decision meetings:** a small committee reviews the outcomes of the first round interviews and makes decisions regarding who will be invited for a second round interview; usually conducted immediately after the interviews

**Step 6 – Second round interviews:** generally take place at the firm's headquarters; usually last three to six hours and involve meeting four to ten different people from the firm; often involve dinner and/or drinks the night before the interviews

**Step 7 – Decision meetings:** a small committee reviews the outcomes of the second round interviews and makes decisions regarding to whom offers will be extended; usually conducted immediately after the interviews

**Step 8 – Offers extended:** offers of employment are often extended via telephone, followed by a formal offer letter sent in the mail; usually occurs within two weeks of the second round interview

**Step 9 – Sell days:** generally take place at the firm's headquarters; meetings are held with a number of people at the firm from different industry and product groups; usually last three to six hours, including dinner and/or drinks the night before or the night of the sell day

**Step 10 – Offer deadlines:** offers usually have deadlines by which recruits must notify the bank of their intent to join the firm; if the offer ceases to be valid after a certain date, that date is known as the **drop dead date** and that offer is called an **exploding offer**

> ### ⏱ Your campus recruiting schedule
>
> Many banks begin recruiting events the first or second week of the school year. As such, check with the campus career center prior to the commencement of classes and pick up a company event schedule to see when particular firms will be on campus. Some banks have recruiting timelines and calendars posted on their websites.

## Targeting Candidates

Analyst and associate hires for an investment bank usually come through one of five channels, listed in order of priority: (1) internal analyst to associate promotions; (2) summer internship programs; (3) diversity internship programs; (4) on-campus recruiting at target schools; and (5) the general applicant pool. What this should tell you is that by the time the banks begin recruiting on campus at target schools, they have already filled a meaningful number of their starting analyst positions. For associates, the banks will satisfy an even larger share of their associate hiring needs from internal promotions and summer and diversity internship programs.

## Summer Internship Programs

Most banks have highly organized summer programs for first year MBAs and incoming college seniors. Landing a summer position, however, is extremely competitive due to the limited number of summer positions available. If you do land a summer position, your chances of securing a full-time position with the firm with which you worked for a summer will be high (assuming you do a good job and work hard that summer). More important than helping you obtain a full-time position, a summer job in banking will give you a preview of the life you can expect, and will help you decide whether you want to be a banker for the next few years.

Unfortunately, second year MBAs are disadvantaged if they do not have a banking or finance internship the summer before applying. If you cannot obtain an internship with a bank, you should do your best to obtain an internship in which you will develop skills that are relevant to banking.

## Diversity Internship Programs

The two most nationally recognized diversity programs are Sponsors for Educational Opportunity or SEO (www.seo-ny.org) at the undergraduate level and The Robert Toigo Foundation or TOIGO (www.toigofoundation.org) at the graduate level. Each program has its own rigorous selection process much like that of the banks, and then places its pool of interns at major firms. These programs offer the opportunity to enter the financial world through an alternative channel. They are very well respected and supported by the investment banks because they help banks accomplish two goals: to identify good candidates and to increase diversity. This is not to say that banks have quotas or hard-and-fast rules with regard to how many women or minority bankers they hire. Banks care about a candidate's talent and drive, not about gender or racial quotas. However, firms actively think about the composition of their analyst and associate classes, and the importance of diversity. This relates to diversity of thought as well as that of gender and nationality. Therefore, banks try to hire candidates with varied experiences and capabilities and these diversity programs help them do so.

## On-Campus Recruiting

Every bank has compiled a list of undergraduate and graduate schools designated as its **target schools,** or schools at which the bank will actively recruit students for analyst or associate positions. This list is fluid and will, to some degree, change every year. But, in general, a select twenty to thirty undergraduate programs and ten to twenty MBA programs are targeted every year by most of the major firms.

Banks select their target schools based on a number of factors, and there is a fair amount of internal debate every year with regard to which schools should be added or eliminated from the target list. In general, banks will want to invest money and time toward recruiting at schools at which: (1) the firm finds many students who are qualified to receive an offer; (2) historically, a high percentage of the students have accepted the firm's offer; and (3) previous candidates from the school have done well at the firm.

The undergraduate programs that tend to receive the most attention from the New York based investment banks are (1) the Ivy League schools such as Harvard, Yale, Princeton, University of Pennsylvania, Dartmouth, Columbia, and Brown; (2) the large universities with well-regarded undergraduate business programs such as the University of Michigan, the University of California, Berkeley, and the University of

Virginia; (3) the larger universities on the East Coast such as Georgetown University and New York University; and (4) some of the smaller liberal arts colleges on the East Coast such as Wellesley, Amherst, Williams, and Colgate.

Although almost every one of the top ten to twenty MBA programs will be an MBA target school, the programs that tend to have stronger and larger finance departments, and consequently more students interested in investment banking, generally receive the most attention from the banks during recruiting season. These include Wharton (at the University of Pennsylvania), Columbia, Stern (at NYU), Harvard, and the University of Chicago.

Recruiting expenses for an investment bank are very high (from the hundreds of thousands to millions of dollars per year) since they include sending many bankers to campuses all over the country and, vice versa, sending students from all over the country to New York City for second round interviews and sell days. Major services firms can spend up to $100,000 per final hire in recruiting and initial training expenses. Because these recruiting costs are very high and a firm is interested in maximizing its acceptance rate, or yield, it is easy to understand why banks spend so much time deciding not only which schools to target, but what their specific recruiting strategies will be for each campus and ultimately which students to target at each school.

Most banks are organized for recruiting by means of **school teams** such that a group of bankers and members of the recruiting staff are responsible for: (1) attending the on-campus presentation for the school; (2) **screening resumes** or reading resumes and identifying recruits to interview; (3) conducting the first round interviews; and (4) communicating with recruits during both the recruiting process and the **sell process,** the period after a firm has extended an offer to a recruit but before the recruit has accepted or declined the offer.

In general, members of a particular school team are either alumni of that particular school or alumni of a college or business school in the same region of the country as that school. Recruits are often more receptive to bankers who have something in common with them. And bankers who attended the target school are best qualified to make recommendations regarding the firm's recruiting strategy at the target school. Members of a school team have significant influence in selecting candidates for first round interviews. At the associate level especially, it is not enough to just have a great resume; it is almost imperative to have made a positive impression on a member of the school team.

^OO^ **Alumni interviewers**

Since most banks organize their recruiting efforts through school teams, your interviewer may well know that your I-Got-An-A class with Professor Famous-For-Easy-Grades was just that. In addition, alumni will know which professors are tough graders. Do not lie or try to pass something off as more than it is; if you are caught, the damage to your credibility in the interview process can be terminal.

During the first phase of the recruiting process, you will generally interact only with members of a bank's school team and members of the recruiting department. If you are invited to participate in a second round interview, the circle of people you meet from a particular firm will widen dramatically.

## General Applicant Pool

Do not be discouraged if you do not attend a target school. The banks target particular schools because they are in the business of finding and retaining qualified candidates and, like any good business practitioner, they are doing what they can to ensure their chances of success. Every year banks make the business decision to focus their efforts and money on particular schools at which, statistically, the likelihood of finding the right people is high. This does not mean that you have no chance of landing a job if you do not go to a target school. It is more difficult, to be sure, but it can be done. Some extremely competent and successful bankers boast degrees from non-target schools such as Millsaps College, Tulane University, University of Rochester, and University of Colorado (alma mater of Richard Fuld, CEO and Chairman of Lehman Brothers).

If you do not attend a target school, try to employ one of the following four strategies: (1) join a diversity program such as SEO or TOIGO if you qualify; (2) find a **sponsor** or someone who can speak on your behalf; (3) try to arrange informational interviews to meet more people in a firm; and/or (4) participate in on-campus recruiting at a nearby target school by checking in with the career center of the closest target school and asking if you can participate in their resume drop. Many large universities will allow students at neighboring schools to do this. As a last ditch effort, some banks have an e-mail address on their recruiting website to which you can submit your cover letter and resume. Do not use this as your only method, though, because banks do not pay much attention to resumes submitted by e-mail; they are just too busy since the number of submissions via a website is very high. Employing multiple strategies will increase your chances of landing an interview. Once you land the interview, you're in the door, and your success or failure in the recruiting process no longer is a function of what school you attended. Instead, like all other candidates who have landed an interview, your fate is in your own hands.

One cannot say that banks never hire someone for a first year analyst or associate position after the candidate has gone to work in another field. It does happen, but it is not common. It is more common to hire laterally from within the industry, broadly defined. A **lateral hire** is a person who is hired as a mid-level analyst, associate, or vice president. Lateral hires are generally people (1) hired away from other banks; (2) people with several years of experience in a particular industry (e.g., healthcare, telecommunications, energy); or (3) people with tangential experience in banking or finance (e.g., M&A or securities lawyers, accountants, and strategic consultants).

## Company Presentations

Most of the large- and medium-sized firms come to their target MBA and undergraduate schools to give a **company presentation** in the fall. These presentations generally last between two and three hours, with approximately forty-five minutes allotted for the formal presentation and the rest of the time allotted for students to meet and ask questions of members of the firm who have come to the company presentation. Banks generally try to have alumni attend the presentation, so there is a high likelihood that the people you meet at your school's presentation went to your school, either as undergraduates or as business school students. Some of them may eventually be your interviewers.

Although these presentations are not likely to be described as "fun," it is important to attend. First and foremost, this will be your first opportunity to meet people at the firm and for them to meet you. Bankers take notes during these events, literally and figuratively, and to the extent that they meet certain students whom they really like or have a good rapport with, it is almost certain the student will get a first round interview with the firm. The school teams usually screen resumes after the company presentation, so making a good impression at these events is important because a strong showing may cause your resume to be taken out of the "Pass" pile and re-filed in the "Interview" pile.

At any company sponsored event, it is important to act naturally while maintaining a professional demeanor. You do not want to come across as being artificial. Chances are you are not going to impress any banker during these events with your knowledge of finance or with that one well-formulated question. The most memorable students are those who are calm but eager, confident but not arrogant, smart and quick on their feet when asked a question, and presentable (we are not talking about fashion or hairstyles, but whether you look like someone who could represent the firm well to a client).

Do not feel obligated to ask questions during the presentation in front of the entire group; save it for smaller group discussions. Do not dominate the conversation if there are other students around. If anything, you should try to incorporate other students standing near you into the conversation while maintaining a lead voice in the dialogue. Also, do not ask boilerplate questions such as, "Which way do you think the market is going?" or "Do you think the Fed will increase rates?" Also avoid questions that could easily be answered on the company webpage. It shows that you have not done basic research. In general, good questions include ones like, "How did you decide to get into banking?," "How did you decide to do M&A, or equities, or *you-name-the product group*?," or "What was it like for you leaving *XYZ town* and moving to New York City?" These types of questions are applicable to any student and prompt the banker to talk about herself and her experiences. When you do talk about yourself, try to distinguish yourself or highlight something unique about your experiences so that if the banker likes you, he or she will remember you. Also, be prepared to have a conversation in addition to preparing a few questions. Forced or odd questions seem stilted, whereas conversations (both good and bad ones) are memorable.

## ˟OˣOˣ Think before you speak

Many less than impressive one-liners occur while attending company presentations, including "I have always wanted to be a banker." Beware of going out on a limb: you don't want to give the impression that you either do not have outside interests or that you are lying, neither of which is likely to reward you with an interview. The most important thing is to appear genuinely interested in the job, the firm, and the banker with whom you are speaking. Just as you are being judged at an interview, so too are you being judged at a company presentation or a recruiting event. Even though the event is labeled as an informational session, do not use it as an opportunity to ask dumb questions. Prepare for the event just as you would for an interview, and be sure to meet with as many people as possible. Most firms keep track of who attends the presentations as well as impressions regarding attendees.

Below are a few things you should do in preparation for and while attending a company presentation:

- Prior to the presentation, review the company's website to read current news and to brief yourself on the company's overall strategy and recruiting process. Website addresses are provided in the Appendix.

- Bring extra copies of your resume to the company presentation in case someone asks for one.

- Ask bankers with whom you spent a good deal of time for their business cards, so that you have a means of following up with them. Follow-up with a thank you e-mail but only to those you spent meaningful time with. Do not shoot off a group e-mail; send individual e-mails.

- Do not spend all of your time talking to just one person; similarly, do not try to meet every banker at the event. Spending ten to fifteen minutes of quality time with three or four bankers is a good target.

> ### ʻOˑOˑ Food and drink
>
> There will likely be food and drinks at the event. Do not gorge yourself with the "free food" – it does not reflect well on you. You may get food stuck between your teeth, end up with bad breath, or be unable to shake hands. Alcohol is often served at MBA events and is unlikely to be served at undergraduate events. Never, under any circumstance, drink too much alcohol at any firm-sponsored event. Think of it this way: for a few free drinks, you may jeopardize your opportunity to get into the firm and profession of your choice.

## Company Sponsored Events

In addition to the company presentations in the fall, some firms host additional workshops or panels, including resume or interview workshops and diversity panels. Firms also may host on-campus case competitions in which case teams are provided with the facts and circumstances of an actual transaction to analyze, and present their conclusions to a panel of bankers. Some firms might choose to host a cocktail hour at a local pub or restaurant or a night of bowling or billiards.

You should consider all of these events as opportunities to meet and talk to a potential employer. They are all terrific venues to learn more about banking and to meet members of different firms. Attend as many of them as possible. The same rules of etiquette apply for all of these events – just because the venue is different does not mean that the rules are different. You should comport yourself at any recruiting event as if you were meeting the firm's decision-maker in her office on a weekday morning and your offer, or lack thereof, depends on that meeting. Think about the number of times that you have heard how much business gets transacted on the golf course. Similarly, many job offers are won at restaurants and other social venues.

## First Impressions

The importance of first impressions cannot be overstated. Each major investment bank meets thousands of students every year who are interested in working for the firm. A bad first impression with even one member of a particular firm can ruin your chances of getting an interview, as could several mediocre or unremarkable first impressions with multiple members of the firm. Also, remember that throughout the recruiting process up until you start working in a particular group, you will be meeting new people. In fact, you will be making first impressions throughout your career. You could make stellar impressions on ten people within a firm but, if one person you interview with has strong feelings against hiring you, you are not likely to get an offer. Do not underestimate the power any particular banker has over your candidacy, regardless of the level or age of that person.

Conversely, if you make a positive impression on ten people in an evening of meet-and-greet, you are likely to get onto an interview schedule, even if your resume on its own would not have passed a screening. Investment banks are, of course, looking for the most qualified candidates, and a 3.7 GPA with a major in finance, Phi Beta Kappa, and a summer internship at a big bank will go a long way. But, if you have a winning personality, are enthusiastic, and get along well with people, you have a good shot at getting an interview. If you are dogged in your determination and well prepared in your interviews, then you are likely to get a job (remember that you only need one job with one firm; if you get ten offers, all the better, but you only need one). And once you get the job, if you work hard, help others, and continue to learn, senior bankers will invest in you and you will become a successful banker. Remember that at every company event you are being evaluated. As a result, people will have certain impressions of you even before your first interview.

## Preparing for the Recruiting Season

In addition to reading about each company before a company presentation, there are other things you can do to prepare for the recruiting season, including reading more and talking to as many people in the business as you can.

***Independent reading:*** An entirely appropriate and important supplement to courses taken in school is independent reading and self-teaching. There are a number of good books on the market that succinctly cover topics in finance, accounting, M&A, and business law (some recommendations can be found in the Appendix). Regardless of whether one is a first year analyst or a seasoned banker who has worked in the business for ten years, one can always benefit from additional reading and studying. You should always be sure that you are reading the most current edition of finance and accounting books as regulations are always changing and innovation in the field takes place at a fairly rapid pace. Not only is continuous self-learning an important discipline to instill in yourself, but there will be many times when you will have a particular question and there will be no one around to answer it. Not surprisingly, the office is fairly empty around 4 a.m. and, if your work is due on a vice president's desk at 9 a.m., you cannot wait until everyone comes back in the morning to get your question answered. During such times your good old accounting and finance textbooks will come in handy. Also, there are a number of books written by ex-bankers which are not only entertaining but provide insight into the world of banking, including: *Liar's Poker: Rising Through the Wreckage on Wall Street* by Michael Lewis and *Monkey Business: Swinging Through the Wall Street Jungle* by John Rolfe and Peter Troob, and books about marquee transactions and important eras in finance, such as *Barbarians at the Gate: The Fall of RJR Nabisco* by Bryan Burrough and John Helyar and *The Predators' Ball: The Inside Story of Drexel Burnham and the Rise of the Junk Bond Raiders* by Connie Bruck.

***Current business news:*** Occasionally, interviewers will encounter a candidate who goes on and on about how interested she is in the markets or M&A. She might say things like "I love banking" or "I was born to be a banker" or "I've wanted to be a banker since I was ten!" Yet when asked to talk about a current event in the market or an M&A deal of particular interest and why it was interesting, this candidate would stare back with a blank look on her face.

If you have a real interest in banking, then you will actually want to (not be forced to, but want to) read things such as *The Wall Street Journal, Business Week, The Economist, Forbes,* or *Fortune.* That is not to say that one who is interested in banking must read every business publication on the market. However, anyone interested in something will naturally choose to read and learn about it, and this applies not only to business but also to people interested in sports, the arts, politics, or any other field. While it is possible to succeed in a field without a strong enthusiasm for it, it is certainly more difficult. The corollary is that you will find it far easier to succeed in a field in which you have a genuine interest than one in which you do not. Said another way, if you do not enjoy reading business literature, you may want to reconsider becoming a banker.

When extremely busy, it is possible to go weeks at a time without reading current news since there are so many demands on your time. Magazines and newspapers can pile up before you have time to sit down and read through them. Although this will happen to you, maintain the discipline to set aside time to stay current on business news. Even ten minutes per day to scan the headlines is better than five hours at the end of the month. It is important both during the recruiting season and once you begin working.

***Talk to people in the business:*** One of the best ways to learn about banking is to spend time with people who are currently, or have at some point been, in the business. Firsthand experience will be the best source of information on a number of important topics. Plus, from talking to and meeting people who are in banking, you will get a sense of whether these are the types of people you want to emulate or with whom you want to spend a lot of your time. Banking, like many businesses, is an apprentice business. This means that you can learn the basics of finance and accounting from a book, but the ins and outs of the business – the knowledge that will distinguish the competent practitioner – come with experience. Learning from a seasoned professional means learning not only the particular skill that she is teaching you, but also a host of other matters that come up when discussing that particular skill. There are many non-academic lessons that seasoned professionals impart to junior professionals, often without the situation even appearing to be a professional one, such as how to comport oneself at a meeting, how to dress appropriately for different types of occasions, and myriad other topics as broad as the scope of human interaction.

# Landing an Interview

## CHAPTER 3

*If you think you can, or you think you can't, you're probably right.*

*Henry Ford*

For many people, trying to land an interview is one of the most frustrating aspects of the investment banking recruiting process because it is something over which they feel they have little control. This is an incorrect assumption. Landing an interview is something over which you have a significant amount of control. As with most things, you control your own destiny. The previous chapter discussed the recruiting season in detail. Your goal should be to use that information to develop your own personal recruiting strategy. Developing networks and contacts in banking and having a strong resume are the building blocks of your recruiting strategy.

There are four primary questions that you should ask yourself in order to construct an effective and persuasive recruiting strategy.

(1) Who do I know?
(2) Which of the school processes are available to me?
(3) What can I do to build additional affiliations?
(4) What resume achievements can I highlight?

| Who Do I know? | Which processes are available? | How do I build contacts? | How do I enhance my resume? |
|---|---|---|---|
| Alumni in banking | Target schools: presentations, resume drop, summer opportunities | Work experience: make each summer count | Strong academics |
| Friends | | | Relevant work experience |
| References (parents' friends or professors) | Non-target schools: use contacts, affiliations, participate with nearby target schools, be persistent | Diversity internship programs | Leadership roles |
| Networks (chance business meetings or introductions) | | Summer internship programs | Interesting background |

## Resume Screening

During the recruiting season each investment bank receives thousands of resumes for analyst and associate positions, and each banker reviews hundreds of them. Usually a banker does not spend more than twenty seconds on each resume and cover letter. The banker is looking for certain clues as to the candidate and, if he does not find those clues quickly and without effort, he will move on and continue looking until a resume is found that is appealing. Since you do not want to have one of those resumes that is passed over, here are some things that you should know.

If you go to a target school, there will likely be a **resume drop date,** which is the deadline to submit your resume or **CV** (curriculum vitae) to a particular firm. In today's environment, resume drops are done electronically either through your campus career center or via e-mail. Each firm's school team will **screen** or review resumes from a particular school and decide which students it wants to invite to first round interviews. Most major investment banks receive anywhere between 200 and 500 undergraduate resumes from a target school and can only invite thirty to ninety students for a first round interview. For MBAs, these numbers are about half. Members of each school team generally screen all of the resumes from the school(s) for which they are responsible.

There are certain universal qualities that the banks look for when screening resumes for analyst and associate positions. Although certain banks may weigh some of these qualities more or less heavily than others, all of the banks will consider your resume and candidacy in light of these characteristics:

- Intelligence and strong analytical skills
- Strong leadership skills and willingness to take initiative
- Attention to detail and accountability for one's work
- Strong communication skills, both written and verbal
- Demonstrated teamwork skills and ability to take direction
- A positive attitude, especially in stressful situations; a sense of humor
- Good judgment, maturity, and integrity
- A willingness to learn; a quick study
- Perseverance, stamina, and ability to multitask
- A clear understanding of the business, the expectations, and the lifestyle
- A long term commitment to banking and a personality fit with the firm

> ### ⏱ Resume drop date
>
> Do not miss this deadline. If you are unclear as to when it is, check with your school's career center. Firms will often collect resumes within twenty-four hours of the drop date and it can be difficult to submit a resume once the firms have already collected them.

Bankers usually screen resumes very late at night, very early in the morning, or thirty minutes prior to the school team meeting, at which the students to be interviewed in the first round are selected. It is during this meeting that your candidacy will be discussed for the first time. Although certain candidates will be high on everyone's list, certain candidates will be on the fence. That is, the group will not be unanimous about whether the candidate should be invited for an interview. Generally, more time is spent discussing candidates who are on the fence than other candidates. If this is your situation, it helps if there is someone in the meeting championing you, arguing why you are a good candidate and why you should be granted a first round interview.

With anywhere between 200 and 500 resumes to review prior to the selection meeting for one school, you can see why someone who is very busy may only spend twenty seconds screening your resume. You neither want to miss this very narrow window of opportunity nor do you want somebody to have a reason not to recommend you. Having a thoughtful, easy-to-read resume that meets the requirements and demands of banking will go a long way toward getting you to the interview stage.

> ### 👓 Formatting your resume
>
> Resume drops are electronic so that they can be collected, assessed, and sent around the firm quickly without the degradation of print which occurs from too much faxing and photocopying. Therefore, if you are submitting your resume electronically, it is important to create it in a standard font and to be mindful of your margins so that, when your resume is downloaded by many different people, it does not overflow onto two pages. If you are allowed, submit a PDF file, which can prevent margin and formatting problems when another party opens the file. Also, stay away from fancy graphics and colors as they may not print out properly, making your resume more difficult to read.

## Critical Parts of Your Resume

For the analyst, there are two ways to demonstrate an interest in finance on paper: (1) course work and (2) relevant work experience. If you have neither, your chances of getting a job or internship are less strong than others with either or both of these. Therefore, the preparation for a career in finance begins in your sophomore or junior year. For the associate, work experience will prove your interest in finance.

*Work experience:* For undergraduates, the preparation for a career in finance begins in your sophomore or junior year. It is important to try to have a business or finance-related internship for at least one summer before applying for full-time jobs your senior year. For the associate, it is equally important, if not more so, that you have finance-related work experience.

Your work experience from the previous summer is the most important part of your resume and should be placed at the top. Describe your experience succinctly and communicate in two to three lines what you did and what the results were. If you worked during the school year after that summer, place your current job first only if it is more relevant than your summer experience. For example, if you worked at General Motors in the Treasurer's Office last summer, that is more relevant than if you worked at the campus pub as a work-study student during the school year. However, the job at the pub may provide fodder for interviews as you discuss your people skills. Time gaps or holes in your resume are red flags, especially if the work experience hole took place when you were out of school. Be sure to fill in these gaps of time with a description of what you did, otherwise the person reading your resume will assume you did nothing.

### ᴼᴼ Previous finance experience

Be especially careful how you represent your work experience if you have had a finance-related internship or job. There is nothing more frustrating than interviewing someone who claims to have investment banking experience but who cannot answer basic questions related to valuation or the capital markets. In other words, do not claim to know more than you actually know. There is nothing wrong with not knowing how to do something. Banks have hired many people with limited or no experience in finance. But claiming that you know how to do something that you do not know will decrease your chances of landing a job.

**School:** For undergraduates, how well you do in school (specifically your GPA) is more important than where you go to school. For MBAs it is the opposite; where you go to school is generally more important than how well you do there since at many business schools it is difficult to measure how well a candidate is doing. What school you attended, or are attending, provides certain clues to the person reviewing your resume. For example, most bankers assume (rightly or wrongly) that receiving strong marks in a computer science class at Berkeley, a finance class at Wharton, an economics class at Chicago or a marketing class at Kellogg is significantly more difficult than receiving an A in a similar class at other schools.

**Major:** You do not have to be a finance major to get an interview, but your choice of major (or minor) does indicate a few important things about you. It indicates what you are interested in, your technical strengths (English majors tend to be good writers, engineering majors tend to be good at math and analytical thinking, pre-med students tend to be good at research and attention to detail), and how rigorous your academic experience has been. Along with your school, your major will help characterize the quality of your GPA (it is believed that a 3.5 GPA in pre-med or engineering is more difficult to attain than a 3.5 GPA in sociology or art history).

### ˆOˆOˆ School performance

Whatever classes you take, business or other, try your best to excel in them. A transcript full of business or finance classes with average grades is less impressive than a liberal arts focused one with stellar grades. An important note, however, is that if you are not a finance or business major, it is critical that other parts of your resume indicate an interest in or talent for investment banking. For example, even if you are not a finance major, you should have taken some accounting or economics courses if you sincerely have an interest in finance.

**GPA:** If you are applying for a job straight out of college, put your overall GPA and, if appropriate, your major GPA on your resume. Do not leave it off; the person screening your resume will assume the worst (that you have a low GPA). Do not use "funny math" either, such as your GPA for the last six quarters because, again, the person screening your resume will assume the worst. Do not put more than two GPAs on your resume; one GPA is preferred. Add your major GPA if you think it will help, but anything more will clutter your resume with useless information. For MBAs a GPA is not necessary and, for some schools, not allowed.

---

### ⌢◯◯ Calculating your GPA

It is imperative that your GPA be correctly computed. If you calculated it yourself, have someone else double check your work. If a computer system calculated your GPA, double check it yourself. Banks will call for your school record prior to making an offer, or will make their offer contingent upon review of final transcripts. They may calculate your GPA and call you to discuss sudden changes in performance, or any confusion. Submitting an inaccurate GPA will make you look careless or, worse, dishonest.

---

*Leadership and teamwork experience:* Anything that points to leadership skills, especially within the context of a large, organized group, is a big plus. Being the president of one club or committee is much more impressive than being a member of ten clubs or committees. The banks are more focused on achievement than the number of activities you participate in. Quantify, if possible, your impact to an organization. Be careful, however, about how you describe your leadership experience because banks are looking for team players with strong leadership skills, not people who always need to be in control or the center of attention.

*Extra curricular activities:* Investment banks look for students who are smart, analytical, and good at communicating, but who are also interesting and fun to be around. You are not likely get an interview if your resume lacks the key characteristics listed previously. However, if you have most of those characteristics, the type of extra curricular activities in which you participate may very well differentiate you from other equally capable candidates. Again, be careful about what you list, and only list activities in which you legitimately participate and can intelligently and passionately discuss.

---

### ⌢◯◯ Extra curricular activities

Do not list that you are fluent in Russian if you have only taken two semesters of Beginning Russian (your interviewer may be Ukrainian and may want to conduct the interview in Russian). Do not list that you have traveled the world if what you have really done is backpacked through Europe. Do not list that you are a computer software specialist if, in fact, the extent of your software experience is Microsoft Office. Remember that the people who will interview you come from all over the world and have varied and often impressive experiences. The likelihood that one of the many people within a firm who may interview you shares some of your experiences or interests is high.

---

*Form, spelling, grammar, and attention to detail:* Many resumes are passed over due to spelling errors, grammatical errors and typographical errors, even if the applicant seemed to have the right type of experience or background. Attention to detail is one of the most important characteristics of a good first year analyst or associate. If a student is not even able to successfully proofread his or her own resume, that candidate is not likely to maintain the attention to detail that is required in investment banking. Also, do not try to put too much on one piece of paper. Resumes that are too cluttered, are in very small font, or have very small margins are difficult to read and, as such, probably will not be read.

*Cover letters:* If you are at a target school, reviewers will spend very little time on your cover letter. Keep it short and sweet and make sure there are no errors in it (especially with regard to the name, gender, and firm of the person you are sending it to). If, however, you are not at a target school, your cover letter is extremely important since it is your opportunity to explain to a bank why you are a good candidate. Focus on your skills and attributes and how you expect to help the bank if hired. Again, keep to a manageable length (ideally a single page).

## Things That Are Less Important

*High school information:* Most people who review your resume will not care about where you went to high school, what your high school GPA was, what sports you played in high school, or what you scored on the SAT. Unless you went to a prestigious school (and even that can be difficult to measure; a school that is well-known in Los Angeles may mean nothing to someone from New York, and vice versa) and are applying for a job in the area where your high school is located (such that there is a high likelihood that alumni of your high school will review your resume), it is best not to include any high school information. If anything, listing your high school (especially if it is a well-known preparatory school) may be seen as arrogant, especially if the person screening your resume comes from a more modest background. If, however, something from high school ties in to why you are interested in banking, that specific experience is worth highlighting.

*Non-related work experience:* If you waited tables or worked at Starbucks in order to finance your college education, that is worth mentioning. And if your part-time work experience can be used to highlight important characteristics, such as leadership skills, ability to work with a team, or ability to multitask, list those experiences but focus on how the experience prepared you for a job in banking. However, college jobs that have done little to prepare you for a job in investment banking will not be of much interest to the person screening your resume. It is okay to list such work experience, but do not waste a lot of space on it.

*Objectives:* Do not spend your time writing an "objective" at the top of your resume.

Your objective is to get a job in investment banking. If not, why submit your resume to an investment bank? Objectives waste valuable space.

***Personal information:*** Do not include any information regarding personal characteristics, such as your height, weight, marital status, or religion. You are applying for a job where none of this information is relevant. Besides, in the United States it is illegal to base hiring decisions on such data.

## Creating Your Resume

In addition to considering the things listed in the previous section, there are some general things to consider when creating your resume:

- Remember that your resume is a reflection of you and may be the only reference point someone has when deciding whether to invite you to a first round interview. Do not give someone immediate reasons to not want to meet you, such as a hole in your work experience or grammatical errors which suggest carelessness.

- More than anything, highlight your interest in finance and why you are qualified for a job in investment banking.

- Keep it simple, professional, and clean. This is a job in banking you are applying for, not a job in graphic design.

- Do not agonize over remembering every club or committee to which you belonged. List only those things that truly reflect who you are as a person and which qualify you as someone who may do well in banking.

- Do not, under any circumstance, oversell yourself. Remember that it may very well come back to bite you later during the interview process. The goal of your resume should be to land an interview; therefore you should highlight your qualifications without endangering your credibility.

- Pay attention to details and be sure you have the basics covered. For example:

  1. Are your phone number and e-mail address easy to find?

  2. Have you spell-checked and grammar-checked your resume several times, even looking up words you are not sure of in the dictionary?

3. Have you checked the salutation of your cover letter and made sure that the spelling of the name of the person to whom you are sending it, that person's gender (especially for gender-neutral names like Chris or Kerry), and the firm's name and address are correct?

4. Have you made sure that your resume is in a standard font and that you are using standard margins so that, if you submit your resume electronically, it will look as you have intended it to look?

- Ask other people to review your resume for you, especially contacts in banking. Take no pride in authorship of your resume and solicit as much feedback and advice as you can. Consider all feedback and use your own judgment in incorporating other people's comments.

- Look at other people's resumes to get ideas about layout and format. Try not to copy other people's words, however, as it may cause your own words to sound stilted.

## Sample Resume

A sample resume is provided in Figure 3.1. Some detailed feedback on the resume is provided immediately after Figure 3.1. Although this is a good resume by most standards, there are a number of items included that may raise questions down the line. Be sure to read the comments in conjunction with the resume.

## Figure 3.1 - Sample Resume

---

**Joseph Brant**
301 East 70th Street, Apt. 5B
New York, NY 10021
(212) 555-1212 (h)
jbrant@columbia.mba.edu

### EXPERIENCE

**KPMG Corporate Finance**      **New York, NY**      6/02-3/05
*Associate, Consumer Group*
- Served as the primary client contact and main execution person on domestic and international mergers, acquisitions, divestitures, joint ventures, and restructurings, with a focus in consumer industries.
- Hired as an Associate after two years as an Analyst at Lehman Brothers.
- Developed financial models and performed valuation analyses supporting M&A transactions.
- Significant experience on sell-side transactions, including conducting due diligence, preparing offer letters, analyzing offers received, and presenting conclusions to company management and boards of directors.
- Drafted management presentations related to M&A transactions.
- Supervised and trained Analysts and Associates; led firm-wide corporate finance and accounting training sessions, covering topics such as 338(h)(10) elections and non-cancelable operating leases; served as an unofficial mentor to various junior bankers regarding professional and personal matters.

**Lehman Brothers**      **New York, NY**      7/00 -6/02
*Analyst, Mergers & Acquisitions Group*
- Worked with domestic and international clients regarding various strategic and financial alternatives.
- Performed financial and strategic analysis on a number of transactions, including a $3 billion merger between ABC and DEF, and the sale of XYZ subsidiary to Big Conglomerate Company.
- Executed numerous buy-side and sell-side transactions in a variety of industries including manufacturing, consumer products, food processing, and financial services.
- Managed various aspects of client engagements on a day-to-day basis.
- Member of Transaction Development Group that worked to identify acquisition targets, develop buyers lists and assess consolidation trends as well as stand-alone transactions for strategic and financial buyers.

**BankOne Securities,**      **Chicago, IL**      6/99 -9/99
*Summer Analyst, Corporate Finance Group*
- Prepared company, industry and financial analyses for various assignments.
- Developed financial models and valuations for corporate transactions.

### EDUCATION

**Columbia University**      **New York, NY**      9/05-6/07
Master of Business Administration, emphasis in Finance
- Dean's List
- Field Study Project: Feasibility study of a high-end resort in Cancun, Mexico.

**University of Michigan**      **Ann Arbor, MI**      9/96-5/00
Bachelor of Arts, History
- Dean's List, graduated Cum Laude; Phi Beta Kappa; Phi Alpha Theta (International History Honor Society)
- Varsity Swimming Team: competed in NCAA championships; member of 1998 National Championship Team

**Universidad de Salamanca**      **Salamanca, Spain**      6/98 - 9/98
- Courses in Economics of the European Community, Spanish Literature and Spanish Civil War History

### ADDITIONAL INFORMATION
- Fluent Spanish. Traveled to over 10 countries. Lived in Australia. Originally from Wisconsin. Certified scuba diver

---

## Comments on Sample Resume

### *Header and Overall Format*

- Name and all relevant contact information appear on top so the candidate can be contacted easily.

- A standard font (Times New Roman) and font size are used, making the resume legible. Standard margins are used to ensure that the resume will print without significant formatting problems.

- The dates are somewhat difficult to read at a rapid glance. The candidate might have written out the months (e.g., June 2002 – March 2005).

- The resume is subdivided into sections from most to least important: (1) experience, (2) education, (3) other.

### *Experience*

- Joseph was hired as an associate at KPMG after working two years as an analyst at Lehman Brothers. A reviewer might assume that he jumped to KPMG either because he wanted the title of associate and did not have it at Lehman or that he was not offered a third year as an analyst at Lehman. Joseph will need to be prepared during his interviews to discuss why he left Lehman, an investment bank, to work for an accounting firm, even though what he did at KPMG was similar, if not entailing greater responsibility, than what he did at Lehman.

- Joseph has described in great detail what he did at KPMG. After two years as an analyst and three years as an associate, he probably did all of the things listed in the bullets. However, he probably was not the "primary client contact" or the "main execution person" on every transaction he worked on at KPMG. Make sure you can back up what you put on your resume, especially with respect to banking and finance-related jobs. The people reviewing your resume will know what general responsibilities you had as an analyst or associate, regardless of the firm.

- The experience of teaching training sessions is a great one. Joseph must be prepared, however, to answer any detailed questions on 338(h)(10) elections and non-cancelable operating leases. If he claims that he taught firm-wide sessions on these topics, he should be able to answer detailed questions about them in an interview. Failure to do so will cause the interviewer to conclude that he is overselling himself.

- Because Joseph was an analyst at Lehman, the interviewer will expect that he knows significantly more about banking and finance than those candidates without the same experience. Joseph must be prepared for more advanced technical questions.

- The Transaction Development Group is interesting but will warrant questions in the interview because it is a marketing function (the act of finding and winning business compared to executing a transaction), which is usually a more senior task. There will be concern on the part of the interviewer that Joseph did not gain much transaction experience while he was an analyst at Lehman. Therefore, he should be prepared to highlight why being part of the Transaction Development Group was beneficial to him and to emphasize that he did gain a significant amount of execution experience even though he was in a marketing-focused group. One easy way for Joseph to address this issue is to put dates regarding his participation in the Transaction Development Group so that it is clear at a glance that he did not spend all of his time at Lehman in a marketing function.

- The BankOne position is good in that it shows that the candidate has been serious about banking for some time, and that makes interviewers and screening committees more comfortable about a candidate both because it shows a candidate's (1) understanding of the job being applied for, and (2) enthusiasm for the business.

### Education

- Columbia's MBA program is strong and Wall Street banks recruit many candidates from there. Most importantly, Joseph is doing well. Any academic distinction, honor society, award, or prize is well worth noting because it is indicative of intellectual horsepower. You will not be asked to develop new algorithms for NASA in investment banking, but banking is not a simpleton's game either.

- The Field Study Project will be of interest and will warrant questions because it relates to real estate and involves international business. The interviewer will want to know whether it was a legitimate field study project or an opportunity for Joseph to party in Cancun for a week.

- The candidate did well academically at the University of Michigan. However, Joseph left off his GPA. The usual assumption, when the GPA is left off (that the GPA is low), will be neutralized somewhat by Joseph's cum laude designation and being on the Dean's list. However, it is better to include your GPA.

- Being on the swim team is a big plus since it shows that the candidate was a competitive athlete at the collegiate level. Banks like athletes and people with military experience since both show a commitment to excellence, a competitive drive, a willingness to work through hard times, an appreciation for and dedication to a "team," and an interest in non-academic activities, all of which are useful skills in banking. Most importantly it shows an ability to balance conflicting schedules and priorities.

- The University of Salamanca indicates a foreign interest, which is good since investment banks operate internationally. However, most interviewers will consider study abroad programs as opportunities for college students to take a semester off (or, in this case, a summer off) to play in a foreign country. In other words, you will not be penalized for it, but neither will you receive extra credit unless you can demonstrate how the experience has made you a better candidate. Joseph should be prepared to talk about how he made use of his time in Spain (e.g., learned to speak Spanish fluently, traveled extensively throughout Europe, etc.).

### Additional

- The comments in the Additional section show that Joseph is an interesting, well-rounded candidate, just the type banks like to hire. He is well-traveled, has lived in other countries, and speaks another language, which is a prized skill in the multinational, multilingual business of investment banking. However, interests listed in "Additional" sections are often the source of left field questions which can trip up a candidate. Remember that your interviewers come from various backgrounds and are accomplished people, and some of them may well speak the language you claim to speak or have expert knowledge of the sport, art, country, or hobby that you list. As such, list only those non-academic, non-professional interests of which you truly have knowledge or experience.

- Unless there is a specific reason you are listing where you are originally from (e.g., applying for a job with a regional bank that is located near your hometown), you should leave off your resume where you are from. If the interviewer has a sense that you may want to return to your hometown, he or she may also draw the logical conclusion that you are considering your job in New York merely as a short term stepping stone in the hope of returning to your hometown. This, especially for associate candidates, is not a positive mark since firms look at associates as multi-year hires (as compared with analyst hires which generally have a two to three year duration).

- Joseph has a five month hole in his resume, from April to September 2005. That is, he finished up at KPMG in March 2005 and began at Columbia in September 2005. This is entirely reasonable and Joseph probably quit his job at KPMG after being accepted to business school in order to travel or pursue some other personal interest. However, since his resume has a resume hole of substantial duration (nearly half a year), Joseph should be prepared to discuss what he did during this period and why. Resume holes of short duration are not likely to attract attention since the assumption will be that the candidate was simply in transition.

## Other Strategies

At the end of the day, remember that if you are a good candidate the firms will want to meet you. It is both possible and beneficial to be persistent without being annoying, and you should try as many different means of meeting people as you can. One caveat: prior to calling someone you do not know, write a letter or send an e-mail. You want to create a positive first impression and a thoughtful letter or e-mail as to who you are and why you will follow up with a phone call in the near future is your opportunity to do this properly. Simply cold calling a busy person who does not know you is the telephonic equivalent of showing up on his or her doorstep without notice, and is likely to receive the same type of response.

*Alumni:* Most people are proud of where they went to school and are often willing to do what they can to help out students from their alma mater (especially if yours is a small college that does not get much attention from the large banks). Check with your campus career center or recruiting office to get a list of alumni who work in investment banking. Call those alumni, introduce yourself, and seek their assistance in being considered for an interview with their firm. Although not everyone you contact will be willing or able to help you, most of them will, at a minimum, help direct your resume toward the person within the recruiting department who is in charge of setting up interviews, and they may even give you some idea of what to say or how to position yourself. Any information that enables you to better prepare for an interview will help you.

*Friends of friends:* If you have friends in banking, know of friends of friends in banking, or know friends of your parents or relatives who are in banking, try to get in touch with them. Similar to reaching out to alumni, if you do not know the person you are calling, just introduce yourself on the telephone, or better yet, send an introductory e-mail first asking for permission to call them. Tell him that you are so-and-so's friend and that you are very interested in banking and getting a job with his firm. If the introduction comes through someone he knows, he will spend some time with you on the phone. Remember, all you are seeking is more information about banking, the firm, and some help getting your resume to the right person. If all someone can spare is five minutes on the phone, this is more information than you began with and ultimately more help toward your cause.

***Informational interviews:*** Assuming you have been able to make contact with someone within a particular firm but you have not been able to set up an interview, ask for an informational interview. An informational interview is an informal meeting in which you come into the banker's office and discuss banking and the firm. It is an excellent way to meet people within the firm and to learn more about the firm. Although not a formal interview, you should comport yourself as if it were. An informational interview has two major benefits: you are likely to learn a lot about banking and that particular firm and, if the banker really likes you, he or she may actively promote your candidacy within the firm. Thus, you may begin with an informational interview and end with the equivalent of a positive, formal interview. Be sure to come prepared with enough questions to last twenty minutes or more; do not waste the person's time by coming unprepared.

***Cold call:*** If you do not know anyone in the firm you are targeting and you do not go to a target school for that firm, do your best to locate the name, phone number, and e-mail address of someone within the recruiting department. Send your resume to the appropriate contact person via e-mail and regular mail, then follow-up with a phone call and another e-mail. If the bank accepts electronic resumes through their website, submit your resume. Recruiting departments are often too busy to respond to resumes that are either not endorsed by someone within the firm or not from a student at a target school, especially during the recruiting season since that is their busiest time. Therefore, you must be persistent. The more persistent you are and the more firms you try, the greater your chances of landing an interview.

# The Interview Process

## Chapter 4

*Whatever you can do, or dream you can, begin it.*
*Boldness has beauty, power and magic in it.*

*Johann Wolfgang von Goethe*

## First Round Interviews

Most investment banks will conduct both a first round and a second round interview. First round interviews usually take place on campus at target schools, whereas second round interviews take place at bank headquarters. The first round interview in investment banking is extremely important and will set the stage for the half-dozen or more interviews you may have with a particular firm. During your first round interview, you will likely meet between one and three people from the investment bank who, as a group, will discuss your candidacy at the end of the day.

The people conducting your first round interview will likely be either bankers who attended your university and/or members of the firm's recruiting department. If your school is on the East Coast or in the Midwest, the interviewer probably had to wake up very early that morning to catch the first train or flight to your school. If your school is on the West Coast, your interviewer probably caught the last flight out of New York the night before, spent much of that flight working, worked in her hotel room when she arrived, and will take the red-eye back to New York at the end of the day. Regardless of your location, it is a safe bet that your interviewer was up early the morning of your interview to travel and/or review voice mails and e-mails, and will be checking in with her office frequently during the day. Your interviewer is likely to be tired and unhappy about traveling to your school to do interviews. Although most bankers care about recruiting, they would prefer that recruiting and interviewing did not take up as much time as it does. They do it because it is important and they recognize it as such, but that does not mean that they enjoy it.

Your interviewer will probably be one of three to six bankers from the firm who is on campus that day. Since each first round interview will likely last twenty to thirty minutes and most interview days will last six to eight hours, your interviewer will likely see ten to fifteen candidates the day she interviews you. A school team will interview thirty to ninety students during on campus interviews. Of these thirty to ninety students, approximately five to twenty (depending on the year and the quality of the candidates) will be invited for second round interviews. This means that of the ten to fifteen candidates your interviewer meets in one day, you must be in the top two to three in order to be recommended for a second round interview.

Try to schedule your interview early in the day. However, try not to be the first interviewee of the day since the bar against which you will be measured will be highest early in the morning (you want to be compared on a relative basis, not on an absolute basis). During the interview do not be distracted if the interviewer's cell phone or Blackberry™ goes off. Pause if you are talking so she can see who is trying to get in touch with her, then ask her if it is okay to proceed or if she needs to take the call. Your consideration will be appreciated.

## Two-On-One Interviews

Due to the cost of sending candidates to New York (or other banking headquarters) for final round interviews, some banks will do two-on-one interviews for the first round. It is easier and less expensive for the bank to send two bankers to screen candidates in the first round than to bring back too many unqualified candidates for second round interviews.

The reasons for two-on-one interviews are simple: to gather an additional viewpoint on each candidate and to see how that candidate reacts to a high-stress situation. Many two-on-one interviews will follow a "good cop, bad cop" formula in which one banker is particularly kind and helpful and the other is particularly unkind and aggressive. While the "bad cop" interviewer is probably pushing it to some extent, there are plenty of people in banking who are like this. If you cannot tolerate her aggressive behavior, investment banking may not be for you.

Both interviewers have power over your candidacy, so treat both well regardless of their titles. Be sure to maintain eye contact with both. You have, in effect, two constituencies whom you are now serving rather than just one, so be mindful of both interviewers' responses to your answers. Lastly, try to engage both interviewers so that they share a little bit about themselves. It will provide you with more information for tailoring your own answers.

## Second Round Interviews

If you are selected for a second round interview, you will be contacted within a few weeks of your first round interview. Your second round interview will likely take place in November or December and require that you fly to New York for a half- or full-day of interviews at the company's corporate headquarters. In order to minimize the disruption of hundreds of college and MBA students visiting headquarters on a weekday, most banks will schedule these second round interview days to take place on Saturday mornings, hence the term **Super Saturday**. Anywhere between five and ten Super Saturdays take place between November and January at each major investment bank and each investment banker is expected to interview or host events for recruits during those Super Saturdays. You can expect your second round interview weekend itinerary to look something like this:

## Table 4.1 - Second Round Interview Schedule

| Day | Event | Comments |
|-----|-------|----------|
| Friday | Arrive in New York City[1] | You will likely fly into New York City on Friday afternoon, unless you live in a town that has direct train service into Manhattan (e.g., Philadelphia, New Haven, etc.). You will fly coach. The firm's travel department will likely make your flight and hotel arrangements for you. |
|  | Check in to your hotel | You will take a taxi from the airport to your hotel. Your hotel will be located near the firm's headquarters and will likely be a very nice four- or five-star hotel. All meals that you eat at the hotel will be paid for by the firm. |
|  | Cocktails or dinner | Cocktails or dinner will take place either at the firm's headquarters, a bar, or a local restaurant. You will likely be accompanied by analysts if you are an undergraduate candidate and associates if you are a business school candidate. |
| Saturday | Interviewing | Interviews begin between 8 and 9 A.M. and end in the early afternoon. You will likely meet with four to seven bankers and each interview will last twenty to forty minutes. |

[1] Or other banking capital such as San Francisco or London

Remember to keep all of your receipts during your trip. The firm will reimburse you for all your business expenses, including the round trip flight, one night at a hotel, taxi rides, meals, tips, and other incidentals. During the recruiting season, your out-of-pocket expenses will increase quickly and it is your responsibility to send in receipts for reimbursement to each of the banks with which you interview. They understand that expenses can be high and add up rapidly, and are generally good about quickly reimbursing candidates for expenses.

## ˆoˆoˆ What should I pack?

- A dark-colored suit, two white or blue shirts, blue or black shoes (recently polished), a conservative looking tie (for men), at least two pairs of hosiery (for women)
- A business-casual outfit to wear to dinner or drinks on Friday night (men should wear a sports jacket)
- One casual outfit for walking around the city
- Updated copies of your resume
- Notes and other reading material you may have about the firm with which you are interviewing and the people you have previously met at the firm
- The letter from the firm inviting you to come to New York for the second round interview, including directions to the firm, the address, a contact name, and your interview schedule
- An alarm clock and a nice wrist watch
- A nice notepad and pen as well as a professional looking bag, portfolio, or briefcase to carry things to and from your interview
- A nice heavy coat and an umbrella if it is fall or winter
- Identification, credit cards, an ATM card, and at least $150 in cash

Remember your entire trip is likely to be only 36 hours and it is a business trip, so there will not be much call for items other than those listed above unless you plan to stay longer on your own tab.

## Friday Night Events

The bank will likely host you for cocktails or dinner the Friday night before the Super Saturday. Make sure that your train or flight to New York on Friday afternoon will get you into Manhattan in time to check in, relax in your hotel, and still arrive for a 7 or 8 P.M. function (including travel time to the location of the event). There will be anywhere from twenty-five to one hundred other recruits in town interviewing with the same firm that weekend. Some banks will have cocktail parties at their headquarters or at a bar, which all of the recruits in town for interviews will attend. Other banks may host school dinners, where smaller groups of candidates from certain schools will go to dinner with alumni from that school. The Friday night events tend to be more casual than the Saturday morning interviews; you should consider them an opportunity to talk more candidly with the analysts and junior associates about their experiences thus far. They are likely to have been in your shoes only a year or two ago.

Although Friday night cocktails or dinner will be more casual than your interviews Saturday morning, always consider yourself to be in an interview and comport yourself accordingly. The recruiting coordinators will ask the bankers who went out with you on Friday night their impressions of you, so if you do anything to turn somebody off, this will be noted in your interview file. Friday night will also be your first opportunity to meet some of the other recruits in town for the Super Saturday. You should treat these other recruits with respect and try your best to get to know them. A recruit who is friendly and outgoing, and who tries to make friends with the other recruits, will be noticed and appreciated by the analysts and associates. Conversely, a recruit who is arrogant, self-centered, and attention-starved will develop a bad reputation. If you want to give people a reason to talk about you, make it for positive reasons. Remember that many of these people will become your colleagues and many others will become analysts or associates at other banks. In investment banking, where information is always at a premium, it is valuable to have contacts in as many places as you can.

You should do your best to be yourself when you are out on Friday night. No one wants to work with someone whose only interest is finance or banking. Analysts and associates get enough of that at the office. When they are out for social events, their goal is to have a good time and, if you spend the entire night trying to make financial small talk with a 23 year-old first year analyst, you are not likely to score high on personality marks. Relax and have fun; just remember to be professional and to exercise good judgment at all times.

Regardless of what you do on Friday night, be sure to be in your hotel room by a reasonable hour so that you can get a good night's sleep. Spend twenty to thirty minutes reviewing your notes and preparing questions for the following morning, paying particular attention to questions that are specific to the firm that will be interviewing you. Also, before you go to bed, be sure that you know how to get to the company headquarters. If you do not know exactly how to get there, walk down to the concierge desk and ask someone to write directions for you and provide you with a map. Then set your alarm and ask for a wake-up call so there is no risk that you do not wake up in time. Wake up a few hours before you need to be at the office for the interview, and spend your morning exercising to be sure that you are awake and having breakfast so that you can review your notes again. Even if you go to bed later than you intended on Friday night, you should get up hours before your interviews to properly prepare. You can always sleep on the trip back home and, besides, if this schedule is too hectic, investment banking may not be for you. If you are in town with someone you know from your school, it is a good idea to plan to meet in the hotel lobby and walk or catch a taxi to the bank headquarters together. If your classmate is late, however, don't wait around too long and risk your own tardiness. Agree that if one is not in the lobby by a specified time, the other will proceed to the interview location alone.

## Super Saturday

You should plan to arrive at the company headquarters fifteen to twenty minutes before the interviews begin. Remember that there is absolutely nothing wrong with arriving too early, but there is a lot wrong with arriving late. While the bankers who interview you will provide the majority of the input on whether you should be hired, recruiting professionals have a fair amount of say on candidates who are at the margin. Arriving early in the morning is a great opportunity to make a positive impression on one or more of these recruiting professionals. When you arrive, there will likely be an orientation for all of the recruits at which someone from the recruiting department will describe the day's schedule and provide you with your specific interview schedule. You will meet with four to seven different people and each interview will last between twenty and forty minutes. The interview schedule generally will include the names and titles of all of your interviewers in addition to the rooms where the interviews will take place. Review this list before you get started so that you can refer to people's names at the appropriate time. In addition, many interviewers will ask you who else you have seen that morning (to see which of their colleagues have met you) and so you should have this information available.

> ### ˆʘ͡ʘˆ Reserve energy
>
> An important bit of advice for your Super Saturday is to reserve energy for your afternoon interviews. Candidates often lose steam after their second or third interview and, unfortunately, the interviews you have at the end of the day are just as important as those early in the day. Maintain energy and enthusiasm throughout the morning and rest on your trip home.

You will be interviewed by bankers of various levels and ages in addition to bankers from various parts of the investment bank (i.e., different product and industry groups). It is not likely that you will be interviewed by one of the bankers you went out with the night before. Some of the people with whom you will interview enjoy recruiting and interviewing, and some of them loathe it and do it only because they are afraid that not doing so will adversely affect their compensation. Some of them were able to get a good night's sleep the night before and some were working until 3 A.M. Some of them have a significant amount of work to do that day (and interviewing is only taking away from their time to do it) and some of them plan to meet friends or family after the interviews are finished. Since each person interviewing you has different things on his mind, you should be prepared for various personality types and interactions.

## General Interview Conduct

You must remember that you are interviewing for a job in investment banking, which is a "professional services" business. While it may sound silly to mention, it is amazing how many people comport themselves in a nonprofessional way during a banking interview. You should do your best to be courteous and respectful while appearing confident and competent. Remember that the "interview process" is an expansive term and includes any time spent with someone at the firm prior to or after the actual interview (i.e., events such as the company presentation, cocktails at a local pub, and your final sell interview are all part of the "interview process"). All impressions are important and each is potentially damaging if you are not thoughtful about your general conduct during all recruiting related events.

Most interviewers will form an impression of you within the first few minutes of meeting you. As a result, be energetic, especially during the first few minutes of your interview. It is difficult not to be drawn to someone who is energetic and passionate about who they are and what they want to do. Throughout your interview, remain enthusiastic about (1) yourself and your accomplishments; (2) the interviewer and her experiences; and (3) your objective, which is landing a job in investment banking.

Below are some basic guidelines when interviewing for a job in investment banking.

*Be enthusiastic:* The point cannot be overstated. Enthusiasm and a great attitude will take you far in life.

*Be polite and professional:* Treat the interviewer with respect and be gracious, earnest, sincere, and confident. The logical corollary is not to be arrogant, overbearing, disrespectful or a know-it-all. Bankers are professionals and should be treated as such. This type of behavior applies to everyone you meet. Assistants in the recruiting office will be administering your day and should be treated the same way you treat the head of the recruiting department.

*Engage the interviewer:* Try not to just answer questions. Instead, try to have a conversation with the interviewer. You can do this by asking the interviewer questions after you have finished giving your response. Or you can ask for clarification if you do not understand something, or circle back on a question and ask if the interviewer is satisfied with the answer.

*The interviewer's name:* Not just in interviews but whenever you are talking to someone, it is a good idea to occasionally use his or her name in the conversation. It will make the person with whom you are speaking feel more comfortable and indicate to them that you are paying attention, just be careful about overdoing it. Refer to your interviewer based on the name he uses when introducing himself to you. Do not use nicknames or truncate the name unless the interviewer introduces himself to you in this way (i.e., do not use Jon for Jonathon unless he introduced himself to you as Jon).

**Handshakes:** Shake your interviewer's hand firmly, look her in the eye and smile when you shake her hand. Be sure your hands are not sweaty before you shake her hand. There is no shortage of recruiting meetings in which certain candidates are referred to as "the guy with the sweaty palms" or something similar. You want to be remembered for your competence, not for your sweaty palms.

**Nervousness:** Even if you are nervous and uncomfortable, do your best to appear relaxed and confident. If a candidate appears nervous during an interview, the interviewer will worry about how the candidate will act during an important client meeting. Even though appearing calm when you are nervous is not easy, smiling often and appearing energetic will usually mask your nervousness. Remember, the interviewer is spending her precious weekend time interviewing you. She wants to like you, so help her do that by being comfortable with yourself.

**Age discrimination:** If the interviewer is noticeably younger than you (which may very well be the case for those interviewing for associate level positions), do not treat the interviewer as younger than you and do not act as if you have more life or work experience than him. You should treat a 25 year-old banker interviewing you in the same way you would treat a 40 year-old banker. There are many young senior associates and vice presidents who started in banking as analysts and were promoted without having gone to business school. These bankers are experienced, very good at their jobs, and often younger than 30 years old.

**Tardiness:** Under no circumstance should you arrive to your interview late. No excuse will help the situation. Most responsibilities as a first year analyst or associate revolve around finishing certain tasks and projects quickly and by a particular day or time.

**Dress professionally:** You want to dress well enough so that no one notices (*i.e.,* so that you fit in), and not so well that anyone notices (*i.e.,* not too flashy). Also, bring a professional looking folder and have extra copies of your resume with you.

**Speak professionally:** Try not to talk too quickly or too slowly. Look the interviewer in the eye at all times. Do not use words such as "yeah," "like," "totally," "you know what I mean," "a lot," "um," or "for sure." Do not be repetitive and overuse the word "really" (*e.g.,* "I really, really want this job because ..."). Do not use banker "buzzwords" such as "comps," "DCF," or "face-time" if you do not know the appropriate context in which to use them. Do not talk about heavy partying, beer drinking, smoking, or drug use.

## What Are They Looking For?

Every interviewer is looking for answers to specific questions when he is interviewing candidates. You should keep these questions in the back of your mind when preparing your interview strategy.

- Is the recruit qualified and capable of performing the job of an analyst or associate?

- Is the recruit hungry for this job? Banking is not for people who sit back and wait for opportunity to come to them; it's for people who seek out and grab opportunity.

- Is the recruit knowledgeable about the position and about the firm? Does the recruit understand the firm's direction and areas of strategic focus?

- Is the recruit confident about his or her abilities, while at the same time humble and willing to learn as much as possible?

- Does the recruit appear to be a giver or a taker? For instance, does the recruit only want to work at this firm because he or she wants to learn and gain from the experience, or does he or she want to contribute to the overall success of the firm as well?

For first and second round interviews, the interviewers fill out a summary of your interview and submit it to the recruiting department at the end of the day. This interview summary and your resume will become the first few pages of your personnel file. The summary may require the interviewer to rank you in addition to writing specific comments. Also, the summary will ask the interviewer whether she recommends inviting you in for a second round interview.

## Developing Your Story

Before getting into the details of specific interview questions, spend some time thinking critically about your qualifications and individual selling points. Draw on these to develop your individual story regarding (a) why you are interested in investment banking and (b) why you are qualified for a job in investment banking. Once you have developed your individual story, you can then begin anticipating the types of questions you will be asked in an interview. Your questions should weave together your individual story as much as possible.

# The Interviews

## CHAPTER 5

*Care and diligence bring luck.*

### *Thomas Fuller*

Various sample interview questions are provided in this chapter. Formulaic answers to these questions are intentionally left out. You are being tested on your knowledge of material, *not* on how well you can memorize black box answers. Professionals strongly dislike books and other resources that spoon-feed answers to potential candidates. The interviewer is trying to peel back the onion to get to know you better and canned answers make it very difficult to do this, not to mention that canned answers make you sound like a robot. You are being judged on how well you think, not on how well you can regurgitate information. Preparing for an interview includes anticipating what questions may be asked. It does not, however, include someone else thinking for you or providing you with answers that interviewers may want to hear. Such resources or crutches are not likely to be available to you when you begin working. Said differently, if you get a job based on someone else's answers, *you* didn't really earn the job. Do your best to find our own voice – in interviews and with all things in life.

---

**ˆOOˆ Getting the answers to interview questions**

At a major investment bank there was a case in which a first year analyst out of ABC College wrote up a list of common interview questions and "good answers to these questions." The analyst then provided these questions and scripted answers to analyst candidates from his alma mater, ABC College. The matter came to the attention of a vice president. The analyst was reprimanded and the investment bank created a new set of interview questions for ABC College. Ironically, by trying to help the cause of ABC College analyst candidates, the analyst did those same analyst candidates a disservice since, from that point on, the ABC College candidates faced a new, more difficult, set of interview questions.

There are certain qualities that signal likely success in investment banking and certain qualities that signal likely failure. The interviewer is looking for clues from you and your resume that indicate whether you possess the qualities they are seeking. Those qualities and some sample questions that are intended to draw out each trait are listed in the following pages. When answering interview questions, it is a good idea to break the question up into three distinct parts: (1) provide some sort of situational summary so the interviewer understands the context of your story or example; (2) answer the question succinctly, describing the actions you took to achieve your goal; and (3) summarize the results.

## Analytical Skills

Most of the work of a first year analyst or associate includes building financial models, performing financial analyses, and creating presentations to be used in client meetings. Analytical skills are critical because much of the model building and analysis involves gathering massive amounts of financial data about a particular company and using or analyzing this data to draw conclusions such as how much the company is worth, whether the company is being properly valued in the marketplace, and or what type of security (e.g., stock or bond) the company should issue to fund a growth strategy. As the job title "analyst" implies, strong analytical skills are a must for anyone interested in a career in investment banking, so be prepared for questions that challenge your ability to think critically as well as your understanding of basic financial concepts. When asked an analytical or technical question, be sure to listen carefully to the question and answer slowly and logically. Be completely honest about your technical experience or financial knowledge. The more knowledge you claim to have, the more your interviewer is likely to challenge that knowledge. Ultimately, when it comes to analytical skills, the interviewer wants to know if you can think through a question critically and come to a conclusion using your existing knowledge base and tools. At its core, this is what you will be doing on the job as an analyst or associate. If you do not have enough information to answer a question, ask questions to better understand where the interviewer is going with it.

When answering an analytical or technical question, it is a good idea to break down your answer into two or three components or points. Summarize those points before you delve into the details, then refer back to those points as you go further into your answer. This will show that you not only understand the material but can also explain yourself logically and clearly. For example, consider the question *"What issues should be considered when valuing a company?"*

There are countless issues that could be considered, but it is best to respond with an answer that allows you to be concise and thoughtful versus an answer that is an unfocused laundry list of potential issues. For instance, a good response would be:

*"Based on my experience at [former employer], valuing a company is not a science. There are countless issues to consider when performing a valuation analysis, some of which will be specific to the industry or the company in question. However, as with all things, there are two to three issues to consider that are fundamental in valuing any company. Based on my previous experience, I believe the three most important factors are (a) the growth prospects of the company; (b) the business risk of the company, especially as it relates to the company's cash flows, and (c) the company's competitive position within its industry. I will further describe each of these three considerations in detail."*

Then you can go on to explain how each of these three factors affects a company's valuation. Obviously there are other factors that are important; however, the interviewer wants to hear how you think and a response that begins like this shows that you (1) understand the question being asked; (2) can quickly access your personal tool chest to answer it; and (3) can systematically and clearly describe your point of view. Once you begin working with clients, you will often be asked your point of view on various things related to the work you are doing, the general financial markets, the likelihood that a particular sports team will make it to the playoffs, or a noteworthy book or Broadway musical. Regardless of the question at hand, the interviewer wants to ensure that you can respond logically and thoughtfully.

### Sample Analytical Questions

- You are starting a copy shop business. What analysis would you perform in order to decide whether it is a good business idea? How would you consider raising funds for your new venture?

- How does a company grow?

- How would you think about selling a plumbing business?

- How can an educational software company with no earnings have a high stock value?

- Do you own any stock? If so, how did you decide to make this investment?

- Assume you are the CEO of a small public company and that you have been approached by a larger competitor who wants to purchase your company for cash. What things would you need to consider in making this decision?

- If you were hired to help open a Starbucks or Krispy Kreme on campus, what would you need to consider?

- If you won $50 million in the state lottery, how much cash will you receive in a lump-sum payment?

- What is a derivative?

- If you had $100 million to invest, what would you do with it and why?

## Communication Skills

Strong written and verbal communication skills are as important as strong analytical skills. A good investment banker is able to simply and eloquently describe to a colleague or to a client his point of view about various types of financial matters. Also, he will be required to write presentations, memos, letters and e-mails, among other things. The analyst or associate who cannot express himself well will have a difficult time with these tasks. It is not enough to be technically gifted with numbers since "quant jocks" without complementary communication skills do not go far in banking. Said differently, it is no use getting to the right answer if you cannot convey it.

Your communication skills will be judged throughout your interview while other skills will be measured based on how you answer specific questions. Always speak slowly and clearly, and pause to consider each question rather than quickly rattling off an answer. It is often a good idea to respond with phrases such as, *"That is a good question"* or *"That is something I have given much thought to"* or *"I don't have much experience with that particular subject matter, however based on what I know about it, I think ..."* Starting off with phrases like these allows you to set the tone for what you are about to say, and pacing yourself is important because it gives you time to clarify what you want to say.

### Sample Communication Questions

- What are your three greatest weaknesses?

- Why should we hire you?

- What other jobs are you interviewing for and why are you considering these jobs?

- Which other firms are interviewing you?

- Why did you not get an offer from the firm you worked with last summer?

- Have you ever been criticized? If so, describe the situation and your response.

- I see from your resume that you speak Russian and Spanish fluently. Do you mind if we speak for a while in Russian?

- If you have so much responsibility at your current job, why do you want to leave?

- What is your GPA and why is it not listed on your resume?

- Why do you think your SAT score from the 11th grade is a relevant indicator of your professional success?

- What experience can you point to which has, in some way, prepared you for a job in banking?

- Do you want to be a banker in ten years?

## Leadership

Bankers must be willing and able to take initiative and control in a challenging situation since circumstances will surely arise when a deal is not going as originally planned and you will need to find a resolution. It is important that you are someone who can take control of a group situation and make decisions that positively affect the team. Soon after you begin working, you will be in situations in which you will need to direct others to do something that affects a client. It is important that, in such situations, you are able to: (1) clearly explain your goal or purpose; (2) delegate tasks; (3) communicate a message; (4) handle yourself well in a high stress situation; and (5) demonstrate other skills that exemplify an effective leader.

Your interviewer will be looking for examples of your leadership skills such as having managed others, having held an elected or appointed office in a club or association, or having been elected captain of an athletic team. Prior to every banking interview, you should have prepared two to three examples of situations in which you displayed leadership qualities so that you can refer to these situations during your interview. Especially helpful are examples in which you found yourself in a challenging situation (e.g., your group needed to deliver a presentation to the department head in two days and nothing had been prepared, or an angry client demanded an emergency meeting the next morning to discuss an error in a financial model) and in which you were able to effectively rise above the situation and guide your team to a successful conclusion.

### Sample Leadership Questions

- Tell me about a situation in which you held a leadership position.

- What is your leadership style?

- Describe a time when your group was faced with a challenging situation. What did you do to remedy the situation?

- Are you better at leading a group or taking directions?

- Describe how you feel about the statement "It is the leader who makes the team."

- Have you ever worked with a team that lacked leadership?

## Integrity and Character

Good character is extremely important to professional services firms, especially in a market environment in which companies ranging from investment banks to accounting firms to insurance companies are being investigated and, in some cases, criminally charged for wrongdoings. As a banker you will be representing the firm in front of clients, other banks, and the general public; the bank interviewing you wants to ensure that the people representing it are respectful, have sound judgment and, if put into a compromising situation, would choose to do the "right" thing even if it meant sacrificing money or business for the firm. Investment banks live and die by their reputations and, as a result, they take all things related to reputation very seriously. Firms have been known to fire perfectly capable bankers if they believe the person's personal conduct is inconsistent with the values of the firm.

Be prepared to discuss experiences in which you were put into compromising situations and how you handled yourself during those situations. The interviewer will look for clues about your character. Do not speak badly about other people or other firms; this may indicate to the interviewer how you may talk in the future about his firm. Even if the interviewer talks badly about another firm, do not follow his lead. Just move on to your next point.

### *Sample Integrity and/or Character Questions*

- Describe a situation in which you were faced with a challenging moral decision and how you responded to the situation.

- Describe a challenging situation in which you did not have the experience to address the problem on your own.

- Whom do you admire and why?

- Have you ever worked with someone you did not like?

- Have you ever worked on something you did not believe in?

- Describe a situation in which you failed in what you originally set out to do.

- Would you report misconduct?

- Would you tell your team if you did a piece of analysis incorrectly rather than hiding it in the hope that nobody finds out?

- Would you advise a client to do what is best for the client rather than what will make the most money for the bank?

## Team Player

Throughout your banking career, you will be working in a team environment; those who do not perform well in a team setting will not do well in banking. The interviewer will be looking for evidence of teamwork experience and your ability to collaborate in a team setting (this includes being both a leader and a follower, depending on the situation). She will be looking for decision-making experiences that involved more than one person and will want to ensure that you are not the type of person who thrives on always being the center of attention. She will also try to determine whether you are the type of person who wants to win for your own sake or for the team's sake.

It is important to display flexibility and openness when working with new people. In looking for evidence of being a good team player, interviewers are fundamentally looking for a good attitude. If you have a good attitude, you will recognize that you are in a client business and need to help out whenever and however necessary to better serve the client. Analysts and associates who often ask what more they can do to help out their deal team are highly regarded. The interviewer will be looking for evidence of your ability to look beyond personal goals in order to advance the goals of the group. Stepping down and doing tasks that are usually done by someone junior to you, working through the night to meet a deadline, and missing an important personal engagement because you did not want to leave your team until the job was done are all good examples of being a team player. Also, your attitude during the interview will be an important signal: if you come across as arrogant or a know-it-all, the interviewer will likely assume that you are not the type to help or perform menial tasks when required to do so.

### Sample Teamwork Questions

- Describe an important situation in which you worked as part of a team.

- Have you been part of a team that lacked direction or did not work well?

- What was your favorite class in college/business school and why?

- In your view, what are the elements of success of a team?

## Attention To Detail

As an analyst or associate, you are being paid to pay attention to the details. This means that the senior people working with you trust that you are taking the extra time to review every document that goes to a client. It may sound ridiculous, but analysts and associates get yelled at for footnotes that are not properly numbered, words that are misspelled, formatting that is incorrect, and commas that are misplaced in numbers, among other things. In fact, some bankers joke that presentation books are like coloring books since much of your time as an analyst or associate is spent taking care of things like formatting, color coordination, and font styles.

But you must remember that any error (regardless of the magnitude) takes away from the *perception* of the quality of advice given to a client. The reason that a senior person will get mad if a word is misspelled is that the work product she is sharing with the client is a reflection of her and of the bank. No client wants to take a chance on a bank that cannot spell check its own presentations.

### Sample Attention to Detail Questions

- What is more important, managing several tasks at once but making a few mistakes, or managing fewer tasks and making fewer mistakes?

- How many classes are you taking this semester and how well are you doing in all of them?

- Have you ever been criticized for submitting reports and/or papers with a number of misspellings or grammatical errors?

## Work Ethic and Dependability

Analysts and associates must be results oriented. They need to be capable of finishing the task at hand, whatever it may be. The interviewer will be looking for examples of situations in which you were presented with a challenge and worked through it to a successful conclusion, regardless of how many hours it took and how many personal engagements you had to sacrifice to get the job done. You should strive to share any particular experience in which your focus and determination led to a successful outcome. Your job in banking will be filled with such challenges and any past experience you have with such situations will help your candidacy.

### Sample Work Ethic and Dependability Questions

- Where are you from and how did you get here?

- Have you ever walked away from a project?

- Do you think like an owner or like an employee?

- What are your expectations of the hours and the lifestyle in investment banking?

- Describe a situation in which you "did what the job required."

## Understanding the Business

Many analysts and associates enter investment banking without fully understanding what they are getting into. As a result, when work becomes difficult and stressful, those who are surprised by the lifestyle become disillusioned quickly. This is why interviewers want to make sure that candidates know what they are getting into with respect to the job they will be doing, the responsibilities that will be placed upon them, and the lifestyle they will be living. It is in neither your interest nor the bank's interest – since it is investing thousands of dollars to interview and potentially train you – for you to quit six months after you take the job. Banks want to be sure that if they hire you, you will stick around. If you do not have a good understanding of the business when you start out, the likelihood of your quitting is higher than for those who know what they are getting into.

### Sample Understanding the Business Questions

- Why do you want to be an investment banker?

- Tell me what you think an investment bank does.

- What product or industry groups are of interest to you?

- Tell me about a recent M&A deal that you thought was interesting and why.

- What is it about Wall Street that interests you?

## Cultural Fit

Every company or organization has a "culture." This is a notoriously slippery concept since there are ten of thousands of employees in each of the major banks and, of course, they are not all the same. Rather, the question of "cultural fit" has to do with the overall tone with which a bank approaches business. A bank's culture, while very real, is nebulous since it is difficult to neatly package thousands of different people into a single adjective such as "competitive" or "hard-nosed" or "patrician." While cultural fit is something that all banks seek to ensure, what it really means in an interview context is whether the interviewer believes that you are the type of person he or she would like to have as a colleague.

### *Sample Cultural Fit Questions*

- Why do you want to work at ABC bank?

- Why did you choose XYZ college/business school?

- What do you think are ABC Bank's greatest weaknesses?

- Which companies do you admire and why?

- Do you prefer to be the star of the show or a supporting cast member?

- Do you prefer to work alone or in a team environment?

- Do you like hierarchy?

- Describe what you did during your summer internship. Did you get an offer? If you did, why are you not going to work for them? If you did not get an offer, why didn't you?

## Preparing For the Interview

Below are additional suggestions for preparing for an interview. Many of these suggestions require significant work up front but, like many things, after the initial investment you will continue to benefit from your efforts without significant additional work.

- Prepare and maintain a running list of possible interview questions. Prior to your next interview, write out your own answers to sample questions and then practice responding to the questions in front of a friend, family member, video camera, or mirror. You will be surprised at how poorly you are likely to answer them out loud on the first try. Don't worry. The purpose of practicing is so that the first, not-so-great effort is in the safety of your own home. More importantly, when you have to do it in a real interview, you will know what you are going to say and how it will sound because you will have practiced. Going forward, spend the first fifteen minutes after each interview writing down the questions you were asked so you can build upon the list you have already created. Do this immediately after an interview, while the questions are still fresh in your mind. Creating flash cards with one question per card is another good way to practice answering questions.

- Know your resume inside and out; anything on your resume is fair game. If you cannot talk about an experience enthusiastically, it does not belong on your resume. Remember that the interviewer does not know you. All he has to go on is whatever you have put on that one piece of paper. You cannot be surprised by any question related to your resume.

- Be prepared to answer basic finance and accounting questions, especially if you are an MBA candidate or a business, accounting, or finance undergraduate. And for those who are non-business majors, you are not expected to know the same level of detail as your peers who have studied accounting and finance in school, but you are on the hook for understanding the basics. Even if you have not taken a corporate finance class in school, if you are interested in working on Wall Street, you should at least be able to talk generally about valuation, capital structure, the market, and the economy. After all, those are elements of the industry for which you are interviewing.

- Know the details about some recent M&A transactions and major securities offerings so that you can speak intelligently about current events in the market and, ideally, some transactions in which the bank with which you are interviewing has participated. Also, if there are major transactions taking place in the market at the time of your interview that much of the financial community is talking about (e.g., the Google IPO in the summer of 2004, the WorldCom and Enron accounting scandals in 2002 and 2003, etc.), be prepared to speak about those intelligently.

- Toward the end of an interview you will be asked if you have any questions. Be sure to have one and be sure that it is not a generic question. Also make sure the question is not redundant, meaning if you already discussed the topic earlier in the interview, do not bring it up again. Instead, ask a question that relates to and is an extension of something you have already talked about. This indicates to the interviewer that you are engaged and paying attention. The most interesting questions are those that relate to the time you and the interviewer spent together because it makes the interview feel more like a conversation than a series of questions.

# Receiving an Offer

## Chapter 6

*Every calling is great when greatly pursued.*

*Oliver Wendell Holmes Jr.*

## Thank You Notes

It is a good idea to send a quick follow-up note or e-mail to the person (or people) who interviewed you. A follow-up note thanking the interviewer for his or her time is both courteous and intelligent; it serves to remind the interviewer who you are and to underscore your good manners and enthusiasm for the job. This is especially important if you get an offer because the more people you know at the bank when you start the job, the better. Since hiring decisions are often made soon after each Super Saturday, send your thank you note via e-mail as soon as possible. An example is provided below.

**To:** alyssa.reiss@bank.com
**From:** henry.peet@university.edu
**Date:** November 15, 2005
**Re:** our interview

Alyssa,

Thank you for taking the time to meet with me today regarding an associate position with your firm. I especially enjoyed hearing about your transition from the West Coast to New York. As we discussed, I believe that my previous experience as a financial analyst in the Corporate Finance Department at PepsiCo provided me with unique insight into the way corporate clients think – just as your experience at Mars did for you prior to business school. I look forward to hearing from you.

Best,
Henry Peet

510-579-2254

## Hiring Decisions

The firm will probably decide whether to extend an offer sometime during the week after your Super Saturday. Each of the bankers who interviewed candidates will get together with a small group of four to seven other bankers (all of whom interviewed the same group of candidates) to discuss and recommend which candidates to hire. If the group interviewed four to seven candidates, one or two of those candidates will likely stand out as excellent, with a group consensus to hire them. Similarly, there will likely be one or two candidates whom the group agrees should not be extended an offer. After those three or four candidates have been singled out, most of the discussion will be spent on the two to three candidates on whom the group is split. Those bankers who are in favor of hiring the "on-the-fence" candidates will make a case for hiring them; those who were not impressed will make a case for not hiring them. If you are an on-the-fence candidate, the specific qualities you exhibited during your interview will be highlighted during this time.

This small group will first submit its recommendations to the recruiting department, then to a small **decision committee**. The decision committee, comprised of recruiting staff and senior bankers from various product and industry groups, will review the recommendations, then decide which candidates from the previous weekend's Super Saturday will receive an offer. This decision committee meeting will likely take place some time during the week after Super Saturday.

## Offers

If you are to receive an offer, most firms will contact you via telephone immediately after the decision has been made. Usually someone from the school team or the recruiting department will call you to share the news. If you are not to receive an offer, the bank may call you or write you with the news. Whether you receive good or bad news, be gracious and professional and take the time to thank the firm for the interview.

Expect to get your formal written offer in the mail within a week or two after your verbal offer and, if you have not received it within two weeks, call the recruiting department to request that it be faxed to you. Do not accept the position until you have read the details of your offer. Remember that this is a contract you are about to sign.

Your written offer should include the following:

- *An invitation to join the firm.* At this stage, it may or may not be for a particular group. For analysts the offer will likely be for two years. For associates the offer will not indicate a finite period of time.

- *Your starting salary.* The language will likely be vague with regard to the bonus portion of your compensation.

- *Your signing bonus.* Which will be sent to you when you agree to join the firm.

- *Health benefits.* Your offer letter will include basic information about benefits.

- *The **drop-dead date*** or the date by which you need to accept or decline your offer. Your offer will expire after this date if you do not accept or negotiate an extension.

- *Information about your upcoming **sell day,*** which is a day you will return to the firm to meet more people and for those people to "sell" you on working for their firm as opposed to accepting a competing offer.

- *A place for you to sign*, thereby accepting the terms of the offer and agreeing to work for the firm. As soon as you have made your decision, sign the offer letter, return the original executed copy to the recruiting department, and keep a copy for your files.

## If You Do Not Receive an Offer

If you do not receive an offer, ask for feedback from those with whom you interviewed regarding what you can do to increase your chances of landing a job either with a different division within the same bank or with another bank. Wall Street is a small place in many ways and both bankers and recruiters are often aware of other opportunities. If the bankers liked you, they may recommend you for another position – in a different department within the same firm (e.g. in Private Client Services or Equity Research) or at another firm. By being consistently upbeat and appreciative, you will give people more reason to want to help you.

Let's assume you have gone through an entire recruiting season and have tried everything possible to land a job with one of the major or regional investment banks, but without success. Do not despair. If you are truly committed to breaking into investment banking, tenacity and persistence will pay off. And you can always wait until a period of robust hiring activity to try to land a job. Lateral hires are not uncommon, especially in boom years when the banks have more business to be transacted than bodies to perform the work. However, gaining work experience that is complementary to banking is a critical first step.

There are countless small to medium sized investment banks and advisory firms across the country. A number of these smaller firms perform advisory services ranging from M&A advice to help on restructurings and bankruptcies. Smaller firms generally work with smaller companies, but the work and analysis performed at a small firm is the same as the work at a large firm.

Landing a job at a smaller or regional firm can also be challenging since fewer positions are available than at the larger firms. In addition, smaller firms generally do not have formal recruiting programs and tend to hire when they need someone as opposed to as part of the traditional recruiting season. Therefore, learning whether a particular firm is looking to hire someone can be difficult unless you know someone at the firm (or know someone who knows someone). Cold-calling and sending in your resume to the smaller firms are the best ways to get in touch with them. Reviewing trade journals and trade press releases to get a feel for which firms are growing and hiring and then contacting a partner or director at the firm are other ways to get your foot in the door. Although landing a job at a smaller firm can be challenging, it can also be worthwhile. The responsibilities are often great and the atmosphere is often less competitive than at the major firms. Many successful bankers begin at smaller firms and transfer to larger firms later in their careers.

## Choosing a Firm

Landing a job in investment banking is not easy, but it is nothing compared to the work you have ahead of you. The job of a banking analyst or associate is challenging and demanding. It will not always be fun and you will not always believe that you made the right decision by coming to Wall Street. That said, working at a firm you are proud of and where you are an integral member of the team will go a long way toward balancing some of the hard times you will inevitably encounter once you begin working.

The projects, deals, training, clients, hours, lifestyle, and compensation for a first-year analyst or associate will be similar at all of the major investment banks. However certain nuances exist at each bank with regard to the people and the general working environment which, as a whole, may allow you to have a different experience at one bank versus another. This is not to say that the decision to go to a particular bank will affect you for the rest of your life. In fact, if you are not happy where you are working, during good economic times it is fairly straightforward to get a job at another firm ("lateral" hires are common at the associate and vice president levels). However, take care and spend time in choosing which firm to join because, if you like the firm and the people with whom you work, the lifestyle and the hours will not seem so painful.

Ultimately, you should go to a firm where you feel most comfortable. You should form your own opinion of each bank based on your personal experiences with the people you meet at each firm, not based on rumors you hear from other people, websites, or trade journals. And do not place a lot of stock in comments bankers make about other banks. They are biased and have an incentive for you to develop negative feelings toward other firms. Since they have chosen to work at one particular firm, they naturally want to believe that their firm is the best. Also, do not pay much attention to **league tables**, or rankings of the investment banks based on criteria like volume of equity offerings and M&A deals advised on, especially if the bank that is trying to hire you shows them to you. Over the course of your career you will learn that it is the people with whom you work, specifically the mentors who take an interest in you and the friends you make, who make the difference with respect to your experience at a particular firm, not the firm's place in the league tables or what you read about the bank in the *New York Times* or the *Wall Street Journal.*

## ʻOʻOʻ League tables

Once you begin working, you will learn that creating league tables is an art, not a science, and a highly edited one at that. All of the major investment banks are leaders in certain products or industries, and it is precisely this that makes them *major* investment banks. Do not be swayed, therefore, by league table positions. One big deal can significantly reorder a league table.

In addition to the people factor, a few other factors can help inform your decision-making process. You should consider programs and policies that each bank offers and decide whether these policies affect your career goals. For instance, for analyst candidates, if you have a strong interest in going to business school, it may not be very important to you that one bank promotes more analysts directly to the associate level than another bank. It may, however, be of interest to you that one bank has a higher percentage of analysts attending top-rated business schools than another bank. It may also be relevant if a particular bank will pay for you to go to business school and guarantee to hold your job for the two years you are away. If you have a strong interest in working in an M&A group and one particular bank has guaranteed you a position in M&A, this may be a factor worthy of consideration. Or, if you have a strong interest in working abroad at some point, you may want to consider a bank that has a formal international rotation program in place versus a bank that does not have such programs or where it may be difficult to transfer out of your group once you begin working.

In summary, you are looking for the firm that is right for *you*, not the firm that is right for your best friend or the firm your older brother chose just a few years ago. Just as the best bottle of wine for *you* is the one which you like the best, not the one most highly rated by a reputable wine magazine or the most expensive, the best firm for *you* is the one which you like the best, not necessarily the "biggest" or "oldest" or "most prestigious." The lesson is that personal fit does matter at a bank. In fact, it is one of the characteristics the bank applied in assessing your candidacy for the firm. You should take the time to consider your options, make an educated decision based on all of the facts and, once you have made your decision, proceed forward without looking back. It is still very early in your career and, if it does not work out for you at any one particular firm, there are many other companies and many other careers out there.

## Accepting Offers

Once you have made your decision, call all the people at the bank (at which you have decided to accept an offer) who played a role in your decision making process to inform them of your decision, to thank them for their help, and to let them know you are looking forward to working with them. Also, if any of these people work in groups that you are considering, now would be a good time to learn more about those groups and to get the names of analysts and associates in those groups whom you can call. Be sure the list of people you call at the bank includes the recruiting coordinator you dealt with most closely and the banker who heads up your school's recruiting team. And don't forget to sign your offer letter. Keep a copy for yourself and send the original back to the firm at which you are accepting a position.

## Declining Offers

You should also call each of the other firms that extended you an offer to let them know you have decided to pursue another opportunity. Thank them for their consideration and tell them that you hope to have the opportunity to cross paths with them again. Call everyone who played a major role in your recruiting process.

Wall Street is very small, so decline offers graciously. You will come across other bankers and recruiters frequently, either working with them as a co-advisor on a transaction, working across the table from them if they are representing the firm with which your client is interacting, or at a campus recruiting function. Also, it may be the case that it does not work out for you at the bank you have chosen and you apply as a lateral hire to those banks that you declined. As such, don't burn any bridges – you never know when you may need to cross them again.

# PART II
## LIFE FOR A JUNIOR BANKER

# The Hours

## Chapter 7

*The heights by great men reached and kept*
*were not attained by sudden flight,*
*but they while their companions slept,*
*were toiling upward in the night.*

### Henry Wadsworth Longfellow

There is no such thing as a typical day in investment banking. In fact, with respect to your schedule and your lifestyle, there is only one thing that you can be absolutely certain of during your first few years as an analyst or associate: you will be working all of the time. This is no joking matter. Books, movies, and recruiters have and will continue to glamorize the life of the young banker, lawyer, strategic consultant, doctor, White House staffer ... the list goes on. The romance they try to sell is that if you work very hard your first few years on the job, your sweat and tears will pay off both personally and professionally.

It is important to understand two very important facts with respect to banking and the hours you work. First, not only are the hours bad, the hours are really bad. And second, the hours do not get substantially better after your first few years; in fact, they get worse. The reason for this is that the pressures and responsibilities increase as you move up the ladder. As a senior banker you report to people who are higher up the food chain and they are invariably more demanding and less tolerant than those down below. Thus, while senior bankers might spend less overall time in the office, they spend just as much time "on the job" and are also more important actors in the overall process, so the expectations are greater.

There really is no average workweek for a junior banker, which is both the best and worst thing about the job. On the one hand you will never be bored, but on the other hand you can seldom plan your schedule. During the first few years as an analyst or associate, you will work anywhere from 70 to 120 hours per week. The following table shows a ninety-hour workweek and, while there is no "typical" week, this table describes fairly well many weeks spent by countless junior bankers.

## Table 7.1 – A Sample Workweek

| Day | In | Out | Hours | Comments |
|-----|-----|-----|-------|----------|
| Monday | 8 a.m. | 12 a.m. | 16 | Monday morning group meeting, needed to be in by 8 a.m. |
| Tuesday | 9 a.m. | 1 a.m. | 16 | Went to the gym for an hour during the day; ate lunch with group members in the building cafeteria |
| Wednesday | 9 a.m. | 1 a.m. | 16 | No time for the gym, but attended a recruiting dinner from 7 to 9 p.m. |
| Thursday | 9 a.m. | 2 a.m. | 17 | Late night, needed to process changes to books for Friday morning team distribution |
| Friday | 10 a.m. | 9 p.m. | 11 | Slept in a little bit; out in time for dinner with friends at 9:30 p.m. |
| Saturday | 11 a.m. | 7 p.m. | 8 | Slept in a lot; out in time for a movie with friends at 8:30 p.m. |
| Sunday | 1 p.m. | 7 p.m. | 6 | Conference call didn't start until 1 p.m.; had brunch with friends before going to the office; conference call ended at 3 p.m.; a few more hours of work to make sure Monday wasn't a disaster lurking; arrived home in time to do laundry, watch TV, and finally go through the week's personal mail |
| **Total** | | | **90** | |

By any junior banker's standards, this 90-hour workweek would be considered normal. During this particular week, although you worked past midnight Monday through Thursday, you were also able to make (and keep) social plans both Friday and Saturday night, in addition to the coveted Sunday morning brunch. As a junior analyst or associate, you relish being able to maintain any semblance of a social life. Although this is a busy workweek by any person's standards, junior bankers live and die by workweeks like this. If this schedule turns you off, banking is not for you. If, on the other hand, it simply scares you, don't worry, you'll get used to it and you'll be so busy most of that time that you'll forget to count how many hours you have worked during a given week. In addition, you'll be learning a highly portable skill set upon which you can depend for the rest of your life.

> ## ʌ‾O‾O‾ʌ What is downtime?
>
> **Downtime** is a period of time when you have nothing to do on your primary projects. There is a lot of downtime in banking. The reason junior bankers in corporate finance or advisory groups work late into the evening or through the weekend is often because they may not have been provided with comments and/or direction from senior bankers until late in the day. Senior bankers spend much of the business day either on the phone with clients or traveling to visit clients. As a result, there can be a multi-hour lag from the time a client asks for something and the time that request is conveyed to the junior members of the team. This means that on some days there is a fair amount of downtime during normal business hours followed by a mad rush to meet a deadline during the evening. This is not the case, however, for junior bankers in groups that are more market-driven, such as capital markets, equity research, or sales and trading. In these groups, there is little downtime during the day.

## A Reality Check

Although working in a corporate finance or advisory group means that you will usually work fairly late into the evening, there are some weeknights when you are out of the office by 7 p.m. or, if not out of the office by 7 p.m., you are able to spend an hour-and-a-half at the gym, an hour in a conference room with colleagues eating dinner, and a half-hour on the phone catching up with the folks at home. There will be some weekends when you do not have to come into the office at all, although you may have to participate in a conference call from home and/or do some work remotely. Also, you will inevitably be checking voicemail every three to four hours throughout the weekend. The flip side is there also will be times when you are in the office all night, you will go home in a car at 7 a.m., have the car wait so you can shower and change clothes, and then return in that same car to the office so that you're ready for an 8 a.m. meeting with your team. And, unfortunately, there are some really ugly nights when you do not even have enough time to run home and shower prior to beginning the next business day. All-nighters are generally occasioned by **fire drills**, which are intense bursts of frenzied work to fulfill a client's or senior banker's urgent request. The all-nighter generally ends by 6 p.m. the following day, which means you will not have slept for nearly 35 hours.

## ʼ◯◯ʼ Do you really pull all-nighters?

All-nighters actually happen, and they happen often. Unfortunately, the all-nighters you pulled in college are not likely to compare to the all-nighters you will pull in banking. Banking all-nighters are stressful and ugly. They can make you sick (usually figuratively and occasionally literally) and cause you to spend the night contemplating your plans to resign once the fire drill is over. Having anywhere between one and five all-nighters per month is not uncommon during your first few years in banking. This number would be toward the higher end in M&A, and toward the lower end for capital markets. All-nighters are a terrible experience, but you get through them, often amazed and proud at how much you and your team were able to accomplish in such a short period of time. And as difficult as any all-nighter is, it is rare for a resignation to emerge the next morning. And even if you were to offer it, the resignation would likely be turned down because your team would recognize that the desire to resign is an outgrowth of a lack of sleep, too much work, and consistent stress. With the right attitude, all-nighters can have a silver lining – sunrises are beautiful from a high-level floor of any big city building!

Regardless of how long you work during any particular day, you are rarely going at 100 percent the entire day if you are working in a corporate finance group. If you are working in a market-driven group, you may be going 100 percent during the day but you will also be able to leave the office much earlier than your friends in corporate finance. For an advisory banker, one day might be extremely hectic, requiring running around and having to get ten things done in the span of two hours, while another day might last fifteen hours but involve a long lunch, a few Starbucks breaks, and a trip to the gym.

The most difficult thing about a banking job is not so much the absolute number of hours but the unpredictability of those hours. It is almost impossible to regularly make plans for a Saturday night, let alone plan for weekend trips or weeklong vacations (nearly every banker has had to cancel vacations – some just days before leaving and some mid-trip, requiring a return trip straight to the office). You simply never know when you will need to work until 2 a.m. and when you will be able to get out at 7 p.m. since your day will depend on your client's or senior banker's day. As a result of this unpredictability, it's almost impossible to have any confidence in plans to see friends, significant others, or family until the day of an event. Some of your friends and family will understand the magnitude of the hours you work and the lifestyle you lead (although many will think you are exaggerating), but many will not understand unless they themselves are also in the business. The hours are punishing and many personal sacrifices are required, but the professional education is outstanding.

## Lifestyle Expectations

Senior bankers will expect you to:

- Always be "on call" and available nights, weekends, and holidays
- Work long hours
- Cut vacations short if they need you back at the office
- Constantly check voicemail and e-mail when you are not physically in the office, so often, in fact, that you can count on rolling over in bed every Saturday and Sunday morning throughout your banking career checking your voicemail and e-mail. You will dread it (there is nothing worse than thinking you have the weekend free and then finding out at 8 a.m. on Saturday morning that you need to be in the office by 10 a.m.), but it will gradually become a part of your existence.

> **◯◯ What is face time?**
>
> **Face time** is the act of staying around the office longer to *appear* busier than you actually are. Junior bankers are afraid to go home before their staffers due to fear of being put on a new project the next day. Whether there is a lot of face time in your schedule depends on the senior people with whom you work.

This emphasis on hours is not meant to scare you but to inform you. More often than not, first year analysts and associates begin careers in banking with a false sense of what their lifestyles will be like. In fact, a high percentage of people ultimately quit after their first or second year precisely because the lifestyle and the personal sacrifice is too much for them, regardless of the potential reward.

The hours described here may seem like a very high price to pay. In return, however, you will gain remarkable business experience and a level of credibility in the business world that you will be able to capitalize on throughout your career. More importantly, you will work with interesting people with varied backgrounds and you will develop lifelong friendships with many of them. Although the hours and the lifestyle are difficult, they will likely transpire into a great investment. Think of it as investing money for retirement: it has a long time to compound, and it's all for your benefit.

# Corporate Policies

## CHAPTER 8

*The whole of what we know is a system of compensations,*
*each suffering is rewarded;*
*each sacrifice is made up;*
*every debt is paid.*

### Ralph Waldo Emerson

This chapter describes the most relevant corporate policies for analysts and associates in investment banking. The chapter is organized into three major categories: (1) in the office; (2) out of the office; and (3) other policies. These descriptions are intended as an overview and to provide a framework for when you begin working. It is important to remember that each bank has its own corporate policies related to these items and that corporate policies evolve over time.

> ### ⏱ Benefits track economic cycles
>
> In times of severe budgetary restraint (i.e., when the market is bad) corporate policies may be somewhat curtailed (e.g., meal allowances are reduced, cars are only allowed very late at night, etc.). Conversely, during times of economic euphoria corporate policies may be enhanced (e.g., concierge services, business or first-class travel allowed for domestic flights, etc.).

## In the Office

***Laptops:*** Laptops are standard issue at almost every bank. You will take your laptop with you when you travel and with it you will conduct most of your work, regardless of your location. Since it is bank property, you are often limited with respect to what you can and cannot load onto your laptop. It should go without saying that you should not download from the Internet (or your personal e-mail account) anything onto your company-issued computer that you do not want your managing director to see.

*Cell phones:* Cell phones make it significantly easier to get in touch with clients and colleagues while traveling. It also makes it easier for people to get in touch with you (hint: that is not necessarily a good thing). Some banks will order the phone for you, while other banks allow you to purchase your own phone and reimburse you for all or part of it. With respect to calls, some banks will allow you to send your phone bill to the firm, while other banks have you pay the bill, then reimburse you for allowed business calls. In general, most banks will only pay for your business calls, but some are more lenient than others when it comes to monitoring which calls are business and which are personal. Again, be prudent. You would not want to lose your hard-earned job over corporate policy abuse.

*Handheld devices:* Handheld devices are convenient and allow you to carry contact information and possibly send/receive e-mail when you are traveling. Blackberrys™, Palm Pilots™ and other electronic hand-held devices are standard issue for some major investment banks while others issue them only to senior bankers. If you get one, the firm will usually pay for the gadget and the monthly bill. Although a Blackberry™ seems like a cool electronic toy and often allows you to travel without your laptop, it is the ultimate electronic leash. If you do not get one, consider yourself lucky.

*Phone calls:* Every phone call you make at the office will be paid for by the firm. Investment banks use so much phone time in so many different contexts that your calls, business and personal, are simply added to the thousands of calls that have already taken place that day. This is not to say, however, that your firm is not monitoring your calls. In all likelihood, there is a report generated daily, weekly, or monthly that details all of the calls that are made from your phone. With respect to personal calls, investment banks recognize that you are at the office for the vast majority of your waking hours, so no one will begrudge you personal calls. However, you were hired for your intelligence and judgment, so use discretion when it comes to personal telephone use (e.g., no "900" numbers or three-hour calls every night to your boyfriend in Hong Kong).

*Assistants:* You will be assigned an assistant, who you will likely share with two to five other people (most of whom will be senior to you and whose work will take priority over yours). In general, your assistant will: (1) help make your travel arrangements; (2) answer your telephone; (3) take messages; (4) find you when people are looking for you; (5) help manage your expense reports; and (6) assist you with administrative tasks, such as making copies, filing documents, and managing large mailings. Basically, assistants allow you to worry about fewer administrative tasks so that you can spend more time focusing on your work. If you are lucky and get a very good assistant, they may also look out for you when you are too tired to take care of yourself ("Yes Mrs. X, your daughter is fine and she called you earlier to wish you a happy birthday" or "It's Lorraine, I'm calling you to wake you up as you asked me to. No, nobody has been looking for you."). Some assistants can function as junior analysts and help you tremendously, whereas others do not take on additional responsibility. As with all things, do not rely on someone else to do something for you if it is important. By doing it yourself you can ensure that it is done in a timely fashion and as you would like it.

> ### ˆOˆOˆ Treat assistants with respect
>
> It is very important to treat administrative assistants with respect. You may not think it, but they have the ear of many senior bankers. Also, news travels fast within the assistant community, and you do not want to be known as the junior banker who is extremely demanding or difficult to work with.

***Offices/Bullpens:*** The analyst or associate "office" is generally a spartan cubicle, approximately four-by-six-feet in size, with semi-permanent walls but without a ceiling so that passers-by can pop their heads in/over whenever they want. This does not bode well for privacy, especially when you are in the middle of a big project and really need some peace and quiet to get your work done. Some junior analysts and associates share real offices, but as attractive as this may sound at first ("Mom, I have an office!"), remember that you are sharing with others. As a result, the enclosed office space can work against you with regard to noise and privacy. This is especially true if you are sharing an office with someone who is exceptionally loud or likes to use the speakerphone (referred to as "the box"). Usually you will not get your own office until you are a senior associate or vice president, and even then such offices are small (ten-feet by-ten-feet), with views of alleys or other high-rise buildings. Also, offices can be lonely (who wants to be by herself in an office at 2 a.m.?). Odd as it may sound, it is often preferable to be in a cubicle than in an office. When in a cubicle, you share in the camaraderie of the office and it is easier to communicate with others when you have questions, which you invariably will. Most junior bankers work in **bullpens**, which are clusters of four to six adjacent cubicles that share an open space. The open space generally makes work fun and enjoyable. Invest in a good pair of headphones, however, so that when you need to drown out or eliminate noise you are able to do so.

***Word processing:*** Every major investment bank will have a dedicated **WP** or word processing and production group, which will help you create presentations (also called books, decks, or stacks). The word processing or production group includes a staff of graphic designers, word processors, editors and copy/production experts whose sole job is to provide support to members of the investment bank. They are basically a dedicated FedEx Kinko's located on your floor (or within a few floors).

> ### ʻOʻOˆ Treat WP professionals with respect
>
> Treat the people who work in WP with respect and you will likely benefit greatly from their services. Conversely, treat them poorly and you may find that your work either does not get finished on time or is completed with a number of mistakes. Many naïve and arrogant junior bankers find themselves in a true pickle (e.g., they need twenty color books printed and bound in less than thirty minutes for a client meeting), without any support staff willing to help because these bankers are not well liked by people in WP (as with the assistant community, a bad reputation among the WP staff travels fast). If you treat people well (regardless of whether they are managing directors in your group or temporary workers in the word processing group) you should not be surprised to find that they, in turn, will treat you well. As with assistants, remember that you are ultimately responsible for the quality of the work. While WP will assist you, their efforts should not be viewed as a substitute for your own efforts.

*Corporate card:* Most firms will provide you with a corporate card or credit card, which you will use exclusively for charging business-related expenses. For example, when you order dinner from the office or when you check into a hotel on a business trip, you will use your corporate card to charge such expenses. You will use your card so often you will probably have the number memorized after a few months. A corporate card allows for easier separation between personal and business expenses and also makes it easier for the firms to monitor and manage your business expenses. American Express is the card of choice for most firms, although since most investment banks are now affiliated with credit card companies and/or commercial banks, more and more firms are urging their employees to use their in-house credit cards. Some firms will pay the corporate card directly so that bankers do not need to worry about paying the bill. Other firms require that bankers pay their corporate card bills directly, and then get reimbursement checks from the banks. Such policies bode poorly, however, for first year analysts and associates. The reimbursement period can take two to six weeks; meanwhile you are **floating** (providing cash up front while waiting for reimbursement) hundreds or even thousands of dollars of expenses for your firm. While a firm's policy on expense reimbursement should not be the driving factor in your decision to join that firm, remember that your cash flow can be at a premium as a young professional. Your rent will be high, your start-up expenses will be high (to buy suits, furniture, and other necessities when you first move to a new city and start a new job) and you may have student loans to pay. Moreover, your bonus will comprise a significant portion of your total compensation, and that money will not be available until the end of the year. You would do better to aggressively manage your personal expenses (i.e., live in a cheaper place and buy less expensive suits) than decide which bank to work for based on expense reimbursement, but it is something to be aware of.

**Free lunch:** JPMorgan ended its free lunch program in the late 1990s and was the last of the major banks to provide a free lunch to employees. Every now and then, however, a free lunch will be provided during group meetings or on Fridays as a means of getting people in the group to spend some time together. Most banks have cafeterias that are partially subsidized and therefore less expensive than the high-priced sandwich and salad shops in Manhattan or London. Many banks have free coffee machines on each floor and some even provide free bottled water and/or soda.

**Dinner:** Since you will be working many late evenings, every major bank will pay for dinner on nights when you are at the office working. The standard limit is $20 to $25 for dinner. Although $25 may sound like a lot of money for dinner, remember that you are working in New York City, London, Tokyo, or San Francisco, the most expensive cities in the world. You will soon learn that after accounting for delivery charges, tax and tip, $25 buys you a dinner of mediocre sushi, greasy Chinese food, or a burger and fries. Some banks will only reimburse food expenses after a certain time at night.

**Entertaining:** Most of your opportunities to dine at the company's expense in expensive restaurants will be related to client and recruiting dinners. Remember, however, that although you will be eating several courses of haute cuisine and drinking expensive wine, you will undoubtedly be *working*. Client dinners are just as much work as building a model in the office, and recruiting dinners can also be trying, especially if you are out with a boring recruit! There will be plenty of times when you will need to return to the office after dinner, so it's not as if you can really enjoy that $50 bottle of wine. The other thing to remember is that you are, at every moment of any kind of dinner like this, representing your firm. Some of the fastest trips from happily employed to unemployed have been as a result of doing something stupid at a client or recruiting dinner (and, not surprisingly, most of these have to do with too many expensive bottles of wine). Fancy dinners are a nice perk, and you should enjoy them if you can, but they are still work, just in a different locale, and you should approach them accordingly.

**Company cars:** All of the major banks have some form of a company car policy. During the week in New York, employees are driven home by a sponsored car company after 8 or 9 p.m. (a line will form outside of the office where the cars are being dispatched). In other cities where town cars are not as common, you will be reimbursed for taxi costs after a certain time. Some New York firms require that you take a taxi if traveling in the city, and they will subsequently reimburse you provided you submit a receipt. Most banks allow you to take cars to and from the office on weekends and holidays. Also, you will generally be able to use a car to get to the airport or client sites that are within driving distance.

## Out of the Office

*Airplane travel:* Most banks only allow business-class or first-class travel on international flights or transcontinental flights (e.g., San Francisco to New York) if the flight is a red-eye. Therefore, for most of your travel, which will be domestic day trips (business travel in which you depart and return on the same day), get used to coach class and learn how to manage working on your laptop during a three-hour flight with people on either side of you. Over time, you will accumulate many frequent flier miles and you will be able to use those miles for personal flights or upgrades in the future. Travel on a private jet is rare. It happens occasionally, but rarely more than a few times within a junior banker's career and, even then, it is usually with a client who is using his company's private jet.

*Rental cars:* Most banks will allow up to a full-sized car rental when visiting a client or traveling on a recruiting trip – although most traveling professionals prefer the convenience of taxis. The likelihood of being able to rent a flashy sports car or convertible is low. Remember, generally you will only need to rent a car for a long period of time when you are working at the client's office and, as such, it is not prudent to pull into your client's parking lot in a brand new car when they are paying your travel expenses. By the way, as the most junior person on the team you will often be driving, so be sure to have directions to where you're going.

*Hotels:* Although you will have the opportunity to stay in your fair share of Four Seasons and Ritz Carltons while traveling on business, you will also stay in a number of Holiday Inns and Motel 6s, and sometimes even less posh accommodations depending on what is available. In a client service business like banking, you go where your clients are and, although you may be able to stay at the Beverly Hills Four Seasons if you are working on a deal for a Los Angeles-based company, there are plenty of clients with whom you will work who are headquartered in small towns with very local hospitality (think Pineville, Louisiana, or Four Corners, New Mexico), cities where your only choice of hotel is a Holiday Inn or perhaps even Joe's Motor Lodge. Although the big, fancy hotels will hold an allure for you at first, you will soon realize that a hotel is merely a place to lay your head (often for only a few hours). After your first few business trips, you will not care where you stay – you will only care that the hotel is located close to where you need to be in the morning (so that you can maximize the number of hours you sleep), that you are able to connect to the Internet, that the hotel serves decent coffee, that it is proficient in performing wake-up calls, and that it offers more than *USA Today* for its newspaper selection. If these requirements are satisfied, you are likely to be happy, regardless of whether you stay at a Four Seasons or a Holiday Inn.

*Food:* All of your food expenses will likely be paid while traveling on business, although some banks may have limits as to how much you are allowed to spend on each meal. Some banks will offer a **per diem** up to $100 per day such that you can spend up to the per diem on food; you get to determine how to allocate that over the day (and perhaps keep what you do not spend). Sometimes you will hear about teams spending ridiculous amounts of money while traveling or when entertaining clients. Although this does happen occasionally, it is not the norm, and it is discouraged.

*Other:* Occasionally you will be asked to travel with very little notice (sometimes a few hours to catch the next flight is all you get) or what you originally expected to be a day trip will turn into a multi-day campout at the client's office. Consequently, you will not be prepared and will need various things, such as clothes and toiletries for your extended stay. In circumstances such as these, your firm will likely reimburse you for any *reasonable* out-of-pocket expenses. Every now and then you will hear stories of someone trying to get away with purchasing $150 Hermes ties and Thomas Pink shirts while traveling because they had to attend a meeting that they did not know about. Often, the purchase is not reimbursed or, if it is, the event leaves such a bad taste in everyone's mouth that the person would have been much better off purchasing the $30 tie or shirt.

## Other Policies

*Health clubs:* If you work at a bank that has a health club on the premises, your gym membership will be subsidized and relatively inexpensive (although the waiting list to become a member of the gym might be long and it could take years to join). However, for most, you will only be eligible for the standard corporate discount offered at many of the city's health club chains. For those moving to New York City, be prepared to spend anywhere between $70 and $200 per month for a gym membership which, sadly, you will only have time to use a few times a week. Given how small New York City apartments are, nice health clubs provide the junior banker a "home away from home."

*Moving expenses:* Most banks will pay for moving expenses when you first move to the city where you will work. Some banks will even pay for your **broker's fee** (fee paid to someone to help you find a place to live). Expect to pay anywhere between 10 and 15 percent of your annual rent to a New York City or London broker. Other banks will give you a larger signing bonus to help cover the cost of the broker's fee. In general, although you will be given some money to cover the costs of moving from Anywhere, USA, to New York City, London, or Hong Kong, the costs of moving to and living in most banking capitals are so high that you will seldom recoup all of your expenses.

*Training:* Some banks offer free classes for you to prepare for graduate school admissions exams or the **Series 7** test (an NYSE-developed and NASD-administered test required in order to sell securities to the public). Some banks will reimburse junior bankers for tuition costs to earn their MBA or other graduate degree, although these programs are not common and are only offered to select employees. Every firm, however, is likely to take training seriously and, in addition to the comprehensive training program you will be required to complete when you begin, you are likely to attend a number of company-sponsored training sessions throughout your career. Some of these will be informal sessions with bankers in your group while others will be firm-wide training sessions with hundreds of colleagues in attendance.

*Free tickets:* The firm you work for is likely to have luxury boxes at local athletic and entertainment venues such as Madison Square Garden in New York City. These are purchased in bulk and are to be used for client entertaining. However, occasionally these tickets are not used by clients and the firm sells them at cost or gives them away to employees so they are not wasted. Occasionally, New York based bankers will be offered free tickets to a Knicks or Rangers game or free tickets to see an opera performance at Lincoln Center. These opportunities do not occur often and, unfortunately, seem to occur only when you cannot accept them due to work obligations. These tickets are generally first come, first served so if your schedule allows you to attend, respond quickly to the offer.

*Off-site meetings or retreats:* Many corporations host off-site activities as a means of improving morale, rewarding employees, or simply having people meet in a new place outside of their normal environment in order to generate new ideas. In a bull market, investment banking off-sites can be particularly deluxe. It should be pointed out, however, that like seminars or conventions that take place in attractive locations, an investment banking corporate off-site is not all fun and games. During off-sites there are a number of meetings to target potential new accounts, identify potential transactions, and encourage greater sharing of ideas by ensuring that most group members get to know each other better. Some banks host ski weekends, sailing weekends, or other types of off-sites with clients which they hope will either provide them with a competitive edge, enable them to invite decision-makers from client companies (and thereby develop better corporate relationships), or both. During bear markets off-sites are far more likely to entail a day at a corporate retreat in the metropolitan area than a Caribbean vacation.

## A Reality Check

Although a job as an investment banking analyst or associate will certainly provide you with a number of perks and benefits that you may not encounter in other professions, they are only provided to help you do your job better. As a first year analyst or associate, you will not be living like Croesus. In addition, although you will be traveling to places all over the world, these are business trips and the main purpose for being in London, Paris, Buenos Aires, Hong Kong, Mexico City or San Francisco is to *work*, not to sightsee, visit with friends, or spend time in the hotel spa. In other words, you are being paid to work, not to have fun.

### ᐟᐤᐤᐟ What is business travel like?

An actual travel schedule for a vice president at a major investment bank included: New York to London on Sunday, London to Paris on Monday, back to London on Tuesday, London to New York on Wednesday, Toronto on Thursday, and New York again on Friday. While the evenings in London and Paris were spent in five-star hotels, during this same week there were two all-nighters, two meals in airports, two meals in hotel rooms, and several meals on airplanes and in the office. Needless to say, this was not a good week, regardless of the fact that this business trip took this vice president to some of the most beautiful cities in the world.

An extended trip for another banker required traveling almost daily for four weeks between Los Angeles and an Indian reservation in the middle of Arizona on one of the smallest propeller planes legally allowed to fly by a commercial airline company. Nights were spent sleeping in a Holiday Inn and meals were either at the local Denny's or International House of Pancakes.

Of course most business travel will not be this extreme and occasionally trips will allow time to see friends or family for dinner or an opportunity for sightseeing. But such opportunities are rare. If a business trip allows you a few hours to walk around Rome, shop for custom made suits in Hong Kong, or sip champagne in Paris, enjoy these small indulgences when they are available to you. Consider opportunities like these perks of your job – just remember to pay for them out of your own pocket.

## Use Your Judgment

You are being hired because several people find you smart, hard working, and capable of good judgment. When it comes to company policies, especially those listed here, apply that same judgment and use discretion with all things related to perks and bank policies. Never try to push the envelope. Serve as a good role model for others when it comes to respecting company policies. Be smart and use discretion with all things related to your job as few things are worth putting your professional career or personal reputation on the line. In essence, "Never do anything during the day that will make it difficult to sleep at night."

More importantly, the real perks of the job are the relationships you will develop and the valuable experience you will gain. Think of your clients and your senior bankers as part of a real-world classroom in which every visiting lecturer is an authority on the topic. This is the bonus that, in the long run, is most valuable; you do not want to jeopardize that.

# Compensation

## CHAPTER 9

*The reward of a thing well done is to have done it.*

*Ralph Waldo Emerson*

Compensation in investment banking includes both a base salary and an end of year bonus. During your first few years in banking, the split between bonus and salary can be approximately 55 percent base salary and 45 percent bonus. As you become a senior associate or junior vice president, the split will migrate toward 25 percent salary and 75 percent bonus. For a senior vice president or managing director, 80 to 90 percent of total compensation is in the form of bonus.

In 2005, total compensation for first year analysts ranged from $75,000 to $100,000 with a base salary of approximately $55,000. For first year associates, total compensation for an associate's first full year ranged from $200,000 to $250,000, which includes a base salary of approximately $95,000. In addition, most first year analysts and associates are provided a signing or moving bonus of between $5,000 and $20,000. The salary increase each year tends to be small (between $5,000 and $15,000) whereas the increase of the bonus can be more significant. Strategic consulting tends to pay entry-level salaries that are competitive with banking salaries and offers year-end bonuses that are generally smaller than investment banking bonuses. Each year certain industry magazines, including *Investment Dealers' Digest*, publish compensation ranges for investment bankers.

Salary is the amount you get paid every two weeks. It is enough to pay for day-to-day living expenses, but it is a relatively modest amount given the cost of living in banking capitals such as New York, London or Hong Kong. Expect your salary the first year out of college to just barely cover rent, student loans, and limited weekend carousing. If, during your first year, you plan to purchase more expensive items such as furniture, designer suits, and flat panel TVs, or if you are particularly social and regularly spend a few hundred dollars when you go out on a Saturday night (easy to do in a big city), you will likely be in debt – either to credit card companies, your parents, or your savings account. For business school graduates, your salary will be about $40,000 more than for a first year analyst, however any business school loans are likely to eat into much of that difference.

Compensation levels track the general financial market. When the market is doing well and the banks are making money, they pay their employees well. When the market is not doing so well, not only do the banks pay smaller bonuses, but they also are quick to lay off employees.

Figure 9.1 tracks the compensation range and median salaries for a second year associate from the period between 1996 and 2003. Notice the cyclical nature of compensation.

## Figure 9.1 – Second-Year Associate Compensation Levels

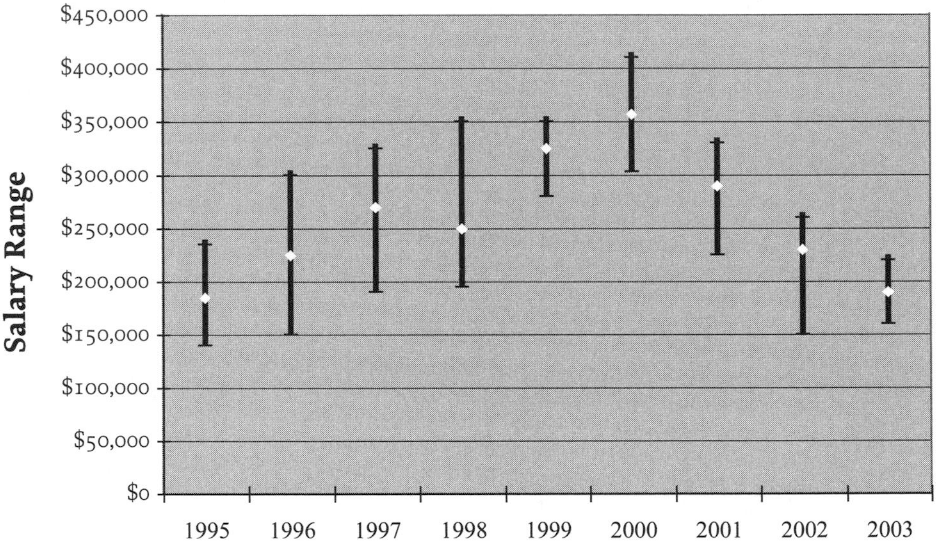

Data source: Hahn, Avital Louria. "Rainmakers Rule." *Investment Dealers' Digest* March 15, 2004: 26-35.

## Performance Reviews

At most of the major banks, bonuses are determined toward the end of the bank's fiscal year (generally November or December) as part of an annual performance review. Bonuses are distributed to employees approximately one month after the end of the fiscal year (December or January). Some banks also review analysts at the end of the fiscal year, although most banks review and pay analyst bonuses during the summer, commensurate with the beginning and ending of the **analyst year** (analysts generally are hired for a two-year program, which begins and ends in July).

Those analysts who have performed particularly well are often invited to stay a third year. Analysts who are performing at the associate level by their third year may be promoted to associate without having to go to business school.

Although many find the time-consuming performance review process to be long and cumbersome, it is extremely important as it not only allows senior bankers to decide how much your bonus should be that year, but it is often the only formal feedback you will receive regarding your performance. There is a lot of sensitivity surrounding the review process, precisely because it is directly linked to people's bonuses and promotion. However, it should be considered an excellent opportunity to speak candidly to people with whom you have worked in order to understand the perceptions of your strengths and weaknesses, and more importantly, what is expected of you for the upcoming year.

Every bank has its own process as it relates to annual performance reviews and compensation. Generally, at the beginning of a performance review cycle you will ask a number of colleagues to review you. Those reviewers will fill out a standard company review form (usually done electronically on a secure web site), which will include opportunities for them to comment on their experience working with you and what they perceive as your strengths and weaknesses. They will also compare you to others in your same class year. Although most of your reviewers will be from your product or industry group, if your work has involved colleagues from other groups they may also review you. Some banks limit the number of reviewers to five or less, while other banks want as much feedback as possible and subsequently your list of reviewers may exceed twenty. If you are an associate, reviewers will be both senior and junior to you; if you are an analyst, almost everyone reviewing you will be senior to you.

## ʹOOʹ Choosing your reviewers

Although at many banks you select the people who will review you, it is assumed that anyone who worked with you for any reasonable amount of time will write a review on you, whether the experience was positive or negative. If you have a bad working relationship with a colleague, it is highly likely he or she will review you. Be prepared for **unsolicited reviews**, or reviews of you submitted by people whom you did not ask to review you. During the review process, you can expect to benefit from the good experiences you had with people and be held accountable for the bad experiences as well.

Once all of the reviews are completed and submitted, a small review committee, generally consisting of senior people in your group, your **line manager** or **staffer** (the person responsible for staffing analysts and associates in your group), and a few select others will go through all of the reviews for everyone within your class and within your group. The committee may review a class year at the product or industry group level, or it may review a broader selection, such as all the analysts within

M&A. Since this review committee has heard all of the feedback on all of the people within a particular class, they will then rank everyone and place each person in one of three to five major groupings. Usually, a sub-committee will then determine what bonuses the different groupings should receive. The review committee will also discuss which of the candidates within the classes eligible for promotion should be promoted (for example, which third-year analysts should be promoted to associate and which fourth-year associates should be promoted to vice president).

A number of issues will be factored into your performance review during the compensation committee meetings. They include the type of deals and experience you had during the year and how well you performed given the projects you were assigned. How well you performed includes not only the quality of your analytical and written work but also your sportsmanship, initiative, and all of the things identified in the recruiting and interviewing sections in which the analyst and associate roles and responsibilities are discussed. One of the most important factors in the review committee will be who spoke well of you or who had issues with your performance. If no one in a review committee meeting is willing to speak strongly on your behalf regarding your accomplishments for the year, it does not really matter how stellar your written reviews are, you will likely be passed over for inclusion in the highest groupings and consequently will not be paid at the top of your class. Banking, like many other parts of life, is a combination of what you know and who you know.

### ʘ‾ʘ Finding your "home"

One of the most important things to do as a junior banker is to find a home. This means you need to find a core team of people with whom you can work. Without a team of people looking out for you, you may get lost in the shuffle regardless of how good you are. It is in your best interest to identify senior people early in your career with whom you want to develop relationships. Choose those people you want to work with because you actually enjoy working with them and believe you can learn from them as opposed to who is most politically aligned. Work very hard for those people and the relationship will be mutually beneficial. Build relationships and your reputation will follow, and try to steer clear of the politics.

Once the review committees have completed their process, your line manager or the head of your group will meet with you to convey your bonus for the preceding year and your salary for the upcoming year, and share with you details of your performance review. If you are up for promotion, this also probably will be communicated at this meeting.

## A Reality Check

The high compensation paid in banking comes with a price. There is no such thing as a free lunch, and in banking you will be working more hours and sacrificing more of your time than in most other jobs. In fact, on an hourly basis, you will probably make significantly less in banking than you would in strategic consulting, accounting or in a managerial position at a corporation. And remember, most banking jobs require that you live in a banking capital, and the cost of living in these cities is very high. As a result, the after tax, after rent salary from your job in banking may very well be lower than your after tax, after rent salary from another job in another city.

> **ʻOʻOʻ Bank your bonus**
>
> Money you earn in investment banking will allow you to buy your freedom in the future. Unfortunately, if you spend all the money you earn, there will be nothing left over in the future. If and when you can, bank your bonus. The financial flexibility will surely come in handy.

Your career choice does not (or at least should not) boil down to an analysis of dollars and cents, especially in the first few years of your career. Although compensation should be a factor in anyone's decision making process, it should only be one of many such factors, including: what you will learn, what experience you will gain, with whom you will work, what contacts you will make, what your lifestyle will be and, most importantly, whether you enjoy what you are doing.

If you decide to enter banking for money alone, you are likely to be unhappy and this will be reflected in your work product. There will be a number of times when you are in the office at 4 a.m. for the fifth day in a row and, during these low moments, if you realize that you are making such sacrifices just for money, you are likely to become discouraged and quit.

If you enjoy what you do and you are good at it, money, success, and personal satisfaction will follow. The compensation in banking can be great, but the personal sacrifice can be as well, so choose a path that excites you, not one that pays you to be excited.

# Training and Mentoring
## Chapter 10

*Keep away from people who try to belittle your ambitions.*
*Small people always do that,*
*but the really great make you feel that you, too,*
*can be great.*

### Mark Twain

Many books and movies depict bankers as loud, arrogant, and capricious. More relevant to you as a junior banker, the general perception is that a lot of screaming takes place in banking and, if you do something wrong, you will be yelled at and ridiculed in front of your peers. It might seem as if banking is a dog-eat-dog world and that only those with thick skin and the ability to also be loud, arrogant, and capricious should apply.

Although it is true that banking is not for shrinking violets and that the environment is more competitive and fierce than many other industries, the environment is certainly not as scary as some have made it out to be, nor is it as scary as it once was. Banking in the 1980s was very different from banking in the 1990s and it is even more different today.

As a junior banker, you will not be thrown into the fire alone. Not only will you go through a comprehensive training program, you are also likely to have ongoing training throughout your banking career. In addition, you probably will be assigned a formal mentor who should regularly check in to ensure that your training and overall experience have been positive. Perhaps more importantly, you will develop relationships with informal mentors. These mentors, although not formally assigned to you as part of your bank's mentoring program, can play a very important role in your career development. For many, mentors will be some of your best sources of advice and guidance during your career.

## ʼOʼOʼ Finding a mentor

Although the firm for which you work may have a formal mentoring program in place, the onus is on you to find a mentor and develop a relationship with him or her. It takes time to develop a candid and honest relationship with a mentor. Once you do, however, you will have someone in the firm with whom you can discuss important career decisions and opportunities. Most relationships with mentors are born from working on projects together. If you work hard and consistently produce good work product for someone, then he will tend to go out of his way to support you professionally or advise you on personal decisions. Also, it is a good idea to find at least one mentor outside of your direct reporting line. In this way, you can candidly discuss issues taking place on your current projects without worrying about how the conversation will affect your working environment. Your boss can be a natural mentor; therefore, try to find someone else with whom you do not work on a regular basis. Also, your mentor should be one or two levels above you so that he can provide guidance on career paths and other advancement issues.

During training, you will be exposed to all of the basics of accounting, finance, financial modeling, M&A, and the capital markets. Also, you will meet a number of people, some your peers, others senior to you, to whom you can reach out when you need help when working. The quality of the analyst and associate training programs at most major banks is excellent. They are mini-MBA programs, specializing in accounting and finance. Top-rated professors from business schools are brought in at the big banks to teach certain modules; they sometimes use the same text books that are used in MBA finance and accounting courses; they have senior people from throughout the bank speak about their areas of expertise; and you are quizzed, tested, and required to give mock presentations to the class.

## ʼOʼOʼ The training program

Treat the training program as your opportunity to meet and make friends with as many new colleagues within the bank as you can. The friends you meet in training could become some of your closest friends and many of them will grow into senior positions either in the firm or at another firm, where they might someday even become a client of yours. During training, it is as important to spend time cultivating relationships as studying the materials and preparing for tests.

Training does not end when the formal training program ends. Once put on-line, individual groups often host mini-training programs to prepare new analysts and associates for working in that group (e.g. the Financial Institutions Group might offer specialized training in accounting for banks and other financial services companies). Also, many groups have teach-ins throughout the year on advanced topics.

> ## ˆОˆ Seeking help
>
> All of the analysts and associates who started before you went through the same learning process that you will go through. Nearly everyone is willing to lend a hand to new people, so do not be shy about asking for help when you need it. The senior people in your group are also a great resource. As with anything, experience is a great teacher. Senior bankers often can put things into context by helping describe the bigger picture. While you should not ask vice presidents and managing directors how to download stock prices (some of the most senior bankers may not even know how to use the Internet), you should not be afraid to ask them questions about strategy, tactics, or timing. Introduce yourself to the senior bankers in your group when you start working and make a point of stopping by their offices or asking them to lunch when schedules allow. You will become more comfortable with those senior people with whom you work, and you should consider all senior bankers to be a source of knowledge and experience.

## Yelling or Screaming

There will be times when someone senior will become angry with you, largely the result of the stress he is under. Depending on the personality, he may even raise his voice, yell, or slam books on the table to make a point. When this happens you must remember that you work in a high-stress environment and people react to stress in different ways. Your firm is being paid substantial fees to perform a particular service; therefore, there is an expectation by the client that the work will be both timely and correct. The bottom line: the stakes are high in banking and, consequently, the stress levels are similarly high. When someone gets mad at you, it is probably because you did something wrong and the deadlines are such that your team cannot afford mistakes at that given moment. When you have an important deliverable, be extremely careful with your work. Triple check your work before handing it to someone for review because during high-stress fire drills, the smallest mistake on your part may worry a senior banker regarding the quality of your work. Worse, they may request that additional analysts or associates be assigned to the team or you may even be removed from the project. Either of these will impair your professional experience and adversely affect your reputation. It is extremely unlikely that you will be fired for making an unintentional mistake. However, there is very little tolerance for repeatedly making the same mistake. As a very senior banker once said, "I don't expect you to know everything, but I do expect you to learn it once I teach you how to do it."

Do not spend a lot of energy trying to justify your errors. Life is too short. The person reviewing your work has more experience and, although you may believe you are correct, you should do the work the way he asks for it. You are much better off diverting your energy to the work that needs to be done than getting angry with the person yelling at you. Realize that his anger will pass (usually when the fire drill is over) and remember that perfection is being demanded of him (from clients and the firm), and therefore he demands the same high quality of work from you. While zero tolerance for a junior banker may seem like an extreme position, remember that banks charge their clients handsomely for their services in the same way that you are being paid handsomely for yours.

> **ᕕ◯◯ᕗ Abusive behavior**
>
> If you work with someone who yells and screams often, without provocation, tell them how you feel about the working relationship. If this does not work (or you are not comfortable having this conversation), bring it up with your line manager. There is a time and place for people to be angry, but abusive behavior generally is not tolerated, regardless of a person's tenure or seniority.

## A Reality Check

You were hired because people who interviewed you believed in your potential to do the job well. They invest in you and want you to succeed. Generally, the behavior that makes senior bankers angry is what should, in fact, make you angry with yourself: an unwillingness to work hard; a bad attitude; a lack of moral fiber or a compulsion to lie about issues; a lack of quality in your work or poor attention to detail; and a general lack of pride in yourself, your firm, or your job. Remember that many other people wanted and applied for your job. Hiring mistakes do happen and to the extent you display any or all of the above characteristics repeatedly, your firm will consider letting you go.

# Diversity

## Chapter 11

*Though all men be made of one metal,*
*yet they be not cast all in one mold.*

### John Lyly

Like law and politics, banking used to be an exclusive old boys network and, as such, it was very difficult for people from outside the network to break into it. Times have changed and today's starting analyst and associate classes at major investment banks look more like a group of United Nations representatives than they do a group of partners at an investment bank twenty years ago.

Although there are more men than women in banking and more Caucasians than minorities, this should not discourage you. The ethnic and gender composition of the starting analyst or associate class at any major bank changes every year, and each year brings more diversity. More and more people from outside of the traditional social classes and feeder schools are entering the field, and all of the banks consider diversity to be a high priority when recruiting and hiring. This is not purely a matter of social science. Business is becoming ever more global. The corollary to business becoming more global is that clients are becoming more global. To service those clients, it behooves the bank to have personnel as diverse as its clients. This means that it is a matter of business savvy as much as anything else that compels banks to try and hire the best and brightest of every race, creed, color, religion and orientation. If you are smart and hard working, banks want you, regardless of what you look like or where you are from. Banks are interested in making money and if you can help them to do that, you have a good shot at getting a job.

Although there are significantly more men than women at senior levels, the reason for this is not a lack of opportunities for women. Rather, fewer women choose banking as a long-term career. Many mid-level female bankers leave mid-career to pursue a path that is more conducive to raising a family. The pressures of raising a family and needing to spend more time at home may make a senior-level banking job less attractive to women than it may for men (although there are certainly plenty of men who leave banking for a better lifestyle as well). Also, because it takes a certain number of years to become a senior banker, the more diverse entering classes of recent vintage are only now making their way into the executive suites.

Due to the lack of senior-level women in banking, there is a lack of senior-level female role models and mentors. However, there are plenty of men who are terrific mentors to women. If you are a woman, you are likely to have to work proportionately harder to find a female role model whom you can emulate than your male colleagues will have to work to find a male role model. Having said that, there is a focus within most banks on grooming more women for senior positions, so you may benefit from an active mentorship program, whether it be formal, informal, or both.

As a minority, do not be discouraged by the ethnic composition of your starting class. In fact, there are likely to be many Caucasian or Caucasian-looking people in your class who have very non-traditional backgrounds, such as being raised in or having gone to school in a foreign country. Once more, remember that banks want quality, in whatever form it may be packaged. Your biggest advantages in interviewing (and doing your job if you are hired) will be intelligence and enthusiasm while your biggest dangers will be carelessness and a bad attitude. You will note that there is no mention in that last sentence about race, creed, color, religion or orientation.

In short, all of the critical factors that can lead to one's long term success in banking are learned and applied, not doled out at birth to a chosen few.

# What Makes a Great Junior Banker?

## CHAPTER 12

*The world is divided into people who do things,*
*and people who get credit.*
*Try, if you can, to belong to the first class.*
*There's far less competition.*

**Dwight Whitney Morrow**
**(U.S. diplomat and politician**
**in a letter to his son)**

Senior bankers believe there are characteristics consistently demonstrated by the very best junior bankers. While these characteristics will lead to success in banking, more broadly they will lead to success in your professional life.

1.  **Have a terrific attitude.** Work hard and unfailingly. Always maintain a great attitude, even in stressful situations. Also maintain a sense of humor and have fun.

2.  **Work intelligently.** Think, write and speak analytically and critically.

3.  **Learn how to do your job.** Know what is expected of you and try to be the best you can be at your job.

4.  **Take ownership of your work.** Pay strict attention to detail, take pride in your work, and always be willing to stand behind it.

5.  **Be a true team player.** Become the go-to junior banker with your deal teams, peers and colleagues. Always be willing to lend a hand.

6.  **Manage your time well.** Complete your work ahead of schedule and try to anticipate what more needs to be done. Remember that it is a marathon and not a sprint.

7.  **Follow directions.** Complete assigned tasks and do what is asked of you. Be someone who only needs to be shown once how to do something.

8. **Be a leader and take initiative.** In your projects and other professional activities, always be willing to learn more and to do more.

9. **Be a teacher and a mentor.** Be the kind of teacher and mentor you would want for yourself. Also find teachers and mentors and develop solid relationships with them. The value of a personal power base cannot be overstated.

10. **Apply the highest levels of integrity.** Use discretion whenever representing the firm. Be unfailing in your judgment. If you are not sure about something, ask.

Sometimes what you *do not do* is as important, if not more important, than what you *do* do. There are certain actions that have tripped up more than a few bankers in the past. Since this is not a club you want to join, we have provided the following list of career-limiting maneuvers (often referred to as CLMs) to avoid when working.

1. **Don't be careless.** There are two defining characteristics regarding work at an investment bank: one, that it is done quickly and two, that it is done correctly. Never compromise the second for the first.

2. **Never divulge confidential information.** If caught, at best you will be fired and at worst you will go to jail.

3. **Never lie.** Whatever the upside of the lie may be, the downside is the loss of your job or, worse, the loss of your reputation. From a risk-reward perspective, that's a bad trade.

4. **Don't complain.** Everyone hates complainers. Don't complain, especially when it comes to how much work you have to do, how many hours you are working, and the type of work you are doing. Everyone you work with has *been there* and they neither need to hear about it from you nor do they want to.

5. **Don't gossip.** Do not talk about people with whom you work and do not spread rumors. Information about who has been saying what has a bad habit of coming around to bite those who are gossiping.

6. **Don't talk about compensation or promotion with your colleagues.** This is personal and confidential information. Be especially careful regarding compensation and promotion discussions in the office.

7. **Try to steer clear of office politics** and don't be a sycophant.

8. **Don't drink too much** at work-related functions.

9. **As best you can, try to avoid face time.** Don't pretend to be busy if you are not. Ask for more work if you need more work or go home.

10. **Only offer your resignation if you are really willing to quit.** Never threaten to resign only to get a promotion or more money. If you are not serious, you may be taken up on it, leaving you without a job. It's a chip you can only play once and, even if you achieve the promotion or obtain the money, it will be a Pyrrhic victory since it will leave a bad taste in everyone's mouth.

# PART III
## PREPARING FOR THE INTERVIEWS

# Financial Statement Basics

## CHAPTER 13

*A good decision is based on knowledge and not numbers.*

### *Plato*

Financial statements are the (secret) language of finance. Any professional involved in making business decisions must develop a facility and ease with numbers, financial ratios and related terminology. Much can be learned by studying the financial statements of a company, but you must first learn how to read them.

Financial statements are used by many parties for different reasons (some of which are described below). This chapter will describe the financial statements, how they interrelate, and introduce financial ratios and terminology commonly used in M&A and corporate finance.

| Constituent | Reasons for using financial statements |
| --- | --- |
| Company managers | Measure performance and make strategic, operating and financial decisions |
| Suppliers and vendors | Measure creditworthiness and liquidity; make credit decisions |
| Equity investors | Value the equity investment; determine solvency; make buy and sell decisions |
| Debt investors | Measure creditworthiness and bankruptcy risk; make buy and sell decisions |
| Regulators | Determine whether the company is operating according to regulations and law |
| Acquirors | Value the company; make investment decisions |

Whereas *historical financial statements* represent what has happened in the past, the *financial projections* of a company attempt to predict what the financial statements will look like in the future. When preparing financial projections, companies make assumptions regarding various items, including future sales and revenues, the costs to achieve those sales, and required capital expenditures. Public companies must follow certain rules when preparing their historical financial statements (some of which will be described in the next section). Whereas historical financial statements are often used by investors, regulators, and outside parties, financial projections are generally used internally to make corporate decisions, and by financial advisors to assist companies in making strategic decisions.

## Financial Accounting Basics

This book is not intended to be an accounting textbook. Instead, the goal is to provide a practical description of how the financial community uses financial statements. On the following pages, a summary of major financial accounting concepts is provided. These are some of the most important and fundamental concepts in financial accounting and some of the first principles in a finance professional's technical tool chest. If you have never taken a financial accounting class, you should supplement this section with a financial accounting textbook and consider taking a college-level accounting class. A list of recommended accounting textbooks can be found in the Appendix.

### *Major GAAP accounting concepts*

1. ***GAAP:*** Generally Accepted Accounting Principles is a set of financial reporting guidelines. The Financial Accounting Standards Board (FASB) is considered by the Securities and Exchange Comission (SEC) and the American Institute of Certified Public Accountants (AICPA) to be the authoritative governing body of GAAP. Public companies must file their GAAP financial statements with the SEC, where they become public record. GAAP is not a fixed set of rules; it is continuously evolving set of principles and there are gray areas in which management has room to use judgment. Since GAAP is not static, be sure to reference current accounting standards whenever in doubt about an accounting rule or issue. FASB's website is www.fasb.org. A list of GAAP reference books is provided in the Appendix.

2. ***Tax accounting:*** In addition to the GAAP books, companies also prepare a separate set of corporate records for tax purposes (tax books), which are used to determine the company's taxable income and tax liability for a reporting period. Material differences might exist between the GAAP books and the tax books. Tax accounting (which has different rules than GAAP accounting) is regulated by the **IRS** (Internal Revenue Service) and other taxing authorities. Whereas GAAP financial records for public companies are publicly available, tax records are not made public.

3. ***Financial statements:*** There are three basic financial statements which companies must prepare in accordance with GAAP - the **income statement**, **balance sheet,** and **cash flow statement**. Companies also provide (1) a schedule that describes **changes in owner's equity;** (2) **footnotes to the financial statements**, which further describe the financial statements; and (3) **management's discussion and analysis** (MD&A), in which management describes key issues and changes related to the financial performance during the period. GAAP financial statements for public companies are filed quarterly

and annually with the SEC based on the company's fiscal year.

4. ***Materiality:*** GAAP only applies to material economic events. The test is, if a reasonable person would make a different decision based on, or would be influenced by, an economic event, the event is material and must be accounted for according to GAAP.

5. ***Revenue recognition:*** In accrual accounting, revenues are recognized when services or goods are delivered and when cash collection certainty is *reasonable*. This means that, technically, a company can only record a sale if it reasonably believes it will be paid for its goods or services. Larger companies use accrual accounting more often than the cash-based method of accounting, which recognizes revenues when cash is actually received or paid.

6. ***Matching principle:*** Any expenses associated with obtaining related revenues should be charged as an expense during the period when the revenues were recognized. If a cost cannot be matched to revenue, it is generally expensed in the period when the cost was incurred.

7. ***Tax deductible expenses:*** Expenses are (generally) tax deductible and are offset against revenues to calculate taxable income. Thus, a company subtracts salaries and production costs, for example, from revenues before it calculates how much tax it must pay.

8. ***Capitalizing assets:*** An asset is anything (except for employees) owned by the company and used in providing or delivering goods or services and used in the generation of future cash inflow. If the asset purchased has a useful life longer than one year, it should be **capitalized** or put on the balance sheet as a long term asset. This means that the total cost of the asset is put on the balance sheet when it is initially purchased and each period a portion of the capitalized asset's value is depreciated for tangible assets or amortized for intangible assets.

9. ***Depreciating assets:*** Assets are depreciated over their useful life and that depreciation is charged through the income statement as an offset to that period's revenues (see matching principle above). The cost of an asset should be depreciated according to a depreciation schedule based on the **useful life** of the asset.

10. ***Fair market value:*** Assets and liabilities are recorded on the company's balance sheet based on **fair market value** (FMV) at the time the item is purchased and added to the balance sheet. Most assets and liabilities are carried on the books based on this **historical cost** minus any corresponding depreciation or amortization. The balance sheet is not routinely adjusted upward

from this historical cost if an asset increases in value. Only when a transaction takes place to sell the asset does the asset's fair market value get captured on the balance sheet (the asset value is recalculated at that time). Conservatism, however, does provide that if there is a material *decrease* in the fair market value of an asset or liability, that item should be written down to the lower fair market value (even in the absence of a transaction). **Write offs** flow through the income statement as a charge and ultimately reduce net income.

11.*Marked-to-market:* Certain assets or investments (e.g., trading securities) are marked-to-market every period, meaning their carrying value on the balance sheet is adjusted up or down to reflect their current market value as opposed to being carried on the balance sheet at historical cost.

12.*Discontinued operations:* Income from discontinued operations and other non-recurring items should be shown separately from income from continuing operations on the income statement.

13.*Management's intentions:* Financial reporting should reflect management's intentions. For example, if management intends to sell an asset in the near term that would otherwise be categorized as a long term asset (and management is fairly certain they will sell it and receive cash proceeds for it), this should be reflected in the financial statements by re-categorizing the asset as available for sale or even as a short term asset.

---

### ˆOˆOˆ  Sarbanes-Oxley Act of 2002

Sarbanes-Oxley was signed into law in 2002 and is considered among the most important U.S. accounting and investor related legislation put into effect since the 1930's. It applies to entities required to file their statements with the SEC.

Sarbanes-Oxley created the Public Company Accounting Oversight Board (PCAOB). It requires that any accounting firm that audits an SEC registrant company must by registered with the PCAOB. Other requirements of Sarbanes-Oxley include greater auditor independence, certifications from a company's CEO and CFO regarding financial reports, stricter regulations over equity analysts and greater accountability for corporations in the event of corporate fraud and criminal action. The scope and importance of Sarbanes-Oxley is vast and someone working on M&A or corporate finance transactions should understand its implications for corporate clients. A summary of Sarbanes-Oxley can be found in most comprehensive GAAP reference books.

## Basic Financial Statements

There are three basic financial statements: (1) the **balance sheet**; (2) the **income statement;** and (3) the **cash flow statement** (also referred to as the sources and uses statement). These statements are generally computed at the end of every **reporting period** (period in which a company's financial performance is measured, such as quarterly, semiannually, or annually) and are used to measure the actual financial results and financial health of a company. Financial statements are used to report actual results, whereas budgets and financial projections are used for future planning purposes.

The following descriptions are used to provide a conceptual framework for understanding the basic financial statements. The best way to learn how to read financial statements is to actually *read financial statements.* That means, after you have reviewed the basic descriptions provided here, you should spend time reading through various annual reports, specifically the financial statements, the footnotes of the financial statements, and the MD&A. The footnotes and the MD&A provide important context that will allow you to better understand the numbers in the financial statements. Financial statements for SEC registered companies can be found at www.sec.gov.

Let's first consider a timeline to understand the time frames of the three statements. Notice in the figure below how the balance sheet is taken at the beginning and end of a reporting period. The reason there are two balance sheets -opening and closing- is because a balance sheet measures assets and liabilities at a *point in time,* whereas the income statement and the cash flow statement are representative of what happens *during* a reporting period. A full set of financial statements includes: (1) an opening balance sheet, (2) an income statement, (3) a cash flow statement, and (4) a closing balance sheet. The opening and closing balance sheets are usually shown together.

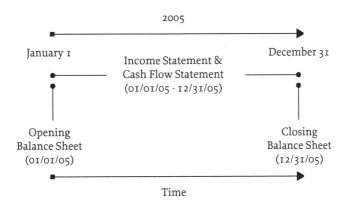

To illustrate important financial concepts we will use the financial statements of SampleCo, a fictional company. We will refer to SampleCo's financial statements throughout this chapter.

## Table 13.1 – SampleCo's Balance Sheet

| Balance Sheet | 2004 | 2005 |
|---|---|---|
| **Assets** | | |
| Cash | $200 | $165 |
| Accounts receivable | 125 | 150 |
| Inventory | 150 | 125 |
| Other current assets | 45 | 50 |
| Total current assets | 520 | 490 |
| Gross PP&E | 1,500 | 1,900 |
| Accumulated depreciation | (300) | (450) |
| Net PP&E | 1,200 | 1,450 |
| Other long term assets | 300 | 300 |
| Goodwill | 250 | 250 |
| **Total assets** | **$2,270** | **$2,490** |
| | | |
| **Liabilities & Shareholders' Equity** | | |
| Short term debt | $125 | $100 |
| Accounts payable | 100 | 150 |
| Salaries payable | 75 | 65 |
| Taxes payable | 45 | 40 |
| Total current liabilities | 345 | 355 |
| Deferred tax liabilities | 200 | 225 |
| Other long term liabilities | 120 | 120 |
| Long term debt | 600 | 700 |
| Common equity | 1,005 | 1,090 |
| **Total liabilities & equity** | **$2,270** | **$2,490** |

## Table 13.2 – SampleCo's Income Statement

| Income Statement - for the year ending | 2005 |
|---|---|
| Revenues | $1,000 |
| Cost of goods sold | (400) |
| Gross margin | 600 |
| Selling, general and administrative (SG&A) | (100) |
| Earnings before interest, taxes, DD&A (EBITDA) | 500 |
| Depreciation, depletion & amortization (DD&A) | (150) |
| Earnings before interest and taxes (EBIT) | 350 |
| Interest expense | (125) |
| Earnings before taxes (EBT) | 225 |
| Income taxes | (90) |
| Net income (earnings) | $135 |
| | |
| Shares outstanding-basic | 100 |
| Shares outstanding-diluted | 105 |
| Earnings per share (EPS) - basic | $1.35 |
| Earnings per share (EPS) - diluted | $1.29 |
| Dividends | 50 |
| Dividends per share (DPS) | $0.50 |
| Earnings to common | 85 |

## Table 13.3 – SampleCo's Cash Flow Statement

| Cash Flow Statement | 2005 |
|---|---|
| *Operating* | |
| Net income | $135 |
| DD&A | 150 |
| Changes in deferred taxes | 25 |
| Changes in working capital | 30 |
| Cash flow from operations | 340 |
| | |
| *Investing* | |
| Capital expenditures | (400) |
| Other changes in assets/liabilities | 0 |
| Cash flow from investing | (400) |
| | |
| *Financing* | |
| Common dividends paid | (50) |
| Changes in short term debt | (25) |
| Changes in long term debt | 100 |
| Changes in equity | 0 |
| Cash flow from financing | 25 |
| | |
| Beginning cash | 200 |
| Total change in cash | (35) |
| Ending cash | $165 |

***Balance sheet***: the balance sheet is a snapshot taken at a point in time. It represents what a company owns (its **assets**) and the claims on those assets (its **liabilities** and **shareholders' equity**) on the date of the balance sheet. The balance sheet may not have the same values the day before the snapshot was taken nor the day after. In addition, the balance sheet always has to "balance," which means that its assets must equal its liabilities plus shareholders' equity.

In the figure below see how SampleCo's assets of $2,490 at the end of 2005 equal its liabilities of $1,400 plus its equity of $1,090.

Assets = Liabilities + Shareholders' Equity

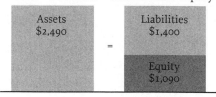

Consider your own personal balance sheet to gain a better conceptual understanding. Let's say you own a house and a car, which together cost $500,000. The value of the house and the car would be listed on the asset side of your personal balance sheet (minus depreciation, which we will touch on later). How did you pay for the house and the car? You might have a mortgage on the house with your local bank and that mortgage has a principal balance of $400,000. And you might have paid for the car with cash. Therefore, your liabilities amount to $400,000 and your shareholders' equity (the value of the owner's portion) amounts to $100,000. Your personal balance sheet would look like this:

| Assets | | Liabilities and Owner's Equity | |
|---|---|---|---|
| Car and house | $500,000 | Debt (bank loan) | $400,000 |
| | | Owner's equity | 100,000 |
| **Total** | **$500,000** | **Total** | **$500,000** |

A balance sheet can be assessed on any given day, although it is generally provided at the end of a **reporting period**, such as the end of a quarter or the end of a **fiscal year**. When a company prepares a full set of financial statements, generally both an **opening balance sheet** and a **closing balance sheet** are provided. They represent the balance sheets at the beginning of the reporting period and at the end of the reporting period, respectively.

---

### ⌐OO⌐ What is fiscal year vs. calendar year?

The **fiscal year** is the annual period for a company's financial reporting. **Calendar year** is from January 1 to December 31. Companies are free to choose their own fiscal year, although many choose a fiscal year that is the same as the calendar year. Certain companies find that having a fiscal year end on December 31 is very difficult, due to the nature of their business. For example, most retail companies are very busy during the December holiday season dealing with sales and customer service related issues. Many of these companies prefer to have their fiscal year end after the holiday season. The company's fiscal year end is listed in its financial statements.

---

**Current assets** and **current liabilities** represent those assets that the company will either receive (e.g., accounts receivable) or those liabilities that are due to a third party (e.g., accounts payable) within an operating cycle. However, if the operating cycle is less than one year, then one year is considered the cutoff between "short term" and "long term." Most companies have an operating cycle that is less than one year.

At the end of 2005, SampleCo has $490 of current assets, including cash of $165, and $355 of current liabilities. Current assets and liabilities are also referred to as short term assets and liabilities.

Items on the balance sheet are listed according to **liquidity** or likeliness that the item will be converted to cash (if an asset) or cash will need to be paid (if a liability). Therefore, current assets are always listed at the top of the asset section of the balance sheet and current liabilities are always listed at the top of the liabilities and shareholders' equity section of the balance sheet. In almost every situation, cash is listed as the first current asset.

*Assets:* the assets of a business are used to run the business and to generate the company's revenues and other cash inflows. Examples of assets include accounts receivable, inventory, and **PP&E** (property, plant and equipment). Employees are clearly assets for many companies, but accounting rules do not recognize "people" as assets. The salaries for those employees are recognized as expenses on the income statement when they are paid, and salaries payable are listed on the balance sheet as liabilities if the employees have earned salaries but the company has not yet paid them.

PP&E is property, plant and equipment. PP&E is often quoted both on a gross basis and on a net basis after accounting for **accumulated depreciation**, which is the aggregate amount of depreciation recognized on the company's assets.

At the end of 2005, SampleCo has gross PP&E of $1,900; however, $450 of it has already been depreciated. Therefore, the net PP&E amount at the end of 2005 is $1,450.

**Depreciation** represents the portion of an asset that is accrued as an expense against the period's revenues.

For example, assume CarCo buys a new car for its car rental business, which costs $20,000. That car will have a depreciable life of five years (meaning it will help generate revenues for five years). Instead of listing the cost of $20,000 as an expense in the first year, the company would first list the item as an asset on the balance sheet (**capitalize** the asset), and then charge off a portion of the $20,000 every year for five years (**depreciate** the asset). If a straight line method of depreciation were being used (such that an equal amount of depreciation is recognized each year during the useful life) and assuming the car has no value at the end of the five years, then $4,000 ($20,000/5 years=$4,000 per year) would be recognized as depreciation expense each year on the income statement. After one year ($4,000 worth of depreciation has been recognized), the net PP&E account for the car would be:

| Gross PP&E (car) | $20,000 |
|---|---|
| Accumulated depreciation | (4,000) |
| Net PP&E (car) | $16,000 |

Many assets that have been fully depreciated from a balance sheet perspective are still useful in terms of their productive capacity. In our example above, although the car is fully depreciated after the fifth year from an accounting perspective, it could still be useful to CarCo after five years.

Other items on the balance sheet include other long term assets and intangible assets. Intellectual property and patents are examples of intangible assets (which are also long term assets). Intangible assets are assets of a company that cannot be felt or touched. Goodwill is an intangible asset and represents the amount paid for a target company above the identifiable book value of assets and liabilities.

*Liabilities and shareholders' equity*: Together **liabilities** and **shareholders' equity** represent all of the claims on the company's assets. They are what "paid" for the assets and include any and all obligations of the company.

Equity holders have claims on the assets after all liabilities have been accounted for or paid; they have rights to the residual interest of a company, net of other obligations including debt. The relationship is similar to ownership of a home in which Alyssa is the owner, but her ownership interest (her equity interest) will not be free and clear until she pays off her entire mortgage. If she were to sell today, the sale proceeds would go first to repay the mortgage and anything left over (the residual interest) would go to Alyssa. Similarly, in a bankruptcy scenario, equity holders are only paid after all of the company's debts have been paid.

Shareholders' equity can be comprised of preferred stock and common stock. Preferred stockholders receive a preferential dividend and are higher in **liquidation preference** than common stockholders (meaning preferred stockholders are paid before common stockholders in the event of bankruptcy). Common stockholders do not receive a preferential dividend, but they do retain all of the residual interest after the debtholders and preferred equity holders are paid. Not all companies have preferred stockholders, but all companies have common stockholders. Within common stock is an account called **retained earnings**.

For example, on SampleCo's 2005 income statement it had earnings of $135 and paid dividends of $50. Therefore, $85 ($135 – $50 = $85) would flow to the common equity account via retained earnings. At the end of 2005, SampleCo had $1,090 of common equity, an increase of $85 from 2004.

Debt is an obligation of a borrower to a lender or an investor to repay borrowed funds with interest by a certain date in the future. Debt is a liability of the company and it is often listed on the balance sheet according to the type of debt. For example, some companies might list **bank debt** (money borrowed from and owed to banks) separate from bonds (debt securities sold directly to investors). Debt that must be paid within one year is considered short term debt and debt that has a **maturity** (the date on which the money must be paid back) beyond one year is considered long term debt. Short term debt is listed separately in the current liabilities section, while long term debt is usually near the bottom of the liabilities section, befitting its long term orientation. Recall that assets and liabilities are listed in terms of liquidity, which is how quickly the asset is expected to be converted to cash or the liability is expected to be paid.

At the end of 2005, SampleCo has $100 of short term debt and $700 of long term debt.

The debt and equity obligations of a company constitute the company's **capital structure** or **capitalization**. Different types of investors have claims to different parts of a company's capital structure. Depending on the type of investment an investor has in a company, the investor can sell her investments or securities in a secondary market (such as the **NYSE,** or New York Stock Exchange) and the value of the investment can rise or fall relative to the balance sheet value, or **book value**. The **market value** of a company's security (which is the price an investor must pay to obtain the security in the open market) might be materially different from the book value of the investment. There are other long term liabilities that are obligations of the company. Examples of non-debt long term liabilities include deferred taxes, and environmental reserves.

At the end of 2005, SampleCo has $225 of deferred tax liabilities and $120 of other long term liabilities.

*Income statement:* The income statement is a measure of financial performance during a period of time (e.g., quarterly, annually). It measures profitability over time as opposed to the balance sheet, which is a point in time measurement.

At the top of the income statement is the company's revenues (or sales) for the period. In 2005, SampleCo had $1,000 of revenues. From those revenues, a series of expenses are deducted to arrive at net income or earnings for the period. Expenses are any costs that were incurred in order to generate the revenues, such as cost of goods sold, salaries, and advertising expenses. Interest expense is an expense since the cost to borrow money is a cost of doing business, as are taxes paid to the government.

DD&A represents the portion of a capitalized asset that is being expensed for the period in question. Note that DD&A is not always separated in a company's financial statements. Sometimes it is included within another account on the income statement (although it will always be disclosed on the cash flow statement since it is one of the non-cash charges that will be added back to net income to calculate operating cash flow).

EBITDA is a commonly used metric and it represents *earnings before interest, taxes, and DD&A*. EBITDA is a proxy for (but not a substitute for) cash flow generated by the assets of a company before debt holders and tax authorities are paid. EBIT is another commonly used metric and it represents *earnings before interest and taxes but after DD&A*.

> ## ʘʘ What is DD&A?
>
> DD&A stands for depreciation, depletion and amortization. Depreciation relates to physical assets, depletion relates to natural resources (except for land, which value is not depleted for accounting purposes), and amortization relates to intangible assets such as intellectual property and patents. Since depletion only applies to natural resources, most companies do not have depletion. Therefore, the financial community uses "EBITDA" and not "EBITDDA."

Earnings (also known as net income) is calculated after adjusting for all of the year's revenues and expenses. Earnings is an after interest and after tax number. **Earnings per share** is the amount of earnings per share of equity (calculated by dividing earnings by the number of shares outstanding). The income statement must also take into account in its EPS calculation the effect of any potentially dilutive securities. For example, a convertible bond is a bond which, under certain circumstances, can be converted into shares of the company; in that event, the same numerator (earnings) will be distributed over a larger denominator (the now increased number of shares); this convertible bond may be a dilutive security because its conversion may dilute (reduce) earnings per share. Calculating fully diluted EPS is described in more detail later in this chapter. It is important to note that "earnings" is not equal to "cash flow." Many non-cash items are included in earnings.

Dividends are a return of capital to shareholders and are paid out of retained earnings. Dividends per share represents the amount of dividends paid per share of equity. Net income less dividends for a period is called **earnings to common.** Earnings to common flows from the income statement into the common equity account on the balance sheet.

The income statement also reflects any gains or losses resulting from the sale of a company's assets. In addition, companies will generally separate any one-time or non-recurring charges on their income statements, including the effects on the company's earnings of a change in exchange rates, changes in accounting policies, and one-time costs associated with mergers or restructurings.

*Cash flow statement:* The cash flow statement reconciles the income statement and the balance sheets at the end of a period to determine the actual cash flow generated by the company or business. The income statement reflects the earnings of the company for a period. However, many non-cash items, such as depreciation, are deducted from revenues to calculate earnings. The cash flow statement is important since it tracks actual cash inflows and outflows. Both investors and creditors care about the health of a company's cash flow since a significant cash shortfall can have serious implications with respect to a company's ability to fund its growth or pay its obligations going forward. A cash flow statement can be created with an opening and closing balance sheet and an income statement.

The cash flow statement is a reconciliation of the opening and closing balance sheet and income statement and is divided into three sections based upon three distinct management actions or decisions.

The first section is called **cash flow from operations** and represents cash flow related to the day-to-day operations of the business. It begins with net income and adjusts for any non-cash charges found in the income statement, including DD&A. Balance sheet changes related to a company's operations, such as changes in deferred taxes and changes in working capital, are also reconciled in this section.

---

### ˆ○○ˆ What are non-cash charges?

Non-cash charges are expenses on the income statement which do not in fact relate to a cash payment. Depreciation is the classic example. Going back to our car example, the car has a depreciable life of 5 years. Thus, for accounting purposes, 1/5th of the depreciable value of the car is charged as an expense on the income statement each year for five years. However, the company paid the $20,000 in cash on Day 1. There is no additional payment of cash in each of the five years which coincides with the annual depreciation of $4,000. Therefore the $4,000 of annual DD&A is a non-cash charge. Other non-cash charges include non-cash restructuring charges related to a reorganization or non-cash charges related to changes in an accounting method.

---

The second section, called **cash flow from investing,** relates to the acquisition of capital goods or assets or long term investments in other companies (these are called capital expenditures or **capex**). Cash received from the sale of assets or subsidiary companies is also included in the cash flow from investing section. Investment decisions relate to how a company chooses to allocate its capital.

The third section, called **cash flow from financing,** relates to changes in how a company finances its assets. It is the section that accounts for any cash changes related to debt and equity holders, including items such as the payment of dividends, the issuance or repayment of debt, and the issuance or repurchase of equity.

**What about investments financed with new debt?**

GAAP requires that a company report the allocation of capital (which is an investment decision) separately from the source of the capital (which is a financing decision). For example, assume a company purchased an asset for $500 but issued debt of $500 to pay for it. The purchase of the asset would be a cash outflow of $500 in the cash flow from investing section and the $500 of new debt would be a cash inflow of $500 in the cash flow from financing section. Although this amounts to a neutral effect on cash, both transactions must be disclosed separately on the cash flow statement.

The amounts calculated from the three sections are added together to calculate the cash flow generated for the period. This cash flow for the period, also called total change in cash for the period, is then added to the cash balance from the opening balance sheet to determine the cash balance for the closing balance sheet.

**The balance sheet and sources and uses of cash**

An increase in an account on the asset side of the balance sheet from the previous reporting period represents a "use of cash," or a negative number in the cash flow statement. A decrease in an account on the asset side from the previous reporting period represents a "source of cash," or a positive number on the cash flow statement. Conversely, an increase in an account on the liabilities and shareholders' equity side of the balance sheet from the previous reporting period represents a "source of cash" and a decrease represents a "use of cash." If you understand this concept intuitively it will make life easier since you will not have to worry about memorizing the "rule."

An example may help clarify this important concept. Let's say you buy a car and therefore an asset account goes up by $30,000. This increase in the asset account represents a use of cash since you had to "pay" $30,000 to the dealer. The increase in an asset account represented a *use of cash* since you now have $30,000 *less cash on hand* because you used it to buy the car. Now let's say you took out a loan of $30,000 from the bank to pay for the car. The new loan would increase your debt by $30,000 and that increase would represent a *source of cash* since the cash was being provided to you by the bank. The increase in a liability represented a source of cash even though you have to pay it back. You have $30,000 *more cash on hand.* The cash flow statement only tracks flows of cash into and out of the company coffers (that is, shown on the balance sheet), it does not account for whether the cash *belongs* to the company.

Additional examples of sources and uses of cash are provided in the following table.

| Sources of Cash | Uses of Cash |
|---|---|
| Decrease in an asset | Increase in an asset |
| • Sale of a manufacturing plant | • Acquisition of manufacturing plant |
| • Reduction in accounts receivable | • Increase in accounts receivable |
| | |
| Increase in a liability or equity | Decrease in a liability or equity |
| • Issuance of new debt | • Repayment of debt |
| • Issuance of common stock | • Decrease in accounts payable |
| • Increase in deferred taxes | • Decrease in deferred taxes |
| • Increase in salaries payable | • Decrease in salaries payable |
| • Increase in accounts payable | • Buyback of common stock |

Let's now discuss how the financial statements are interrelated. First, let's discuss those items on the income statement that are also related to the balance sheet. The cross-references between SampleCo's balance sheet and income statement are highlighted in Table 13.4.

## Table 13.4 – Ties Between the Income Statement and the Balance Sheet

| Balance Sheet | 2004 | 2005 | Income Statement | 2005 |
|---|---|---|---|---|
| **Assets** | | | Revenues | $1,000 |
| Cash | $200 | $165 | Cost of goods sold | (400) |
| Accounts receivable | 125 | 150 | Gross margin | 600 |
| Inventory | 150 | 125 | Selling, general and administrative | (100) |
| Other short term assets | 45 | 50 | EBITDA | 500 |
| Total short term assets | 520 | 490 | DD&A | (150) [1] |
| Gross PP&E | 1,500 | 1,900 | EBIT | 350 |
| Accumulated depreciation | (300) | (450) [1] | Interest expense | (125) |
| Net PP&E | 1,200 | 1,450 | Earnings before taxes | 225 |
| Other long term assets | 300 | 300 | Income taxes | (90) [2] |
| Goodwill | 250 | 250 | Net income (earnings) | $135 |
| **Total assets** | **$2,270** | **$2,490** | | |
| | | | Shares outstanding | 100 |
| **Liabilities & Shareholders' Equity** | | | Earnings per share - basic | $1.35 |
| Short term debt | $125 | $100 | Earnings per share - fully-diluted | $1.29 |
| Accounts payable | 100 | 150 | Dividends | 50 |
| Salaries payable | 75 | 65 | Dividends per share | $0.50 |
| Taxes payable | 45 | 40 | Earnings to common | 85 [3] |
| Total short term liabilities | 345 | 355 | | |
| Deferred tax liabilities | 200 | 225 [2] | | |
| Other long term liabilities | 120 | 120 | | |
| Long term debt | 600 | 700 | | |
| Common equity | 1,005 | 1,090 [3] | | |
| **Total liabilities & equity** | **$2,270** | **$2,490** | | |

See corresponding footnotes on next page.

1. DD&A from the income statement is added to accumulated depreciation from the previous period's balance sheet to arrive at the new accumulated depreciation.

| | |
|---|---|
| Accumulated depreciation (2004) | $300 |
| Add: 2005 DD&A | 150 |
| Accumulated depreciation (2005) | $450 |

2. Differences in cash taxes paid (the actual amount of cash paid to taxing authorities this year), as opposed to taxes on the GAAP or book income statement, result in a mismatch in cash. A deferred tax liability is created when the tax liability calculated for the GAAP books is greater than the actual taxes paid. You can think of the deferred tax liability in this circumstance as an IOU to Uncle Sam (a tax payment has been recognized in the GAAP books that will be paid to Uncle Sam in the future). For SampleCo $25 of the $90 in taxes is deferred and deferred taxes increased by $25 from 2004 to 2005. A cash adjustment must be made to the cash flow statement to adjust for any cash differences based on taxes.

3. Common equity increases based on net income earned during the period and decreases based on dividends paid during the period. The amount of earnings less dividends is the amount contributed to retained earnings. Also, equity issuances during the year are an increase to the common equity account and repurchases of equity are a decrease to the common equity account. We will assume no equity issuances and no equity repurchases in 2005 for SampleCo.

| | |
|---|---|
| Common equity (2004) | $1,005 |
| Add: 2005 net income | 135 |
| Less: 2005 dividends paid | (50) |
| Add: equity issuances | 0 |
| Less: equity repurchases | 0 |
| Common equity (2005) | $1,090 |

Now we will describe how the cash flow statement is tied to the balance sheets and the income statements. The comments are listed after Table 13.5.

## Table 13.5 – Creating the Cash Flow Statement

| Cash Flow Statement | 2005 | |
|---|---:|---|
| **Operating** | | |
| Net income | $135 | [1] |
| DD&A | 150 | [2] |
| Changes in deferred taxes | 25 | [3] |
| Changes in working capital | 30 | [4] |
| Cash flow from operations | 340 | |
| | | |
| **Investing** | | |
| Capital expenditures | (400) | [5] |
| Other changes in assets/liabilities | 0 | [6] |
| Cash flow from investing | (400) | |
| | | |
| **Financing** | | |
| Common dividends paid | (50) | [7] |
| Changes in short term debt | (25) | [8] |
| Changes in long term debt | 100 | [8] |
| Changes in equity | 0 | [9] |
| Cash flow from financing | 25 | |
| | | |
| Beginning cash | 200 | |
| Total change in cash | (35) | [10] |
| Ending cash | $165 | |

1. The cash flow statement begins with net income from the income statement. Be careful to start with net income and not net income *after dividends*. Dividends are captured in the section Cash Flow from Financing.

2. DD&A is a non-cash charge on the income statement and therefore it is added back to net income in the cash flow statement.

3. We have assumed that SampleCo's deferred taxes increase by $25 from 2004 to 2005. This is a source of cash since the company is paying less in cash taxes than its tax liability on its GAAP books.

4. Changes in working capital represents the total change of both current assets and current liabilities. Neither cash nor short term debt is included in the working capital calculation because, like dividends, short term debt is captured in the section Cash Flow from Financing and cash is what you are solving for. An increase in a current asset from one period to the next represents a use of cash and an increase in a current liability from one period to the next represents a source of cash. The $30 change in working capital on SampleCo's cash flow statement is calculated as follows:

| Changes in working capital | 2004 | 2005 | Source/(use) |
|---|---|---|---|
| Current assets [1] | | | |
| Accounts receivable | $125 | $150 | ($25) |
| Inventory | 150 | 125 | 25 |
| Other current assets | 45 | 50 | (5) |
| Sub-total | $320 | $325 | ($5) |
| Current liabilities [2] | | | |
| Accounts payable | $100 | $150 | $50 |
| Salaries payable | 75 | 65 | (10) |
| Taxes payable | 45 | 40 | (5) |
| Sub-total | $220 | $255 | $35 |
| Total change in working capital | | | $30 |

1. An increase in an asset is a use of cash. A decrease in an asset is a source of cash.
2. An increase in a liability is a source of cash. A decrease in a liability is a use of cash.

5. Capital expenditures represents the amount spent on new assets and investments during the period. Since SampleCo did not sell or retire any assets during the year, the amount of capital expenditures is also equal to the difference in gross PP&E from 2004 to 2005.

6. There were no other changes in other assets and other liabilities for SampleCo from 2004 to 2005.

7. Dividends paid to common stockholders is a financing action; therefore, it is captured as a cash outflow in the section Cash Flow from Financing.

8. An increase in debt represents a source of cash (since the new debt is cash flow that the company can now use). A decrease in debt is a use of cash.

9. Changes in equity represents any change in the common equity account *excluding* net income or dividends. A change in equity would occur if the company issued new common stock or if it repurchased common stock.

10. Total change in cash is the sum of Cash Flow from Operations, Cash Flow from Investing, and Cash Flow from Financing.

## Financial Ratios and Terminology

Like many things, financial statements can be meaningless without a method of reading or analyzing them. For example, if a company earns $50 in net income, is that good or bad? What if it earned $50 million, or $500 million? Financial ratios and financial terminology provide readers of financial statements with the ability to compare a specific company's financial performance to that of other companies using a shorthand method or language. We will discuss some of the most commonly used terms here. Many of the calculations and ratios described here are used in performing M&A analysis, including comparable company analysis and comparable transaction analysis. The rest of this chapter will refer to the financial statements of SampleCo.

***Market value***: Shares in a public company can be bought and sold in a secondary market and the value of a share in the secondary market can be significantly different from its accounting book value. The market value (also known as **equity value**) represents the aggregate value of stockholders' equity based on the current stock price. It is calculated by multiplying the number of diluted shares outstanding by the current stock price.

Diluted shares outstanding    ×    Stock price    =    Market value

Market value is usually quoted based on fully diluted shares outstanding. The closing stock price on a given day should be used for the calculation and the day on which the stock price is taken should be noted with the market value (since prices change from day to day).

Assuming a current stock price for SampleCo of $20, its market value would be calculated as follows:

105 diluted shares outstanding    ×    $20 stock price    =    $2,100 market value

*Basic shares outstanding* and *fully diluted shares outstanding*: Basic shares outstanding are the total number of shares issued and outstanding by a company. The issued and outstanding shares may be significantly fewer than the shares *authorized* in a company's charter or bylaws. **Treasury shares** (shares that have been repurchased by the company in the open market) are considered issued, but they are *not* considered outstanding and, therefore, are not included in the calculation of shares outstanding. The basic shares outstanding for a public company can be found on the first page of its most recent 10Q or 10K.

Fully diluted shares outstanding represents a company's shares outstanding, adjusted for any stock options and/or potentially dilutive securities such as the equity component of **convertible debt** (which is debt that can be converted into equity under certain circumstances).

The **treasury stock method** of accounting is used to calculate fully diluted shares outstanding for options and the **if-converted method** is used for convertible debt or preferred stock. In the treasury method, the options are assumed to have been exercised and the proceeds from the sale of shares are used to repurchase shares in the market at the current market price, thereby partially offsetting the number of new shares issued from the options. Similarly, the if-converted method assumes that potentially dilutive securities are converted to equity. Therefore, the number of shares outstanding increases, but the amount of debt or preferred equity on the balance sheets declines, as does interest expense (in the case of convertible bonds) or dividends paid (in the case of preferred equity), reflecting the fact these securities no longer "exist" since they are assumed to have been converted into common equity.

*Options:* An option is a security that allows the owner to buy a share of common stock at some predetermined price. The predetermined price is called the **strike price** (also known as the **exercise price**).

Assume that SampleCo has 20 options issued with a strike price of $15. This means that the owner of one of these options could exercise her option to purchase a share at $15 from the company. If the current market price is $20, she could also take the share that she just purchased at $15 and sell it in the public market for $20, thereby making a $5 profit just by exercising the option. Options are often provided to employees as a form of compensation. Options to purchase shares that are issued with debt securities or preferred stock are called **warrants**.

For SampleCo, the fully diluted shares would be calculated by adding the basic shares to the additional shares that could be issued from the options. To calculate the additional shares from the options using the treasury method, calculate the available cash based on the difference between the strike price and the current stock price and determine the number of additional shares that could be repurchased with this cash.

| | | | | | |
|---|---|---|---|---|---|
| 20 (options exercised) | × | $15 (strike price) | = | $300 (proceeds from sale) |
| $300 (proceeds) | / | $20 (current price) | = | 15 (repurchased shares) |
| 20 (shares from options) | - | 15 (repurchased shares) | = | 5 (net shares from options) |
| 100 (basic shares) | + | 5 (additional shares) | = | 105 fully diluted shares |

Once you understand the theory behind the treasury stock method, you can apply a shortcut formula to calculate the additional shares. This formula is:

$$\frac{\text{Current stock price} \quad - \quad \text{Strike price}}{\text{Current stock price}} \quad \times \quad \text{Number of options} \quad = \text{Additional shares}$$

For SampleCo, the calculation would be

$$\frac{\$20 \quad - \quad \$15}{20} \quad \times \quad 20 \quad = 5 \text{ additional shares}$$

100 basic shares + 5 shares = 105 diluted shares

If the exercise price of an option is less than the current price, then the option is considered to be **in the money**. If the exercise price of an option is greater than the current price, then the option is considered to be **out of the money**. The SEC and FASB believe that investors are rational and that options will only be exercised if, in fact, they are in the money. If they are out of the money (strike price is greater than market price), then rational holders of the options would not exercise them and, therefore, there will be no additional shares to issue as a result of the options. If, in our example, the current stock price were $10, no rational investor would exercise his option with a $15 strike price. If he did, he would pay $15 for a security that is only worth $10 in the open market. On day one he has already lost $5 per share in value. Thus, if options are out of the money (the strike price is greater than the current price), the options are **anti-dilutive** and no adjustment would be made to the shares outstanding for a fully diluted shares outstanding calculation. Public companies disclose options outstanding in their 10k SEC filings.

> ### ⏱ Expensing options
>
> In December 2004, FASB issued a revision to FAS-123 Accounting for Stock-Based Compensation. The newly revised GAAP requirement is that companies are required to expense the value of their options on the income statement based on the fair value of the option as of the grant date. The fair value of the option must be expensed during the time that an employee is required to provide service to the company. The argument is that companies should recognize the value of the options as an expense since the options do have value when companies issue them to employees (else why would companies issue them to employees?). All companies are required to use the Fair Value Method. Historically, companies used the intrinsic valuation method which allowed them to bypass the income statement if the options were out of the money at the time that they were issued.

***Convertible securities:*** Convertible securities (often called "converts") are debt or preferred securities that can be converted into a predetermined number of shares (either at the company's option or the investor's option). They are hybrid securities that are part debt and part equity and offer the upside of equity with the defensive characteristics (fixed-income and liquidation preference over common equity) of debt. A convertible security has a maturity date and, if it is not converted prior to the maturity date, the security falls due for repayment (just like debt).

To calculate the effects of convertible securities for fully diluted shares outstanding using the if-converted method, you must determine if the convertible is in or out of the money. If it is in the money, then you would calculate the number of shares that would be issued if the convert were exercised. The steps to calculate the new shares issued for a convertible bond are as follows:

1. Nominal value of bond issue / par value (for bonds par value is usually $1,000, but not always) = number of bonds

2. Issue price × (1 + conversion premium) = conversion price (usually 20-40% premium, but not always)

3. Par value (usually $1,000, but not always) / conversion price = conversion ratio

4. Par value (usually $1,000, but not always) / conversion ratio = conversion price

5. Number of bonds × conversion ratio = number of new shares issued

6. If conversion price < stock price then convert is "in the money"

7. If conversion price > stock price then convert is "out of the money"

8. If conversion price is close to the stock price then convert is "at the money"

Let's consider an example in which a company has $350 million 2-percent convertible bonds outstanding. The bonds have a par value of $1,000 and a conversion ratio of 33.333. The current stock price is $40. In this example we are given the conversation ratio and so we must calculate the conversion price. Other times, companies will disclose the conversion premium and you must calculate the conversion price and then the conversion ratio, as described in steps 2 and 3 above.

1. $350,000,000 / $1,000 = 350,000 bonds

2. $1,000 / 33.333 = $30.00 (conversion price)

3. Conversion price of $30 is < current price of $40, so the converts are in the money

4. 350,000 bonds x 33.333 conversion ratio = 11,666,550 new shares

In addition to calculating the new shares that would be issued if the converts were exercised, you must also calculate the after tax interest expense that you would save if the security were converted from debt into equity (since if it were equity, the company would no longer have to pay the interest expense associated with the convertible when it was considered debt).

Assume the corporate tax rate is 35 percent.

1. $350,000,000 × 0.02 = $7,000,000 (pretax annual interest)
2. $7,000,000 × (1 − 0.35) = $4,550,000 (after tax annual interest)

Now let's apply this understanding to SampleCo. Assume that $200 of SampleCo's $700 of long term debt is comprised of 15 convertible bonds. The convertible bonds pay a 5 percent coupon and the conversion ratio is 1.0. We must calculate the effect on net income of eliminating the bonds and the effect on the shares outstanding of converting the bonds.

Recall that SampleCo has net income of $135:

$$\text{Basic EPS} \quad = \quad \frac{\$135}{100} \quad = \quad \$1.35$$

Diluted EPS using the if-converted method:

$$\frac{\$135 + \$6.5^{\text{(note 1)}}}{100 + 15^{\text{(note 2)}}} \quad = \quad \frac{\$141.5}{115} \quad = \quad \$1.23$$

Where:
1.  After tax interest = face value × coupon × (1-tax rate) = ($200 × 0.05 × (1 − 0.35) = $6.5)
2.  New shares = convertible bonds × conversion ratio = (15 × 1.0 = 15)

**Total debt:** Total debt represents the aggregate amount of debt that a company has outstanding at any given point in time. Cash is subtracted from the debt to determine **net debt**. Ideally, the market value of debt would be calculated and used in performing financial analysis. However, since most companies have debt whose book value is similar to its market value, the book value is often used based on the company's most recent balance sheet. Be careful, however, in using book value of debt if you are dealing with a company whose debt is likely to have a market value significantly less than its book value (for example, this is the case with companies that are in the process of a bankruptcy restructuring).

The total debt for SampleCo for 2004 is $800 (based on $100 of short term debt and $700 of long term debt). The net debt for SampleCo is $635 (based on $800 of total debt and $165 of cash).

### ^OO^ Why is net debt calculated?

Excess cash is subtracted from total debt to calculate net debt because investors assume that cash on the balance sheet could be used to pay down debt. If the cash were used to pay down debt, then the debt would be reduced by the amount of cash available. This is also why it is assumed that companies with significant levels of cash are vulnerable to a takeover – because a would-be acquirer could buy the company with debt and, once in control of the target, use the company's own cash to pay down the acquisition debt.

**Enterprise value:** Enterprise value (also known as **firm value**) represents the value of both the equity (common equity and preferred equity) and the debt of a company, based on the current market value of common equity. The market value of equity is added to the book value of the preferred stock and the net debt to arrive at the enterprise value. Minority interest is usually subtracted to arrive at enterprise value.

Market value + Net debt + Preferred equity - Minority interest = Enterprise value

Since the market value for SampleCo is $2,100, its net debt is $635, and SampleCo has no preferred stock and no minority interest then the firm value or enterprise value (based on diluted shares outstanding) is $2,735.

*SampleCo Enterprise Value*
$$\$2,100 \ + \ \$635 \ + \ \$0 \ - \ \$0 \ = \ \$2,735$$

### ◠◠ Why is calculating enterprise value important?

Enterprise value is a proxy for asset value. By calculating the enterprise value, an Acquiror can determine whether it is paying a fair price for the operating assets of a business. As a buyer, inherited debt liabilities should be considered a dollar-for-dollar offset against the value Acquiror is willing to pay to obtain control of the equity of a target company.

Recall that a company's assets are paid for by its liabilities and shareholders' equity. If you wanted to buy a company (including all of its assets), could you get away with just buying the owner's equity? No. What would happen to all of the liabilities and debt of that company?

Consider SampleCo, which for 2005 has book values of $2,490 in assets, $800 in debt liabilities, $600 in other liabilities and $1,090 in shareholders' equity. The market value of equity for SampleCo is $2,100 (based on a $20 current stock price and 105 diluted shares outstanding). Could Acquiror take over the assets of SampleCo just by paying the market value of equity of $2,100?

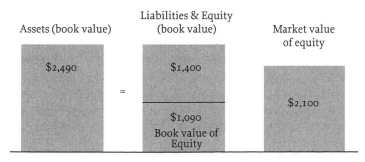

| Assets (book value) | Liabilities & Equity (book value) | Market value of equity |
|---|---|---|
| $2,490 | $1,400 | |
| = | | $2,100 |
| | $1,090 Book value of Equity | |

No, because that $2,100 is only enough to buy the equity in the public market. Acquiror still would have to *assume* (take responsibility for) the liabilities before it could assume control of all of the assets. In essence, Acquiror would have to pay $2,900 to acquire the assets of SampleCo (comprised of $2,100 to the equity holders and $800 in assumed debt). Acquiror would also assume $600 of other non-debt liabilities. Note that this simple example does not take into consideration control premiums, which will be covered in more detail in later chapters.

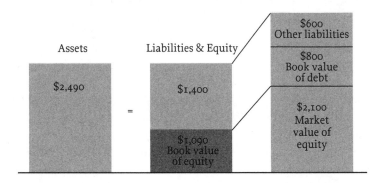

***Earnings per share or EPS***: EPS is calculated by taking the net income (also known as earnings) for a period, and dividing it by the number of basic and fully diluted shares for the same period to calculate the basic EPS and fully diluted EPS, respectively. Usually, EPS is quoted for a company's fiscal year (e.g. $1.00 for 2005), although public companies will also report quarterly EPS during the year (e.g. $0.25 for Q1 2005). FAS-128 of GAAP governs the proper accounting for basic and fully diluted EPS. Since EPS is such an important metric for investors, the rules governing the calculation of EPS are very specific. Consult FAS-128 if you have any questions regarding the calculation of EPS.

EPS is calculated based on the **weighted average shares outstanding** for the period in order to account for any shares that were issued or repurchased during the period. For example, assume a company with 200 shares outstanding issued 50 shares on June 30, 2005. Since the company had 200 shares outstanding as of January 1, 2005, then the weighted-average number of shares for the year would be 225, and this number would be used to calculate the EPS for 2005.

| | | | | |
|---|---|---|---|---|
| 200 | × | 50% | = | 100 (200 shares weighted for ½ the year) |
| 250 | × | 50% | = | 125 (250 shares weighted for ½ the year) |
| 100 | + | 125 | = | 225 (weighted average shares for year-end EPS) |

## ʘ̈ Remember to use weighted average shares

A common error is to calculate EPS based on the shares outstanding at the end of the period, instead of calculating EPS based on the *weighted average* number of shares for the period. This is especially true when calculating the effects of various transactions. Be sure to watch out for this common error. In addition, be sure to watch out for **stock splits** when reviewing a company's shares outstanding. A stock split occurs when a company decides to literally split its shares in two (or whatever ratio it determines) such that the owner of one share becomes the owner of two shares (if there were a 2-for-1 stock split, resulting in twice as many shares outstanding after the stock split).

## ʘ̈ What is quality of earnings?

Investors are particularly interested in the **quality of earnings.** In other words, is the earnings per share sustainable (high quality of earnings) or is it based on non-recurring or one-time items (low quality of earnings)? Investors take special care to determine whether earnings include **non-recurring items** (items that are special and are not part of the company's regular course of business), which will not or cannot be replicated in future years. In general, non-recurring items would be excluded from the earnings or EPS number an investor uses to make investment decisions. Investors are also especially interested in how fast a company's EPS will grow over time. This metric is referred to as the company's **growth rate** and generally represents the compound annual EPS growth over a five-year period. For example, a company with Year 1 EPS of $1 and a 10 percent growth rate would be expected to have Year 2 EPS of $1.10, Year 3 EPS of $1.21, Year 4 EPS of $1.33 and Year 5 EPS of $1.46, with each year's EPS being 10 percent greater than the year before.

Public companies will generally provide investors and equity analysts some guidance as to what they believe their EPS will be for a given year. In certain cases, they might even provide guidance for the following year's earnings. Investors will factor this guidance into their investment decision making and are especially critical of situations in which a company's actual earnings are materially different from the company's previously provided guidance, since investment decisions earlier in the year were predicated on those numbers.

*Price-to-earnings multiple or P/E:* a P/E multiple represents the market value of a stock relative to its EPS. It is the most commonly used multiples-based valuation metric. It is calculated by dividing the current stock price by the annual earnings per share, based on diluted shares outstanding.

$$\frac{\text{Market price}}{\text{EPS}} \quad = \quad \text{P/E}$$

A P/E multiple is usually calculated based both on the **LTM EPS** (the EPS for the latest twelve months) and on a **forward** basis (EPS for the upcoming fiscal year) in order to capture any disparity between the last year's and the coming years' performance.

For example, if the LTM EPS for a company is $2.00 and the current year's EPS (also referred to as FY1 EPS) is projected to be $2.25 and the current stock price for the company is $40, then the LTM P/E = 20x ($40 / $2) and the FY1 P/E = 17.8x ($40 / $2.25).

For SampleCo, the P/E based on 2004 EPS would be calculated as follows:

$$\frac{\$20.00}{\$1.29} \quad = \quad 15.5\text{x}$$

Since the P/E multiple is calculated based on the current stock price and the current stock price represents the market's perception of the company and its future growth prospects, the P/E of a company is generally correlated to the growth prospects of the company. As such, companies with higher growth rates tend to trade at higher P/E multiples and companies with lower growth rates tend to trade at lower multiple levels.

If SampleCo has a five year growth rate of 10 percent, that would imply an EPS in FY2 (forward year 2) of $1.42 ($1.29 × (1+0.10) = $1.42) and a FY2 P/E of 14.1x ($20 / 1.42 = 14.1x).

*Book value of equity:* The book value of equity is the accounting value of the shareholders' equity and it is often used to establish the base level value of equity for a company. Since it is based on a company's accounting records, it is a historical-based method of considering value as opposed to other methods which are based on future earnings power. In general, the book value of equity is stated for the common equity and excludes preferred stock. The challenge with using book value of equity as a metric is that it does not take into account the market value of the equity as reflected in the stock price.

For SampleCo, the book value of equity at the end of 2005 is $1,090. As with most balance sheet-related items, it is common to refer to the most current balance sheet information.

***Price-to-book ratio or price/book multiple:*** Price/book (also known as market/book) is another commonly used multiple. It represents the market value of equity as a multiple of the book value of equity. Most companies have a market value which is higher than their book value. The price/book multiple is calculated by dividing the market value of equity by the book value of equity.

$$\frac{\text{Market value of equity}}{\text{Book value of equity}} \quad = \quad \text{Price/book multiple}$$

For SampleCo, the price/book ratio would be calculated as follows:

$$\frac{\$2,100}{\$1,090} \quad = \quad 1.9\text{x}$$

---

**ᴼᴼ Do you include or exclude preferred equity?**

In general, the book value of equity refers to a company's common equity and, therefore, preferred equity should be excluded when calculating a price/book multiple. Be careful, however, when reviewing a company's financial statements since companies often will include preferred equity as part of their summary equity section.

---

***Enterprise value to EBITDA:*** Like P/E, the EV/EBITDA multiple is commonly used to measure a company's relative valuation. Unlike P/E, however, which is related to the market value of equity of a company, an enterprise value to EBITDA multiple is related to the enterprise value (or the firm value). It is calculated by dividing the enterprise value by EBITDA.

$$\frac{\text{Enterprise value}}{\text{EBITDA}} \quad = \quad \text{EV/EBITDA multiple}$$

For SampleCo, the EV/EBITDA multiple would be:

$$\frac{\$2,735}{\$500} \quad = \quad 5.5\text{x}$$

> ### ʻOOʻ Enterprise value vs. equity value multiples
>
> When calculating multiples, be careful to differentiate between when to use enterprise value and when to use equity value in the numerator. In general, the numerator should match the denominator. For example, EBITDA is a pre-interest or pre-debt number, meaning it represents a value to the firm and not just to the equity holders. That is why enterprise value is used with EBITDA when calculating multiples. Net income, on the other hand, is an after interest or after debt number. It is a value that flows only to equity holders, which is why P/E is calculated using equity value and not firm value.

**Return on equity (ROE):** Return on equity represents the earnings power of the shareholders' equity and is calculated by dividing the earnings by the shareholders' equity. It is stated as a percentage:

$$\frac{\text{Earnings or net income}}{\text{Book value of equity}} = \text{Return on equity (ROE)}$$

ROE is often used as a measure of financial performance. Since earnings is an after-interest number, ROE is considered a metric for leveraged returns (or returns after accounting for debt). Similar calculations such as return on invested capital (ROIC), return on investment (ROI), and return on assets (ROA) are used in conjunction with ROE. Since these other metrics relate to the assets of a company (as opposed to just the equity component), these are considered metrics for unleveraged returns.

For SampleCo, the ROE would be calculated as follows:

$$\frac{\$135}{\$1,090} = 12.4\%$$

**Dividend per share (DPS):** Dividends per share represent the amount of dividends paid per each share outstanding. They are calculated by dividing the total amount of dividends by the number of basic shares outstanding.

$$\frac{\text{Dividends}}{\text{Shares outstanding}} = \text{Dividends per share (DPS)}$$

The dividend per share for SampleCo would be calculated as follows:

$$\frac{\$50}{100} \quad = \quad \$0.50$$

***Dividend yield:*** Dividend yield represents the amount of dividends received per share of stock owned relative to the current stock price. It is calculated by dividing the DPS by the current stock price and is stated as a percentage.

$$\frac{DPS}{Current\ stock\ price} \quad = \quad Dividend\ yield$$

Dividend yield is an important number since it provides investors with a proxy for how much cash flow they will receive each year for holding the stock relative to the investment price. Dividend yield is often considered in combination with a company's growth rate to calculate the **total return** for a company (dividend yield plus earnings growth), since earnings growth is a proxy for stock price appreciation. Generally, slower growth companies have higher dividend yields compared to higher growth companies in order to compensate for their slower growth and therefore slower stock price appreciation. Some companies, especially higher growth companies, do not pay dividends.

For SampleCo, its dividend yield would be calculated as follows:

$$\frac{\$0.50}{\$20.00} \quad = \quad 2.5\%$$

Assuming a 10% EPS growth rate, total return would be calculated as follows:

2.5% (dividend yield)   +   10.0% (EPS growth)   =   12.5% (total return)

***Payout ratio:*** the payout ratio represents a company's dividends per share as a percentage of earnings. It is calculated by dividing DPS by EPS.

Higher growth companies tend to have lower payout ratios because they are reinvesting cash back into the business. More mature, slower growth companies tend to have higher payout ratios since – with fewer calls on the cash to grow the business – they return more of the cash to shareholders.

The payout ratio for SampleCo is calculated as follows:

Based on basic shares

Based on diluted shares

$$\frac{\$0.50}{\$1.35} \quad = \quad 37\%$$

$$\frac{\$0.50}{\$1.29} \quad = \quad 39\%$$

# Strategic Transactions

## Chapter 14

*Better one safe way than a hundred on which you cannot reckon.*

*Aesop*

## Strategic Planning

Every company, big or small, should have a strategic vision or **strategic plan**. One of the primary goals of that strategic plan should be to:

> Improve, maintain, and/or accelerate the market leadership, profitability, and growth trajectory of a company, thereby leading to enhanced shareholder value.

A strategic plan goes beyond geographic expansion plans and new product ideas. It also goes beyond the financial projections for the company. Rather, a company's strategic plan is a roadmap addressing a fundamental question: What type of company does it aspire to be and how does the company expect to achieve that goal in the next five to ten years.

A strategic plan must balance the desires to grow shareholder value, and thereby appeal to equity investors, with a complementary financing strategy that appeals to debt investors as well. A **strategic transaction** is any action that helps implement a company's strategic plan. That action can be on a small scale (such as the sale of one manufacturing plant) or a large scale (such as a corporate merger with another company). In addition to building, buying and/or selling assets, a strategic action can be related to financing, such as the decision to implement an aggressive stock buy-back program or recapitalization. The value of a strategic transaction is measured by many metrics, the most important of which is a company's stock price.

The product of any strategic planning exercise is usually a "base case" financial forecast for the next five to ten years. The base case forecast should incorporate the most likely operating and financial strategy. Alternative scenarios as well as upside and downside cases are usually prepared as sensitivities to the base case. The strategic plan is usually updated once a year after a company wide effort to capture the most likely operating and financial scenario. Throughout the year, the base case strategic plan and financial forecast are used as planning tools.

## Strategic and Financing Transactions

A company can maximize shareholder value using both strategic transactions and financing transactions. Strategic transactions are further divided into two main categories: (1) transactions to enhance or grow a business, such as a strategic acquisition, and (2) transactions to clarify a business, such as the sale of a non-core division. Financing transactions are also further divided into two main categories: (1) transactions to fund growth such as a major equity offering and (2) recapitalization transactions, such as a share buyback program.

### Figure 14.1 – Maximizing Shareholder Value

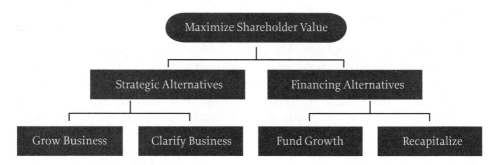

Specific examples of transactions to grow, clarify, fund and recapitalize a business are provided in Figure 14.2. To maximize flexibility, many companies consider more than one strategic option at any given time. When a company pursues a **dual path**, it prepares for two or even three options and follows each path as if it were going to be executed. This way, the company is prepared to execute a number of strategic options and can decide on one or two depending on market conditions as the time for a final decision approaches. Because many companies pursue dual path processes, it is important that advisors be well versed in all of the strategic options shown in Figure 14.2.

## Figure 14.2 – Strategic Options to Maximize Shareholder Value

| Strategic Alternatives | Financing Alternatives |
| --- | --- |
| **GROW BUSINESS** | **FUND GROWTH** |
| Organic growth | Private placement |
| Invest in research and development | Issue bank debt |
| Strategic alliance | Issue public debt |
| Joint venture | Issue public equity |
| Acquire assets | Issue private equity |
| Strategic merger | Manage liabilities |
| **CLARIFY BUSINESS** | **RECAPITALIZE** |
| Sale of major subsidiary | Special dividend |
| Spin-off or split-off of major subsidiary | Change dividend policy |
| IPO of major subsidiary | Large share repurchase |
| Tracking stock | Ongoing share repurchase |
| Sale of company for cash | Major recapitalization |
| | Leveraged buyout |

## Buy vs. Build

To grow a business, a company's management must decide between buying and building. Buying allows a company to satisfy certain strategic goals in a shorter period of time, whereas building allows a company to develop products or services exactly as it wants. Buying and building are not mutually exclusive, and many successful companies are both aggressive buyers *and* builders. Some of the advantages of building and buying are described below.

*Advantages of building*

- Full control over how the work is performed, how the products are made and how customers are treated
- No need to pay a control premium for another company
- Pride of ownership (e.g., Apple)
- Protection of proprietary technology (e.g., The Coca-Cola Company, Procter & Gamble)
- Maintenance of corporate culture, as desired (e.g., IBM)

*Advantages of buying*

- Opportunity to enter a new geographic or product market immediately (e.g., Deutsche Telekom/Voicestream to create T-Mobile USA)
- Acquisition of an irreplaceable asset (e.g., a patent or market-leading brand)
- Elimination of a competitor
- Reduction or elimination of execution risk inherent in trying to build the business from scratch
- Acquisition of an existing distribution network (e.g., Federal Express/ Kinko's)

## Strategic Rationale

A transaction should only be considered if it makes good strategic sense for a company. Buying a non-strategic company on the cheap (just because one can profit from the deal) is the business of leveraged buyout and private equity companies; it is not the business of a strategic player. The first litmus test of any transaction should always be: what is the strategic rationale of the transaction?

Examples of strategic rationales are listed below. Either independently or in conjunction with others, each might provide a good reason for undertaking a transaction. They are organized into one of three categories: (1) revenue growth, (2) cost savings and margin improvement, and (3) technology enhancements. In addition to these strategic rationales, you may be able to think of others.

*1. Revenue growth*

- Gain access to a faster growing customer base or product market
- Benefit from cross-marketing opportunities among various products and/or markets
- Better manage and utilize strategic assets
- Improve penetration in core markets
- Strengthen brand portfolio with a complementary but growing business
- Elevate a business or brand to a regional, national or global scale by leveraging customer or distribution channels

*2. Cost savings and margin improvement*

- Improve manufacturing and operating margins (achieve economies of scale)
- Reduce risk by reducing volatility of earnings and cash flow
- Leverage purchasing power
- Leverage sales force and/or distribution infrastructure
- Reduce work force

- Enhance sourcing capabilities
- Fill an operating gap

*3. Technology Enhancements*

- Gain access to proprietary intellectual property or technology
- Complement and leverage core skills and technology
- Combine technology and R&D functions and reduce operating costs
- Increase flexibility to accommodate product innovation (may also produce revenue benefits)

## Increasing Shareholder Value

If a transaction makes strategic sense for a company, then the next important question is: *Does the transaction increase shareholder value?* Shareholder value is literally the value *created* for the shareholders of a company. Value creation for a public company is measured most transparently by the company's stock price. Ultimately, however, the most important consideration is whether a transaction increases the intrinsic value of a company (even if not immediately reflected in share price appreciation).

To measure whether a transaction increases shareholder value, the financial impact of a transaction must be considered. Attractive financial impact occurs if the transaction:

- Provides earnings per share accretion and accelerates growth
- Diversifies credit risk and reduces cost of capital
- Achieves strategic objectives and financial targets more rapidly
- Increases financial return metrics such as return on equity (ROE) or return on invested capital (ROIC)
- Provides for trading multiple expansion

The main factor that drives the value of a company's stock price is growth, of both earnings per share and cash flow per share. For start-up companies, revenues or sales growth is a key indicator since many start-ups do not have earnings and may even have negative cash flows. Investors look for a return on their investment, and earnings and cash flow appreciation are proxies for shareholder return. The faster a company grows, the faster value and/or capital may be returned to shareholders in the form of stock price growth or dividends.

*If a company's stock price is a measure of a company's ability (or inability) to increase shareholder value, and if stock prices are driven by an investor's expectation of growth, then how do strategic transactions play into the quest for value creation?*

Two variables factor into a company's stock price (when using a multiples-based valuation method). The first is the company's earnings and/or cash flow, and the second is the valuation multiple that investors use to price the stock. Ideally, strategic transactions will affect both of these variables in the stock price equation. An important consideration in determining which strategic transaction(s) to undertake, therefore, is to identify on a per share basis which transaction(s) will increase the earnings and cash flow side of the equation and/or the company's valuation multiple.

The impact of a transaction on earnings per share and cash flow per share depends on a number of items, including: (1) the price paid for Target, (2) the consideration used (e.g., stock vs. cash), (3) the accounting treatment of the transaction and (4) any synergies generated from the transaction. **Accretion/dilution analysis** considers all of these factors to calculate a pro forma EPS for the transaction. Accretion/dilution is a fancy way of saying "Does a transaction increase (accrete) or decrease (dilute) the earnings per share (or other financial metric) of acquiror?"

Earnings and cash flow per share are just one part of the valuation calculation. If a strategic transaction causes a company to be valued in the market at a higher multiple than its current multiple, then the stock price will increase even if no incremental earnings or cash flow are generated. This in itself is value enhancing. The act of a valuation multiple increasing is called **multiple expansion** and the act of a valuation multiple decreasing is called **multiple compression**.

For example, if a company's EPS is $1.50 and its current P/E multiple is 15x, the implied stock price is $22.50.

$$\$1.50 \text{ EPS} \times 15\text{x P/E multiple} = \$22.50 \text{ stock price}$$

However, assume the company undertakes a transaction that is consistent with its strategic plan and enhances the company's future growth prospects (but does not actually increase EPS in the current year). The transaction also minimizes the company's financial risk and credit risk, and the transaction repositions the company to become the market leader in its sector. All of these things would be viewed positively by the market and the market might subsequently "re-rate" the company with a higher P/E multiple. Let's say the market re-rates the company at a 17x P/E multiple. Even with the same EPS of $1.50, the new stock price would be $25.50, or 13 percent greater than the status quo stock price of $22.50.

$$\$1.50 \text{ EPS} \times 17\text{x P/E multiple} = \$25.50 \text{ stock price}$$
$$(\$25.50 / \$22.50) - 1 = 13.3\% \text{ increase}$$

It should be noted that price to earnings is not the only valuation multiple that investors care about. Enterprise value to EBITDA (EV/EBITDA) and price to cash flow (P/CF) are also important, among others.

It is never easy to determine with certainty the multiple at which a company will trade in the future. A company's trading multiple will be driven not only by its own performance but also by the performance of its peers, the state of the overall market and interest rates, and the market liquidity of the stock, among other factors. However, certain transactions will be viewed positively by investors if the transaction is consistent with the company's strategic plan and will be viewed even more positively if the transaction also provides an attractive financial impact. Conversely, a transaction that is not consistent with a company's strategic plan, even if the transaction provides an attractive financial impact, is likely to be viewed negatively by the financial community and investors. This might result in the company's trading multiple being re-rated down (multiple compression), so that even with a higher EPS from the proposed transaction, the Acquiror's stock price might be lower.

$$\$2.00 \text{ EPS } \times \text{ 10x P/E multiple } = \$20.00 \text{ stock price}$$
$$(\$20.00 / \$22.50) - 1 = 11.1\% \text{ decrease}$$

As Table 14.3 shows, a benefit to *either* Acquiror's EPS *or* its P/E multiple leads to an increase in stock price (or shareholder value) at a percentage rate equal to the change in *either* EPS or P/E. Accretion/dilution analysis should be performed for any contemplated transaction because, as shown in Table 14.3, it is a proxy for share price accretion or dilution on a pro forma basis (post transaction).

## Table 14.3 – EPS and P/E Multiple Impact on Stock Price

*Scenario:* *Status quo*

| | |
|---|---|
| Earnings per share (EPS) | $1.50 |
| P/E multiple | 12.0× |
| Status quo stock price [1] | $18.00 |

*Scenario:* *Earnings change*

Note what happens to the implied value per share for the company when its earnings per share increases or decreases by 10 percent but the P/E multiple does not change

| | | |
|---|---|---|
| Percentage change in EPS | 10% | (10%) |
| Earnings per share (EPS) [2] | $1.65 | $1.35 |
| P/E multiple | 12.0× | 12.0× |
| Implied stock price | $19.80 | $16.20 |
| Percentage change in stock price from status quo [3] | 10% | (10%) |

*Scenario:* *Multiple change*

Note what happens to the implied value per share for the company when its earnings per share does not change but the P/E multiple increases or decreases by 10 percent

| | | |
|---|---|---|
| Percentage change in P/E multiple | 10% | (10%) |
| Earnings per share (EPS) | $1.50 | $1.50 |
| P/E multiple [4] | 13.2× | 10.8× |
| Implied stock price | $19.80 | $16.20 |
| Percentage change in stock price from status quo [3] | 10% | (10%) |

*Scenario:* *Earnings change and multiple change*

Note what happens to the implied value per share for the company when its earnings per share and the P/E multiple both increase or decrease by 10 percent

| | | |
|---|---|---|
| Percentage change in EPS and P/E multiple | 10% | (10%) |
| Earnings per share (EPS) | $1.65 | $1.35 |
| P/E multiple | 13.2× | 10.8× |
| Implied stock price | $21.78 | $14.58 |
| Percentage change in stock price from status quo | 21% | (19%) |

---

1. EPS × P/E multiple = stock price

2. $1.50 × (1 + percentage change)

3. (Implied stock price / status quo stock price) - 1

4. 12 × (1 + percentage change)

## Table 14.3 continued

*Summary table*

|  | Share price | % change from status quo |
|---|---|---|
| Status quo | $18.00 | 0% |
| EPS change only (+ 10%) | $19.80 | 10% |
| EPS change only (- 10%) | $16.20 | (10%) |
| Multiple change only (+10%) | $19.80 | 10% |
| Multiple change only (-10%) | $16.20 | (10%) |
| EPS change (+10%) and multiple change (+10%) | $21.78 | 21% |
| EPS change (-10%) and multiple change (-10%) | $14.58 | (19%) |

## Synergies

**Synergies** are either reduced costs or increased revenues created by a merger or other strategic transactions. **Cost synergies** are efficiencies created through improved operating practices, the elimination of redundant functions, and greater economies of scale. For example, if two companies with separate call centers merge and eliminate one of the call centers without affecting productivity or customer service, this is a cost synergy since the two companies can achieve the same level of revenues with reduced costs, thereby improving margins. **Revenue synergies** result from the ability to generate greater revenues through the merger of two companies, such as Acquiror selling its products through Target's distribution network.

Because synergies are subject to uncertainty, it is often informative to analyze synergies as a range of values as opposed to targeting one particular value or estimate for synergies.

Common categories of synergies include:

*Cost Synergies*

- Consolidated purchasing
- Selling, general and administrative (SG&A) reductions (e.g., back office, marketing, corporate administration)
- Manufacturing and/or plant consolidation
- Distribution benefits
- Better management
- Lower cost of capital
- Synergies from filing consolidated taxes
- Removal of duplicate public company administrative costs

*Revenue Synergies*

- Access to partner's customer or geographic markets (if different)
- Cross-selling to partner's customers
- Improved market penetration

Synergies are a critical component of the value creation in a strategic transaction because, in theory at least, in an efficient market there is no value creation without synergies. An example may help clarify this concept.

Let us assume that a company is available for sale. Acquiror values Target at $500 million and purchases it for $500 million in cash. Acquiror has paid "fair value" for Target meaning Acquiror purchased an asset worth $500 million by paying $500 million in cash. Has Acquiror created *value* for itself with this transaction? No. Acquiror added a $500 million asset to its business portfolio, it is true, but it *paid* fair market value for it. Acquiror has not created any value since the transaction has a net present value of zero (NPV=0). That is, there is no additional value created after the purchase price of $500 million has been paid to the Sellers.

Let us now change our assumptions slightly. It turns out that this company for which Acquiror paid $500 million has a contiguous distribution area to its own, and Target has underutilized capacity in its sales and distribution system. In addition, Acquiror already has a top-notch management and corporate development team that can assume a number of new responsibilities in addition to their current responsibilities. As a result, Acquiror is able to eliminate the Sales, Distribution, Executive, and Corporate Development functions of Target. All told, those services cost about $20 million annually, which will now flow to Acquiror's bottom line (to earnings). This $20 million of annual cost savings are the pretax synergies created from the transaction. Ultimately, if Acquiror pays "fair value" for Target, then the value creation for Acquiror is the capitalized "value" of all future synergies arising out of the transaction which Acquiror does not give to Target in the form of an increased purchase price.

> ## ʻOOʻ "Paying away" synergies
>
> If Acquiror paid more than "fair value" for Target on a standalone basis, then Acquiror actually paid away to Target some of the value of the transaction synergies rather than keeping the value of those synergies for itself. If there are competing bidders for Target, paying away some of the synergies might be necessary in order to win control of Target. It is important, however, for bidders not to pay Target *more than* fair value plus synergies because if this is done, the transaction will have a net present value of less than zero (meaning it will be a value-losing

**👓 "Paying away" synergies (continued)**

transaction from day one). In Figure 14.4, notice that the maximum price Acquiror should pay for Target is $620 million, which is the sum of the standalone value for Target of $500 million plus the value of the synergies of $120 million. If Acquiror pays more than $620 million, Acquiror will pay more than the combined value of (1) Target's value on a standalone basis and (2) the capitalized value of the synergies. If Acquiror pays $500 million for Target, Acquiror will keep the $120 million of synergy value for itself. If Acquiror pays Target somewhere between $500 and $620 million, then Acquiror will pay away some of the synergy value and keep some of the synergy value for itself.

## Figure 14.4 – Components of Value

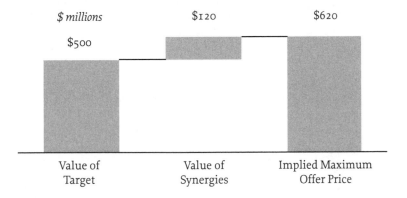

How is the $120 million of synergy value actually calculated? By virtue of Acquiror's ability to absorb this new company without needing to absorb much of its cost structure, it will have $20 million of cost synergies per year that Target does not have on a standalone basis. Assuming Acquiror's current P/E multiple is 10x and a 40 percent tax rate, this $20 million of annual savings should generate $120 million of additional value (further assuming P/E is the appropriate method to value this company). The calculation of the $120 million is shown in the following table.

## Table 14.5 - Capitalizing Synergies

| | | |
|---|---|---|
| Savings | = | $20 million pretax synergies each year |
| Tax rate | = | 40% |
| After-tax savings | = | $20 × (1 − 0.4) = $12 million each year |
| Incremental earnings | = | $12 million each year |
| P/E multiple | = | 10x |
| Capitalized synergies | = | Incremental earnings × P/E multiple |
| | | $12mm × 10 = $120 million |

### ⌐OO⌐ Why is P/E such a commonly used metric?

Many people wonder why P/E is such a commonly used valuation metric. Refer to the example above in which a merger generates an additional $20 million of pretax earnings and, as a result, implies additional value of $120 million using a P/E multiple method of valuation. Consider this incremental savings of $20 million per year, or $12 million after tax per year, in the context of basic corporate finance. What does this stream of cash flows look like? Since these are incremental earnings that will continue forever (or as long as the company is in existence), we can think of this as a perpetuity in which the annual after tax cash flow is $12 million. The way to value a perpetuity is to apply the formula:

$$PV_{perpetuity} = \frac{Cash\ Flow}{Discount\ rate} = \frac{CF}{r}$$

In this example, CF = $12 million and the present value = $120 million. Applying the perpetuity formula, you can calculate an *implied* discount rate of 10 percent.

$$\frac{CF\ (\$12\ million)}{r\ (unknown)} = PV\ (\$120\ million)$$

To solve for $r$, divide $12 by $120
$12 / $120 = 0.10, or 10 percent

The implied discount rate in this example is 10 percent, and the inverse of 10 percent is 10 (1 / 0.10 = 10), which is the P/E multiple. Therefore, the inverse of the P/E multiple is the implied discount rate using the perpetuity method of valuation.

## ◠◯◯ Why is P/E such a commonly used metric? (continued)

Investors use P/E multiples for valuation purposes because it is a proxy for a perpetuity discount rate and therefore is a shortcut cash flow based method of valuation. If the inverse of the P/E multiple represents a perpetuity discount rate, then multiplying earnings per share by a P/E multiple is effectively using the perpetuity method of valuation.

| EPS | × | P/E multiple | = Present Value |
| $12 million | × | 10x | = $120 million |

*Which is the same as*

| EPS | / | Discount rate | = Present Value |
| EPS | / | Inverse of P/E multiple | = Present Value |
| $12 million | / | 10% or 0.10 | = $120 million |

Since P/E is a method to value the stock or equity of a company, the assumption is that earnings is a proxy for cash flow to equity holders and the inverse of the P/E multiple is equal to the discount rate for an equity holder.

Or, if you consider a growing perpetuity formula in which you divide the cash flow by the result of $(r - g)$, where $r$ is the discount rate and $g$ is the perpetual growth rate, the inverse of the P/E multiple is equal to the difference between $r$ and $g$. In the example above, we might assume that the long term growth rate $(g)$ is 1 percent or 0.01 and therefore the discount rate $(r)$ is 11 percent or 0.11, so that the implied $(r - g)$ is equal to 0.10 (0.11 − 0.01 = 0.10).

Valuation using P/E multiples is often employed by investors due to its simplicity. It is a short cut method of cash flow valuation to equity holders using the perpetuity method or growing perpetuity method of valuation. And it is simple to use because all that is needed to perform the present value calculation is EPS and a P/E multiple.

It is important to remember that while many synergies are positive, there are usually some offsetting costs as well (sometimes referred to as "negative synergies" or "costs to achieve synergies"). Thus, synergies analysis must include the costs to achieve the projected synergies (such as severance expenses for headcount reduction; facility shutdown costs for plant closures, including environmental cleanup; relocation expense; etc.).

Synergies analysis must also include all negative synergies, such as SG&A to replace services formerly provided by a parent company (legal, treasury, audit, etc.), lost sales at either Acquiror or Target due to customer or product cannibalization, transition issues, the potential for disruption to Target's and/or Acquiror's business, and the renegotiation of contracts with change of control provisions.

When a transaction is announced, financial markets will generally give more credit to forecasted cost synergies than to forecasted revenue synergies. The reason is because cost synergies are more easily quantifiable and because they are considered more likely to be achieved.

For example, if a redundant production facility is to be closed as part of a transaction, and that plant has 500 employees with a fully loaded cost per employee (cost of salary plus all benefits) of $67,000 per year, that is $33.5 million of annual pretax cost savings (500 × $67,000 = $33.5 million). This $33.5 million is an identifiable number because the company knows how many employees work at the plant and it also knows what it pays to each of these 500 employees. Because these items are known, there is a high likelihood that the annual pretax cost savings will be close to $33.5 million once the 500 employees are laid off.

A challenging aspect of revenue synergies that is sometimes overlooked is the impact on operating margins from the increased sales. For example, assume a merger of two beverage companies increases output from 75 million bottles to 95 million bottles on a bottling line with a capacity of 100 million bottles. This occurs because Acquiror operates in different markets than Target and therefore has the ability to sell 20 million more bottles than Target did on a stand alone basis. Because this increase of 20 million bottles is on an existing production line, there is no increase in fixed costs. In the following table notice how the increase from 75 million bottles to 95 million bottles increases the gross margin percentage from 78 percent to 81 percent by reducing the production cost per bottle.

## Table 14.6 – Revenue Synergies and Gross Margin Increase

*Assumptions*

| | |
|---|---:|
| Fixed operating costs | $9,000,000 |
| Variable costs (per bottle) | $0.10 |
| Selling price per bottle | $1.00 |
| Maximum bottle capacity per plant | 100,000,000 |

| | Existing | Post transaction |
|---|---:|---:|
| Bottles produced | 75,000,000 | 95,000,000 |
| | | |
| Fixed operating cost | $9,000,000 | $9,000,000 |
| Variable cost at 10 cents per bottle | 7,500,000 | 9,500,000 |
| Total costs | 16,500,000 | 18,500,000 |
| | | |
| Cost per bottle (total costs / bottles produced) | $0.22 | $0.19 |
| Capacity utilization (bottles produced / maximum capacity) | 75% | 95% |
| Selling price per bottle | $1.00 | $1.00 |
| Gross margin per bottle (selling price – cost per bottle) | $0.78 | $0.81 |
| Gross margin percentage (gross margin / selling price) | **78%** | **81%** |

Now assume Acquiror can sell 40 million more bottles (as opposed to 20 million more bottles) so that post transaction 115,000,000 bottles would be produced. Since the existing production line can only handle 25 million more bottles (because its capacity is 100 million and it currently produces 75 million), changes would be required in order to handle the additional capacity. In order to sell the additional 40 million bottles, let's assume the company adds an additional production line to the factory. The new production line would increase fixed costs by another $9 million but would add another 100 million of bottling capacity, increasing the total capacity to 200 million. Notice in this situation that, even though the number of bottles sold increases by 40 million, the gross margin decreases from 78 percent to 74 percent.

## Table 14.7 – Revenue Synergies and Gross Margin Decrease

*Assumptions*

| | |
|---|---|
| Fixed operating costs ($9,000,000 × 2) | $18,000,000 |
| Variable costs (per bottle) | $0.10 |
| Selling price per bottle | $1.00 |
| Maximum bottle capacity per plant | 200,000,000 |

| | Existing | Post transaction |
|---|---|---|
| Bottles produced | 75,000,000 | 115,000,000 |
| | | |
| Fixed cost | $9,000,000 | $18,000,000 |
| Variable cost at 10 cents per bottle | 7,500,000 | 11,500,000 |
| Total costs | 16,500,000 | 29,500,000 |
| | | |
| Cost per bottle (total costs / bottles produced) | $0.22 | $0.26 |
| Capacity utilization (bottles produced / maximum capacity) | 75% | 58% |
| Selling price per bottle | $1.00 | $1.00 |
| Gross margin per bottle (selling price – cost per bottle) | $0.78 | $0.74 |
| Gross margin percentage (gross margin / selling price) | **78%** | **74%** |

This type of change in gross margin is very important to consider and incorporate into a model for valuation analysis or financial impact analysis. Thus when analyzing a potential transaction and considering revenue synergies, be sure to understand the impact of the additional revenues on the Target's operating cost structure and margins.

# The Role of Valuation

## CHAPTER 15

*Bought a cheap horse, $16 ... he is blind.*

### Henry John (H.J.) Heinz

Valuation analysis is the act of determining how much an asset, portfolio of assets, stream of cash flows or business is worth. It is performed by corporations, investors, analysts and bankers for a wide range of situations. Examples of when valuation analysis should be performed include: (1) when an investor needs to determine what price should be paid for an investment - the investor could be an individual purchasing securities, or the investor could be a company or group of investors buying another company; (2) as a tool in making strategic decisions; (3) when a company is preparing for an initial public offering in order to determine a valuation range for its stock; (4) when prospective partners are creating a joint venture in order to know how to split the partnership fairly; (5) by investment bankers when providing a fairness opinion; (6) by management when issuing stock options to determine the proper strike price for the options; and (7) in litigation work in order to determine potential damages. This chapter will provide both a conceptual discussion of valuation and an overview of the most commonly used valuation techniques.

## Value is Relative

Value is a *relative* concept, not an *absolute* one. An asset or business may simultaneously be worth a certain price to one buyer and a different price to another buyer, or one price to a buyer at one point in time and a significantly different price to the same buyer two years later. For a seller, that means there is a range of values (not one absolute value) that represents a fair price for the asset or business. In addition, the nominal value of an asset or business can be affected by prevailing macroeconomic conditions, such as the interest rate environment. Specifically, low interest rates lower the cost of capital for a company. A low cost of capital allows buyers to afford higher purchase prices because return thresholds are easier to achieve. The opposite holds true in a high interest rate environment -- with high interest rates, a buyer's cost of capital increases, which drives purchase prices down.

When performing valuation analysis, those new to M&A often try to find one correct answer or one correct number. There is no absolute correct answer or number when it comes to valuation. Instead, a range of values is more appropriate. This is partly because the same asset is worth different amounts to different buyers, and partly because valuation is based on assumptions. Each change in assumptions leads to a different valuation result. It is impossible to know with certainty which assumptions will ultimately prove correct since assumptions relate to the future. Therefore, it is impossible to know with certainty what the "correct" valuation is since it is based on assumptions which have a natural margin of error built into them. As a result, analytically rigorous valuation analysis must recognize that buyer preferences, prevailing conditions and margin of error all play a role in valuation. The only way to capture such disparities is to provide a range of values rather than a specific value when performing valuation analysis.

A business owner or executive might think his business or asset is worth a certain amount -- perhaps someone told him his company was worth a certain value in the past and that particular number has stuck in his mind, or perhaps the company has a team that regularly performs internal valuation analysis. Regardless of how someone has come to believe what his company is *worth*, it is important to remember that no seller can decide independently what her business or asset is *worth*. Nor can a buyer decide independently what an asset or business is *worth*. It takes a willing buyer *and* a willing seller to determine a market value. Also, a buyer cannot buy if the seller is not ready to sell; and a seller cannot sell unless a buyer is ready to buy.

Consider the price you might pay for a home. You cannot go to a "home supermarket," select the home you want with a nonnegotiable sticker price on it, and walk to the checkout counter to pay for it. When selling a home, sellers have listing prices that represent the price or value they want for the home. When buying a home, buyers make offers based on (1) what they think the home is worth and (2) what they can afford. Imagine that your friend Steve is a prospective buyer. He has searched and searched and finally found a New York City apartment that he likes which is listed at $800,000. However, given the apartment's size, features, associated liabilities (e.g. plumbing and electrical issues), and the neighborhood, he does not think it is *worth* $800,000. So he makes an offer for $730,000. The seller considers Steve's offer, but decides she would like to hold out for a higher price. A few weeks later, Marc, another buyer, makes an offer for $780,000 and the seller accepts it. They sign a legal agreement binding each other to the sale.

In this example (which is not at all uncommon), two independent buyers came to a different conclusion as to the value of the home. Is one of them right and one of them wrong? No. The same apartment was simply *worth* more to one party than to another. Perhaps Marc works only a few blocks from the building and therefore ascribed a significant amount of value to location. Regardless of the reason, there was $50,000 of value ($780,000 - $730,000 = $50,000) that existed for Marc that did not exist for Steve and, as a result, Marc was willing to pay more for the same apartment.

And the seller who thought her apartment was worth $800,000 realizes that it is only worth $730,000 to $780,000 (which is the range of values offered by interested buyers for the apartment).

While more complex, selling a business or a company's asset is not very different in theory from selling a home. Different buyers will come to different conclusions regarding value. Some buyers will be emotional about the company or asset whereas some buyers will make their decision based solely on the financial and strategic merits of the transaction. The goal of a seller is to find the buyer who is willing to offer the highest value <u>and</u> who can deliver the best contractual terms (including, importantly, the greatest certainty to closing).

> ## ˆ𝗈𝗈ˆ Valuation tenets
>
> When performing valuation analysis it is important to remember:
> 1  There are no absolute prices, only relative values;
> 2. Different buyers will allocate different values to different components based on how they plan to run the company or use the asset; and
> 3. Prevailing factors, such as interest rates, industry growth rates, and consolidation trends, will affect valuation levels.

## Valuation Methods

The best indicator of value for a public company is the current stock price. The market provides the best leading indicator of fair value because it reflects the price an investor is willing to pay at any given moment for a non-controlling share of the company. However, the current market price must be tested to see if the market price reflects the intrinsic value of the company (i.e., to check if the market is correctly valuing the company). Also, with a private company, there is no current stock price to refer to so other valuation methods must be used.

So how do people agree on a value for a non-controlling interest or a controlling interest in a company? Agreed upon valuation methodologies provide a common language for buyers, sellers, advisors, analysts, creditors, lenders and courts. While there are many valuation methods, the five listed below are the most commonly used in M&A and corporate finance analysis:

1. Comparable company analysis
2. Comparable transaction analysis and premiums paid analysis
3. Discounted cash flow analysis (DCF)

4. Leveraged buyout analysis (LBO)
5. Breakup analysis

Some of these methodologies are more appropriate in certain situations than in others. Most often, some combination of these five valuation methodologies is used to triangulate to a valuation range. This means that many or all of these analyses are performed and then a valuation range is determined based on the conclusions from each of the analyses. There are also specialized valuation techniques such as recapitalization analysis and liquidation analysis that are used in specific circumstances. In addition, certain industries, including natural resources, financial institutions, and real estate, have specialized industry-specific valuation methodologies that are regularly used.

## Multiples Based Methods

**Comparable company analysis** and **comparable transaction analysis** are *multiples* based analyses, meaning that the value of an asset or company is calculated as a multiple of a metric, such as earnings per share, cash flow, revenues, or EBITDA. The primary characteristic of comparable *company* analysis is that it is based on current stock prices and generally reflects the value for a **minority interest** (or non-controlling interest). The primary characteristic of comparable *transaction* analysis is that it is based on prices paid in acquisitions for control of the company and therefore includes a **control premium** (or price paid in order to take control of the company, as opposed to a minority share whose owner cannot determine on his or her own how the company is run). Thus, in an efficient market, the only difference in valuation using comparable company analysis and valuation using comparable transaction analysis should be the control premium.

---

### ʘʘ What is a multiple?

If a candy company sold for $100 million and the company had revenues of $50 million for the year ending 2005, then the company sold at a *sales multiple* of 2x 2005 sales.

$100 million purchase price / $50 million in sales in 2005 = 2x 2005 sales

A sales multiple is just one type of multiple; there are many types of multiples that are used in valuation analysis.

---

### Comparable Company Analysis

- The premise behind comparable company analysis is that a non-controlling interest in companies within the same industry or companies exhibiting similar underlying business fundamentals (e.g., growth, profitability, risk, volatility, etc.) should be valued in the equity market on the same relative basis as a multiple of financial and operating metrics.

- Comparable companies (the "trading comp set") are selected and financial multiples are calculated for each of the companies in the trading comp set based on the current stock price of each company in the peer group. Examples of multiples include price to earnings (P/E), enterprise value to EBITDA (EV/EBITDA) and price to book (P/B).

- Multiples from the trading comp set are then applied to the data of the company being valued in order to determine an implied valuation range for the company being valued.

- Comparable company analysis is the best method for valuing a minority interest or for pricing an IPO (initial public offering of a company's stock). It is not as useful of a method in a sale context since comparable company analysis does not include a control premium.

- Comparable company analysis is also referred to as comparable trading analysis.

## Comparable Transaction Analysis

- The premise behind comparable transaction analysis is that a controlling interest in companies within the same industry or companies exhibiting similar underlying business fundamentals (e.g., growth, profitability, risk, volatility, etc.) should be acquired (in a change of control transaction) on the same relative basis as a multiple of financial and operating metrics.

- Companies within an industry or peer group that were acquired in a change of control transaction are selected (sometimes dating back many years if there has not been much M&A activity in a sector). Financial multiples are calculated for each of the transactions in the comp set based on the sale price of each company in the peer group.

- The types of multiples used in comparable company and comparable transaction analysis are the same – the difference is that comparable company analysis is based on the stock price in the public market and represents a non-controlling share whereas comparable transaction analysis is based on the price an acquiror paid for control of a company and includes a control premium. Examples of multiples include price to earnings (P/E), enterprise value to EBITDA (EV/EBITDA) and price to book (P/B).

- Multiples from the transaction comp set are then applied to the data of the company being valued in order to determine an implied valuation range.

- Premiums paid analysis is often performed in conjunction with comparable transaction analysis. In premiums paid analysis, premiums paid per share of stock in comparable change of control transactions are applied to the stock price of the company being valued. For example, assume that in the telecom sector, the average premium paid during the last two years in M&A transactions was 25 percent. Assume you are valuing TelecomWest which is currently trading at $30 per share. You could apply the average 25 percent premium to a share of TelecomWest stock to estimate the implied M&A value per share of TelecomWest.

$30 per share × (1 + 0.25 average premium) = $37.50 M&A value per share

- Comparable transaction analysis is also referred to as precedent transaction analysis.

---

### ᴼᴼ What does it mean to "spread comps?"

In finance parlance, the verb "to spread" generally means to prepare a financial analysis using Microsoft Excel. Spreading comps means to prepare a set of comps -- the data is literally spread across the columns of an Excel spreadsheet.

---

## Cash Flow Based Methods

**Discounted cash flow analysis** and **leveraged buyout analysis** are cash flow based methods of valuation which use time value of money fundamentals. With discounted cash flow analysis and leveraged buyout analysis, value is determined based on the projected cash flows that the company or asset generates, discounted by the company's (or asset's) cost of capital. Since DCF and LBO analyses are based on forward looking projections, they are valuation methods which allow a company's operating strategy and growth strategy to be included in the analysis. Valuation using DCF and LBO analysis is determined *intrinsically*, based on what the asset or company generates itself, not based on multiples or metrics from comparable companies or comparable transactions.

A derivation of DCF analysis is **discounted equity value analysis** or DEV. The difference between DCF and DEV is that DEV considers only the cash flows to and the value for equity holders, whereas DCF considers cash flows to and the value for both debt and equity holders. LBO analysis goes a step further and makes a determination of value based on how much leverage (or amount of debt) the asset or business can support, thereby maximizing returns to the equity holders.

## Discounted Cash Flow Analysis

- The premise behind discounted cash flow analysis is that the firm value or enterprise value (which is the value to both the debt and equity holders of a firm) should equal the present value of the perpetual free cash flows of the company, discounted by the company's weighted average cost of capital. Free cash flow represents all of the cash inflows and outflows of a company excluding any financing related charges such as interest payments to debt holders or dividend payments to equity holders.

- Since DCF analysis is based on projected free cash flows, great care must be taken in developing projections which are reliable, reasonable and which accurately reflect the most likely operating scenario for the company.

- Discounted cash flow analysis is considered the best method for calculating the intrinsic value of a company since value is calculated based on internally generated cash flows of the company, and those cash flows are then discounted based on the inherent risks of those cash flows. There are no "outside" forces in effect such as prices paid for other companies (as is the case with multiples based analysis) or the return required by a private equity investor (as is the case with leveraged buyout analysis).

## Leveraged Buyout Analysis

- Leveraged buyout analysis is based on the assumption that a company will be purchased by private investors and the company will become privately held. The buyout will be paid for with debt and private equity.

- Acquiror will raise the highest allowable levels of debt (given the target credit ratings and the market appetite for the company's debt) such that the equity investors contribute the minimum amount of equity practicable, thereby maximizing equity returns.

- The LBO value of the company is the maximum offer price at which the equity investor earns his minimum required equity return. In today's market, most private equity investors require an annual equity return between 15 and 30 percent. Historically, private equity investors would only consider transactions with an annual equity return greater than 25 percent.

- LBO analysis is often used to determine the "floor" value for a company since it represents what a financial buyer would be willing to pay. Since strategic buyers are usually able to generate more synergies than a financial buyer and since strategic buyers tend to have lower return requirements than financial buyers, strategic buyers are generally able to pay more for the same company than a financial buyer.

## Breakup Analysis

- The question in breakup analysis is: "What is a company worth if I break it up and sell off the pieces?" It is generally used only if a company operates in more than one major line of business.

- All four of the other methodologies are applied in breakup analysis.

- It is, however, important to consider the tax consequences of breaking up a company and selling off the component pieces, since adverse tax consequences can nullify any additional value that otherwise might have been created in a breakup scenario.

## Valuation Ranges

Once various valuation analyses have been performed, it is important to review the valuation ranges derived from various methods and use all of that information to triangulate a valuation range for the company. Investment bankers often create a page called a **football field** to graphically depict the various valuation ranges derived using different valuation methodologies. An example of a valuation football field can be found in Figure 15.1.

In general, a football field will show that the valuation range from comparable company analysis is lower than that of comparable transaction analysis (because comparable transactions include a control premium). This is not always the case, however, especially if there has not been M&A activity in the industry for many years.

## Figure 15.1 – Example of a Valuation Football Field

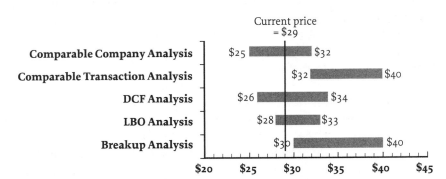

In Figure 15.1, the current stock price of $29 is within the comparable company analysis range of $25 to $32. The comparable company analysis range is less than the comparable transaction analysis range of $32 to $40. This is generally to be expected since comparable transaction multiples include a control premium whereas trading comparables (from comparable company analysis) do not. The comparable company analysis range in Figure 15.1 is generally in line with the DCF analysis range, which means that, currently, investors are properly valuing the company in the public markets relative to its intrinsic value. The breakup analysis range in Figure 15.1 is wider than some of the other methods. This is not uncommon because there is less certainty in the values of several component pieces compared to a single company (because there is execution risk involved with each of the individual sale transactions and also because there may be uncertainty as to the range of values for some of the component pieces).

If the company in Figure 15.1 were for sale and a would-be Acquiror were to offer $38 per share, the offer is likely to be considered "fair" from a financial point of view due to the fact that:

1. $38 represents a $9 per share or 31 percent premium to the current price of $29;

2. $38 is on the high end of the comparable transaction analysis range of $32 to $40 ; and

3. $38 is greater by $4 per share than the high end of the DCF analysis or "intrinsic value" range of $26 to $34.

This means that, assuming the markets were to properly value this company based on a DCF valuation, the highest value a public investor should be willing to pay for a non-controlling interest is $34 per share. If Acquiror were to offer $38 per share, the offer price would exceed the standalone intrinsic value of the company. The only reason a potential acquiror should be willing to pay $38 per share for a company that is, at most, worth $34 on a standalone basis is because the potential acquiror can create *more than* $4 per share of synergy value (such that a price of $38 per share is still a value enhancing transaction for Acquiror *even after* paying away $4 in synergy value in order to gain control of Target).

If, in this same example, the DCF analysis range were $35 to $45, as shown in Figure 15.2, as opposed to $26 to $34, as shown in Figure 15.1, Target might not want to accept an offer of $38 per share. If the company believes in the integrity of its strategic plan and its projections, it might want to try and realize its strategic plan and then allow time for the market to reward it with a higher stock price. Assuming the market ultimately does recognize the intrinsic value of the company (assumed here to be the DCF analysis range of $35 to $45), it is possible that this company could be worth more in the public markets than the $38 per share offered by Aquiror.

## Figure 15.2 – Example of a Valuation Football Field

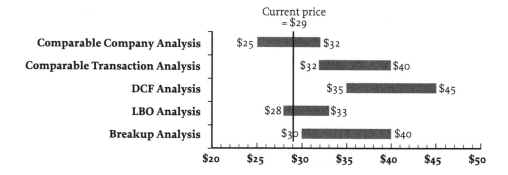

# ACKNOWLEDGMENTS

*The Practitioner's Guide to Investment Banking and The Recruiting Guide to Investment Banking were conceived and written at the same time. As a result, it would be extremely difficult to distinguish between contributions to one book, the other or, in some cases, both. Out of necessity, the following full set of acknowledgments appears in both books.*

We are grateful to many people for their unflagging editorial, strategic, and emotional support in bringing these books to fruition. If these books are useful it is only because so many extraordinary friends, colleagues, mentors, and family members helped make them so. Collaborating with all of you on this multi-year project has been a remarkable experience for us both professionally and personally. We are humbled by your knowledge, experience, insights, and willingness to help. On behalf of those whom we hope to help with these books, we thank you.

A few individuals, in particular, were instrumental in this project. It is difficult to capture in words the appreciation we have for Jimmy Elliott, Edward McAniff, Bert Valdman, and Roger Wood. Their imprimatur is felt throughout this work. These books are as much theirs as they are ours.

> Jimmy Elliott, head of JPMorgan's North American M&A Group and one of the finest practitioners we know, instilled in us a love for banking and taught us the importance of building the tool chest, step by step. Jimmy never asks anyone to work harder than he works himself. From him we have learned a tremendous amount about winning, the business of investment banking, being an advisor, and that being a teacher is an important element of being a leader. The most important lesson he imparted to us is that there is absolutely nothing to fear if you know what you're doing.

> Edward (Ted) McAniff, senior partner at O'Melveny & Myers, law professor and counsel to us on all things personal and professional, contributed immense time and energy toward this project not to mention all of our other endeavors. Ted significantly improved a number of sections, provided us thoughtful direction along the way, and field tested material with his students. Ted's commitment to teaching served as inspiration for this project in the same way that his commitment to excellence inspires us every day.

> Bert Valdman, chief financial officer of Puget Energy, played a major role in bringing these books to completion. Were it not for Bert, these books might not have been finished. For almost ten years Bert has been a mentor and friend, encouraging us to challenge ourselves and to stay focused on the end-goal while

reminding us to enjoy the journey. Bert was always willing to review sections of the books and many times gave us invaluable advice on both direction and tone.

Roger Wood, head of Power Investment Banking at Rothschild North America and longtime mentor, was tireless in his support of and help on reviewing and editing major sections of the books. Roger taught us the importance of keeping one's eye on the details as well the need to keep true to oneself in spite of what can be immense outside pressures. An outstanding banker, Roger provided comprehensive feedback and detailed comments on how to improve multiple sections of the books.

The M&A, corporate finance, and valuation sections benefited greatly from the wisdom and expertise of some of the most competent finance professionals we know. We hope we have faithfully reflected their knowledge and insights. For reading countless review packages, answering repeated phone calls and e-mails, and for greatly improving this work, we are deeply grateful.

Greg Annick, founder and managing director of Pasadena Capital Partners and former partner at Leonard Green & Partners, was instrumental in editing the leveraged buyout and financial sponsor sections. Greg's exceptional integrity and steadfast commitment to doing what is right inspire us more than he will ever know.

Souren Ouzounian, managing director at Merrill Lynch, provided comments, criticism and suggestions on the capital markets, financing and credit sections. A constant source of strength and a trusted confidante, Souren serves as role model to us in many ways.

Steve Raftopoulos, managing director and head of middle market M&A at JPMorgan, provided meaningful comments to the M&A and valuation sections. Steve's sense of humor and down-to-earth manner keep us grounded and focused on what is most important.

Marc Castellani, vice president at JPMorgan, was especially helpful in reviewing and editing the valuation sections. In addition, Marc's commitment to training junior colleagues serves as a model for what we want these books to accomplish.

Richard Wong, vice president at Banc America Securities, probably responded to more left-field questions than anyone. One of Richard's greatest virtues, as a friend as well as a banker, is his ability to make anyone comfortable in his presence. His friendship has long been a source of support.

Gavin Wolfe, managing director at Credit Suisse First Boston, provided valuable contributions to various M&A sections. Gavin and his wife Hope helped support this project in ways they might never fully appreciate.

Peter Cimmet, director of strategic planning at Arysta LifeScience, provided suggestions which greatly improved the M&A sections. He regularly reminds us that laughter is an important component of success in banking and in life.

Richard Ford, managing director at Royal Bank of Canada, devoted significant time to the accretion/dilution chapter and also shared some of his own writings on the subject, which proved to be very useful as we grappled with simplifying this important and often confusing topic.

James Lind at Berkshire Bridge Capital offered valuable suggestions on the leveraged buyout and financial sponsor sections. Always available for a quick phone call, Jim served as an important sounding board on our many private equity questions.

Julie Bell, director at JH Partners, graciously and tirelessly responded to a regular deluge of e-mails asking her opinion on numerous topics. Julie was deeply involved in helping shape the glossary and also contributed to the corporate finance and recruiting sections.

Jonathan Adler, partner at Fried Frank, committed an enormous amount of time to review and substantially improve the deal mechanics section. Clients and colleagues alike benefit from his gentle good humor and sheer competence.

Craig Adas, managing partner of the Menlo Park office of Weil, Gotshal & Manges, was unfailing in his willingness to help us improve the legal sections. He has clarified concepts and answered legal questions for nearly ten years now and we are grateful to him for it.

Derek Whang, associate at The Halifax Group, made valuable contributions to the valuation, leveraged buyout, interviewing, recruiting, and life for a junior banker sections. Derek's signature laugh is priceless as is his friendship.

Ram Seethepalli, director of business development in Asia for Cendant, has offered help in many ways and on many levels. While his work on the books consisted of reviewing M&A sections, his influence is felt far more broadly.

Maya Tichio, vice president at Deutsche Bank and one of the most detail-oriented and thoughtful people we know, was particularly helpful in developing the glossary as well as the financial statement and corporate finance sections.

Kaoru Ogihara, associate brand manager at DelMonte Foods and always gracious and good hearted, provided feedback on the valuation, corporate finance, interviewing and recruiting sections.

Todd McKenzie, executive vice president at Countrywide Financial, was particularly helpful in reviewing the due diligence and deal mechanics sections, sharing anecdotes and clarifying concepts to greatly improve these sections.

John Morris, managing director and co-head of ratings advisory at Lehman Brothers, was tremendously helpful as we wrote and rewrote the credit and sources of capital sections. A thoughtful and pragmatic advisor, John has helped many clients and colleagues learn the intricacies of credit analysis.

Charles Freeman, vice president at JPMorgan, significantly improved the credit sections and clarified a number of challenging concepts. One of the most conscientious and candid professionals we know, Charlie is extremely effective as a credit analyst and as a mentor.

Thomas Musante, managing director at AIG SunAmerica, read through numerous sections and characteristically provided helpful feedback at every turn, including the covers and introduction.

John Whelan, vice president at JPMorgan, provided sage advice and feedback on the sources of capital and credit sections. Financial sponsors are fortunate to have John work on their behalf, as are we.

Todd Guenther, managing director at Lehman Brothers, asked difficult questions which served to improve the M&A and valuation sections. Todd has served as a confidante and sounding board on multiple matters over the years.

Marc Junkunc, Ph.D. and assistant professor of management at the University of Miami, was integral in the development of the corporate finance sections. Marc's sensitivity as a teacher and experience as an analyst helped improve these sections tremendously.

Samuel Thompson, Jr., professor of law and director of the UCLA School of Law Center for the Study of Mergers and Acquisitions, helped us correct and considerably improve the tax sections. He also provided insight and advice on the writing process arising out of his many published articles and books.

Alex Panos, managing director at TSG Consumer Partners, made significant contributions to the leveraged buyout, private equity, and discounted cash flow sections and we appreciate his advice on how to market and sell these books.

Lotti Chi, associate at Primus Asset Management, reviewed the financial statement and corporate finance sections and provided meaningful feedback on a number of things along the way including illustrations and charts.

Will Morris, partner at American Industrial Partners, reviewed and improved the leveraged buyout and private equity sections and also serves as a role model as someone who successfully balances a professional career with a love for the outdoors.

John Tjia, managing partner of TMG & Associates, spent considerable time reviewing the accretion/dilution chapter. John also provided encouragement and advice on the process of writing and publishing which helped us tremendously.

Jim Morris, managing partner of TMG & Associates, was integral in improving the merger accounting and accretion/dilution sections. Jim also shared insights and advice arising from his own experience as an author.

Dan Collin, principal at Monomoy Capital Partners, read through the M&A sections and provided helpful suggestions based on his experience as an analyst and associate.

Philip Arra, vice president at Hunt Investment Group, considerably improved the corporate finance sections.

Joseph Brant, who has one of the hardest jobs of anyone we know, was helpful in ensuring that the corporate finance sections were clear, accessible, and written in layman's terms.

Jon Rezneck, associate at Greenhill, provided a number of useful suggestions which served to greatly improve the valuation and financial statement sections.

Robert Tichio, private equity associate at Goldman Sachs, provided helpful feedback on the corporate finance sections and served as a sounding board as we developed the investment banking sections.

Tina Chan, former analyst at JPMorgan, reviewed the accretion/dilution chapter in detail and always reminded us of the virtues of returning home to California.

Richard Casavechia, managing director at JPMorgan, taught us a great deal about the structuring aspects of M&A through his advice over the years.

Patrick Walravens, managing director at JMP Securities, was helpful in improving various M&A sections.

Catharina Min, partner at Squire, Sanders & Dempsey, reviewed and improved the merger agreement and deal mechanics sections.

Ben Benjamin, former partner at O'Melveny & Myers, reviewed the tax section and clarified a number of concepts.

Marc Jones, former partner at McDermott Will & Emery, provided constructive comments and suggestions on a number of legal sections.

Don Weil, longtime entrepreneur, provided advice and perspective at multiple points along the way.

Steve Kopff was helpful in improving the tax and accounting sections.

Henry Gosebruch, vice president at JPMorgan, sets the standard and we are all better for it.

Lance Bylow, senior vice president at Lehman Brothers, has long been a thoughtful and selfless friend. His encouragement during difficult periods is particularly appreciated.

A number of colleagues made meaningful improvements to the recruiting, interviewing and life on the job sections. As any experienced banker will tell you, interviewing for and landing the job are as difficult and frightening as any M&A or capital raising transaction. We gratefully acknowledge those who played a seminal role in the development of these important sections.

Martin Atkin, former head of recruiting and junior resources at JPMorgan and now senior portfolio manager at Sanford Bernstein, was instrumental in developing the voice and tone of the recruiting and interviewing sections. His additions to the recruiting section improved the work well beyond where it might have been without his input. British by origin, a world citizen by choice and a class act in every respect, Martin has long been a role model for us.

Nelson Shing, senior vice president at Nicholas-Applegate and trusted friend, whose counsel has led us on the right path many times. He has long been an extension of the family and also prepared Jerilyn for her very first banking interview many years ago.

Jon Menor, investment analyst at Brandes Investment Partners, reviewed various sections of the book and also served as Jerilyn's better half on many complicated transactions at JPMorgan. He may be the only surfing Hawaiian who can build an Excel model that would make Bill Gates proud.

Lex Miron introduced us to his colleagues at Savvian, which enabled us to field test material from the book. Lex also provided anecdotal additions to the life on the job sections with the perspective of an older sibling or trusted friend.

Steve Matloff, former associate at Morgan Stanley, made suggestions which caused us to significantly rewrite various sections and we thank him for the encouragement to take this entire process slowly and steadily.

Matthew Rho, vice president at SV Investment Partners, was extremely helpful in editing the recruiting and life on the job sections and enthusiastically supported the project early in the process when we needed encouragement the most.

Christian Charnaux, former analyst at JPMorgan and one of the best at having fun but never letting it get in the way of being competent, provided terrific comments to the life on the job and interviewing sections.

Chris Bell, marketing manager at Intuit and characterized by his love of finance, was helpful in reviewing and editing the recruiting and interviewing sections as well as the corporate finance sections.

Peter Lee, associate at Tiger Management and a great example of a classic American success story, helped us as we first crafted the recruiting and life on the job sections.

Anshuman Vohra, associate at Carl Marks Advisory Group, provided substantial comments for the life on the job sections. Anshuman's extraordinarily positive attitude has always distinguished him personally and professionally.

Kerry Dolan, senior editor at Forbes Magazine and lifelong friend, served as an extremely helpful sounding board throughout the project, assisted with the introduction and covers and responded to our many questions regarding editing and writing.

A heartfelt thank you to those people who touched the book in more ways than they will ever know. For their help, support, and commitment to this project, we are deeply grateful.

Rachel Castillo, sister, friend, and superb at the vastly underrated skill of simply getting things done. From helping edit, to fact checking, to navigating the publishing world, to creating the glossary and bibliography, Rachel's contributions to this project and to our lives are immense. If it weren't for her talent in film production, we would steer her toward a career in banking.

Mary and Edward Kresky often served the role of counselors and surrogate parents. The quintessential New York couple, whose entertaining stories about New York politics and business provide us with immense pleasure, we greatly appreciate the many pep talks, invitations and home-cooked meals

Our outstanding interns, Allen Kogan, Marcello Pantuliano, Ross Fox, Yvonne Lin, Candace Jackman, and Maria Pablo, were tireless in their reading, editing, and fact-finding missions. We never would have been able to handle all of this without them.

Sonny and Gloria Kamm for giving us countless ideas about the book and for assuring us that a little irreverence is a good thing.

Jeanne Leinhardt and Leslie Gardner, managing directors at JPMorgan and, more importantly, colleagues and friends, have long been supportive and willing to go the extra mile on behalf of clients and colleagues.

Julia Min, executive director, MBA Program at the Haas School of Business at UC Berkeley, was enthusiastically supportive of the books and provided excellent marketing ideas borne of her experience working at Haas and NYU's Stern School of Business.

We are deeply indebted to our employers, JPMorgan, Lehman Brothers, Banc America Securities, and the Office of Ronald Reagan for giving us an opportunity. We are proud to have been involved with such outstanding institutions and impressive people.

Much of our desire to pursue careers in investment banking started in the classrooms of two influential finance professors. We thank William Cockrum, professor at the Anderson School at UCLA and former vice chairman of A.G. Becker & Co., and Stephen Etter, longtime finance lecturer at the Haas School of Business at UC Berkeley and partner at Greyrock Capital Group, for bringing their love of finance and banking into their respective classrooms. We hope these books do for others what Professors Cockrum and Etter did for us years ago.

The production of these books is a major undertaking, especially for investment bankers who were neophytes to the world of publishing. These books would not have been possible without the creative expertise of a number of specialists who were generous and patient as we came up the curve. In particular, we would like to thank Alejandro Paul, our fantastic and talented graphic designer who probably suffered with us more than anyone else on the actual creation of these books. Gracias por toda su ayuda, su paciencia y su amistad. Thank you to our editors Meghan Ward and Suzanne Young for improving our work literally one page at a time. Our illustrator Jeffrey Bean was terrific at taking our scribbled ideas and translating them into art.

Catharyn Martz provided expert indexing, a formidable task in books like these. Candace Hinkle and Laurie Houghton of Sheridan Books were helpful in sharing their book production expertise. And Tracey and Nat Bolton of Bolton Designs and Sarah Sloboda were wonderful to work with as we developed electronic media for this project.

To those colleagues who, though they may not have contributed specifically to these pages, were nonetheless instrumental in our professional development and therefore a *sine qua non* for these books. From them we learned a tremendous amount about investment banking and without their mentorship we would not have had the capability or confidence to embark on a project like this. Thank you to the following current or former managing directors at JPMorgan: Laurence Whittemore, Paul Dabbar, Jamie Grant, Sarah Nash, Avi Lewittes, Rick Escherich, Jim Bold, Hernan Cristerna, David Jeffries, and Walter Hulse. Also, for being role models and for leading by example, thank you to Bill Williams, senior partner at Sullivan & Cromwell, Judge Alfred T. Goodwin, Senior Judge, Ninth Circuit Court of Appeals, Jose de la Torre, dean of the business school at Florida International University, and Tom Labrecque, former chairman of Chase Manhattan Bank.

To those friends and colleagues with whom we have shared memorable and often comical experiences in and out of the office, thank you for ensuring that the real benefit of banking is our lasting friendships. In addition to the colleagues who helped with the book, thank you to Paul Ward, Nathan Craig, Dave Blechman, Hala Ataya, Martin Kurtz, James Baker, Eddy Allegaert, Howard Rhee, Jamey Spencer, Ladell Robbins, Edouard Metrailler, Sylvia Son, Jay Koval, Helen Shan, Kristin Williams, R.A. McDonough, Greta Kessel, Hank Romaine, James Tashjian, Ian McAllister, Steve McKenna, Norm Gretzinger, Brett Pickett, Brad Nii, Derek Idemoto, Rich Lark, Yancey Spruill, Christiana Voskarides, Chris Martell, Peter Kuhn, Lowell Strug, David Kramer, Luis Galeano, Eileen Smith, Luis Castro, Jon Secor, Chris Reale, Doug Gonsalves, Lori Lancaster, Megan Taylor, Redic Thomas, Thomas Donnelly, James Smith, Ed Hikmet, David Brakoniecki, Alison Dolan, Anu Aiyengar, Sheru Chowdry, Kelly Hampaul, Karen Wong, Raymond Junior, Fifi Chan, Vera Tzenova, Carl Vevle, Jakeym Hubert, Vielcka Mansukhani, Diana Chen, Sakura Takano, Rohit Mohindra, Tom Miles, Yezan Haddadin, Alejandro Vicente, John Bates, Alex Allgood, Jay Ferguson, Caleb Hsieh, Randal Klein, Stephanie Ng, John Overbay, Tim Panos, David Stonberg, and Chris Winchenbaugh.

Ted Craver, Peter Lersey, Russ Harding, Sandra Seville-Jones, and the rest of the Edison International team, thank you for teaching us that being an advisor is as much about being a good friend as it is being a good banker.

Thank you to the many other clients with whom we were fortunate to work so closely, in particular, Gerald Luterman and Ann Jordan and the rest of the KeySpan Energy team, the Strategic Planning team at Puget Energy, in particular Jim Sant and Don Gaines, and Mark Greenbaum, Emily McNeal and the analysts and associates at Savvian.

We would not have survived New York without the aid, assistance, humor, and occasional ministrations of Lorraine Friedman, Tammy LoCascio, and Jeanne Meehan. We have been and always will be their biggest fans.

Jared Kieling, editorial director at Bloomberg Press, offered encouragement at a critical time in the development process of these books.

Lou Paget, best-selling author and longtime friend, helped us navigate the perils of writing and publishing and offered advice and words of experience along the way.

A heartfelt and sincere thank you to those who have been a pillar of strength for us these last few years, including Ross and Cynthia Peet, Elaine and Mike Darer, Dan Zohar, Amyra Rand, Nicole Smelzer, Carlos Madrazo, Andy Wilcox, Meredith Kenny, Chaco Clotfelter, Greg Warnick, Roxanne Castillo, Sid Wales, John Fish, Matt Tysler, Kacie Stratton, James Scott, Greg Zimmer, Steve and Tami Holsten, John Savarese, Neils Bergquist, Bill Thomas, Roger Minami, the Franks, Joan Liechty, Chip and Sarah Blaufuss, Ross Higuchi, Gary Waldron and Sunny Foster, Ann Longyear, the Ryan family, Chip Cushman, Carla de Cervantes, David Rauch, Tom Goepel, Alejandro Ogarrio, Thomas Kelly, Lisa Brant, y nuestros amigos en Buenos Aires: Fernando y Paula Lopez, Gabriel y Florencia Lopez, y Frank y Fabiana Almeida. Their friendship helped us reach the finish line.

Our wonderful and supportive families, the McAniffs, Castillos, Peets, Armases, Reisses, Judillas, Carvers, Grahams, and Aquinos, who in spite of sometimes not knowing exactly what it is we do or where we are doing it, always provided assurances that these books would be worth it. We thank them for their unlimited supply of encouragement.

Our parents, for always believing in us. It is a pleasure to be their friends and an honor to be their children.

Our siblings, Jennifer, Rachel, Alyssa, and John, Maura, Nancy, Seana and Kathleen, for keeping us honest and reminding us never to take ourselves too seriously.

To all involved in this journey, thank you for waiting patiently for the conclusion of a process which occasionally seemed interminable. Your good humor, vast reserves of patience, and unwavering support buoyed us on many occasions when the proverbial light at the end of the tunnel seemed far, far away. We hope you are as proud of your contribution as we are grateful for it.

JC and PJM

# APPENDICES

# Investment Banks and Advisory Firms

Firms are listed alphabetically. For firms with headquarters outside of the U.S., the New York headquarters are provided.

## ABN Amro
Park Avenue Plaza, 55 East 52nd Street, New York, NY 10055
(212) 409-1000, www.abnamro.com

## Banc of America Securities
IB Headquarters: 9 West 57th Street, New York, NY 10019
(888) 583-5800, www.bankofamerica.com

## Barclays
200 Park Avenue, New York, NY 10166
(212) 412-4000, www.barclays.com

## Bear, Stearns & Co.
383 Madison Ave., New York, NY 10179
(212) 272-2000, www.bearstearns.com

## The Blackstone Group
345 Park Avenue, New York, NY 10154
(212) 583-5000, www.blackstone.com

## Brown Brothers Harriman & Co.
140 Broadway, New York, New York 10005-1101
(212) 483-1818 , www.bbh.com

## Citigroup Global Corporate & Investment Banking
388 Greenwich Street, New York, NY 10013
(800) 285-3000, www.citigroupgcib.com

## Credit Suisse First Boston
11 Madison Avenue, New York, NY 10010
(212) 325-2000, www.csfb.com

## CIBC World Markets
245 Park Avenue, New York, NY 10017
(212) 856-4000, www.cibcwm.com

## Commerzbank
1251 Avenue of the Americas, New York, NY 10020
(212) 703-4000, www.commerzbank.com

## Deloitte & Touche Corporate Finance
1633 Broadway, New York, NY 10019
(212) 489-1600, www.deloitte.com

## Deutsche Bank
60 Wall St, New York, NY 10005
(212) 250-2500 , www.db.com

## Dresdner Kleinwort Wasserstein
1301 Avenue of the Americas, New York, NY 10019
(212) 969-2700, www.drkw.com

## Friedman Billings Ramsey
1001 Nineteenth Street, Arlington, VA 22209
(703) 312-9500, www.fbr.com

## Goldman Sachs
85 Broad Street, New York, NY 10004
(212) 902-1000, www.goldmansachs.com

## Greenhill & Co.
300 Park Avenue, New York, NY 10022
(212) 389-1500, www.greenhill-co.com

## Houlihan Lokey Howard & Zukin
1930 Century Park West, Los Angeles, CA 90067
(310) 553-8871, www.hlhz.com

## HSBC Corporate, Investment Banking and Markets
New York, NY
www.us.hsbc.com

## Jefferies & Company
520 Madison Avenue, 12th Floor, New York, NY, 10022
(212) 284-2300, www.jefco.com

## JMP Securities
600 Montgomery Street, Ste. 1100, San Francisco, CA 94111
(415) 835-8900, www.jmpsecurities.com

## JPMorgan
277 Park Avenue, New York, NY 10172
(212) 270-6000, www.jpmorgan.com

## Lazard Frères & Co.
30 Rockefeller Plaza, New York, NY 10020
(212) 632-6000, www.lazard.com

## Lehman Brothers
745 Seventh Avenue, New York, NY 10019
(212) 526-7000, www.lehman.com

## Morgan Keegan
50 North Front Street, Memphis, TN 38103
(901) 579-4539, www.morgankeegan.com

## Merrill Lynch & Co.
4 World Financial Center, 250 Vesey Street, New York, NY 10080
(212) 449-1000, www.ml.com

## Morgan Stanley
1585 Broadway, New York, NY 10036
(212) 761-4000, www.morganstanley.com

## Needham & Co.
445 Park Avenue, New York, NY 10022
(212) 371-8300, www.needhamco.com

## Oppenheimer & Co.
125 Broad Street, New York, NY 10004
(212) 668-8000, www.oppenheimer.com

## Pacific Growth Equities
1 Bush Street, Suite 1700, San Francisco, CA 94104
(415) 274-6800, www.pacificgrowthequities.com

## Perseus Group
150 California Street, San Francisco, CA 94111
(415) 318-3600, www.perseusgroup.com

## Peter J. Solomon Company
520 Madison Avenue, New York, NY 10022
(212) 508-1600, www.pjsolomon.com

## Piper Jaffray
800 Nicollet Mall, Suite. 800, Minneapolis, MN 55402
(612) 303-6000, www.piperjaffray.com

## Raymond James
880 Carillon Parkway, St. Petersburg, FL 33716
(727) 567-1000, www.raymondjames.com

## Robert W. Baird & Co.
777 East Wisconsin Avenue, Milwaukee, WI 53201
(800) 792-2473, www.rwbaird.com

## Rothschild
1251 Avenue of the Americas, New York, NY 10020
UK 44 20-728-05000, www.rothschild.com

## Royal Bank of Canada
200 Bay Street, Toronto, ON, Canada M5J 2W7
(416) 842-2000, www.rbc.com

## SG Cowen & Co.
1221 Avenue of the Americas, New York, NY 10020
(212) 278-6000, www.cowen.com

## SunTrust Robinson Humphrey Capital Markets
3333 Peachtree Road Northeast, 10th Fl, Atlanta, GA 30326
(404) 926-5217, www.suntrustrh.com

## ThinkEquity Partners
600 Montgomery Street, 8th Floor, San Francisco, CA 94111
(415) 249-2900, www.thinkequity.com

## Thomas Weisel Partners
One Montgomery Tower, San Francisco, CA 94104
(415) 364-2500, www.tweisel.com

## Toronto Dominion
66 Wellington Street West, Toronto, Ontario, Canada M5K 1A2
(416) 982-6160, www.tdsecurities.com

## UBS Securities
299 Park Avenue, New York, NY 10171
(212) 821-3000, www.ubs.com

**Wachovia Securities**
> 301 South College Street, Charlotte, NC 28288
> (704) 590-0000, www.wachovia.com

**Wells Fargo**
> 600 California Street, Suite 1600, San Francisco, CA 94108
> (415) 645-0800, www.wellsfargosecurities.com

**West LB**
> 1211, Avenue of the Americas, New York, N.Y. 10036
> (212) 852-6000, www.westlb.com

**William Blair & Company**
> 222 West Adams Street, Chicago, IL 60606
> (312) 236-1600, www.williamblair.com

**WR Hambrecht & Co.**
> 539 Bryant Street, Suite 100, San Francisco, CA 94107
> (415) 551-8600, www.wrhambrecht.com

# GLOSSARY OF TERMS

Throughout the glossary, the terms Acquiror, Target, and Seller are capitalized and refer to the acquiring company, the target company, and the selling shareholder(s), respectively, in an M&A transaction. All of the glossary terms provided here are described in detail in the ScoopBooks title *The Practitioner's Guide to Investment Banking, Mergers and Acquisitions, Corporate Finance.* Some terms are described in *The Recruiting Guide to Investment Banking.*

## A

**ability-to-pay analysis:** M&A analysis used to assess the maximum price Acquiror can pay for Target based on various financial metrics, including EPS accretion/dilution, balance sheet impact, and credit impact.

**accelerated depreciation:** Any depreciation method that provides for greater depreciation in earlier years than the comparable amount of depreciation during that time using the straight line method of depreciation. Modified Accelerated Cost Recovery System (MACRS), sum of the years' digits, and double-declining are accelerated depreciation methods and are often used for tax accounting purposes whereas straight line depreciation, which is not an accelerated depreciation method, is often used for GAAP accounting purposes. See also **Generally Accepted Accounting Principles.**

**accelerated marketing transaction:** When marketing a securities offering, the company meets only with targeted investors. This is in comparison with, and in contrast to, a fully marketed transaction in which the company meets with a broader group of investors. An accelerated marketing transaction is executed on a faster time frame than a fully marketed transaction, usually in recognition of strong investor demand. See also **fully marketed transaction**.

**acceleration clause:** A covenant found in debt agreements and loan indentures. The clause usually states that the total amount of debt is due in full immediately if the borrower fails to make a scheduled interest or principal payment on the specific debt. Most loans and some bonds also have cross default provisions (also referred to as cross acceleration rights) whereby *all* of the company's outstanding debt comes due if the issuer or borrower misses a scheduled interest or principal payment on *any* outstanding debt.

**accretion/dilution analysis:** A financial impact analysis that compares a company's financial results before a transaction to the company's pro forma financial results after the transaction. Accretion/dilution is most commonly performed for earning per share (EPS), but it can also be performed for other financial metrics including cash flow per share and dividends per share.

**acquisition:** The purchase of a division, subsidiary, or stock of a company or the purchase of individual assets.

**acquisition currency:** The consideration (e.g., cash, stock, notes, or some combination thereof) paid by Acquiror to Seller(s) in an M&A transaction.

**additional consideration:** Additional payment offered to Seller in an M&A transaction, in addition to cash, stock, and/or notes. Examples include earnouts, contingent payments, and contingent securities.

**advance notice provision:** Requires that notice be given to management regarding proposed shareholder initiatives in advance of a shareholder meeting in order to provide management and the board of directors with sufficient time to react to the proposed initiatives. If it exists, this provision is found in a company's bylaws or corporate charter. Companies choose whether or not to have an advance notice provision.

**affirmative covenants:** Covenants in a legal agreement that require a party to take a certain action. See also **negative covenants.**

**agreement and plan of reorganization:** Legal agreement used in a merger, if the merger is structured as a tax-free reorganization under the Internal Revenue Code (IRC).

**American depositary receipt (ADR):** A special type of security that represents shares of foreign companies but is itself a U.S. security, and which trades on a U.S. stock exchange.

**amortization:** Similar to depreciation, but for intangible assets such as intellectual property. As of 2001, goodwill is no longer amortized but is periodically tested for impairment. See also **depletion, depreciation, goodwill.**

**amortizing debt:** Debt in which the principal is gradually repaid over the life of the debt. In comparison, debt with a bullet payment has a one-time repayment of the entire principal at the end of the term. Most loans are amortizing whereas bonds are generally bullet payments. Bullet payments may also be called balloon payments. See also **bullet payment, sinking fund.**

**analysis at various prices (AVP):** An M&A analysis used to calculate implied transaction multiples over a range of offer prices.

**anti-greenmail provision:** Requires that before a would-be Target can make a greenmail payment to a Raider, a specified percentage of non-Raider shareholders must approve the payment. A greenmail payment is money paid to a Raider in exchange for Raider's shares in Target and is essentially money paid to make Raider go away. If it exists, this provision is found in a company's bylaws or corporate charter. Companies choose whether or not to have an anti-greenmail provision.

**arbitrageur:** A person or firm who enters into and seeks to profit from transactions when the same security or commodity is trading at different prices in two or more markets at the same time. See also **risk arbitrage.**

**asset-based lending:** A form of secured financing in which assets are used as collateral for bank loans or other debt such as bonds. Examples include the securitization of a company's accounts receivable, mortgages secured by underlying real estate, and loans secured by a company's assets. See also **secured lending.**

**asset purchase agreement:** see **purchase and sale agreement**.

**asset swap:** The exchange of assets between two parties. If structured in accordance with applicable IRS provisions and subject to limitations, an asset swap can be a tax-deferred transaction.

**asset write down:** A reduction in an asset's book value (for GAAP purposes) to fair market value. Occurs when an asset's fair market value is less than its book value and the lower fair market value is deemed to be a permanent change. In the absence of an acquisition, assets can be written *down* to fair market value, but they cannot be written *up* to fair market value (though in the context of an acquisition, assets can be written up or written down to whatever their fair market value is). An asset write down is a non-cash event. See also **Generally Accepted Accounting Principles.**

**asset write up:** A GAAP accounting event related to purchase accounting. In an acquisition, if the fair market value of an acquired asset or liability is greater than the book value, the asset or liability is written up from the book value to the greater fair market value. Asset write ups only occur in acquisitions whereas write downs can occur in an acquisition as well as in the normal course of business if there has been a permanent reduction to the value of the asset. See also **Generally Accepted Accounting Principles.**

**available for sale method:** A GAAP accounting method used to account for investments in other companies when the investor corporation does not exert significant control over the investee corporation, and when the fair value of the investee's security is readily available. See also **Generally Accepted Accounting Principles.**

# B

**balance sheet**: A financial statement that represents what a company owns (its assets) and any claims on those assets (its liabilities and shareholders' equity). A balance sheet is a point in time measure, meaning it measures the balance of accounts on one particular day. Most companies prepare annual and quarterly balance sheets. See also **cash flow statement, income statement.**

**bank debt:** Money borrowed from banks. In form, most bank debt is either a loan or a line of credit.

**basic shares outstanding:** Total number of shares issued and outstanding by a company. Basic shares outstanding exclude the dilutive effects of options and convertible securities. Earnings per share (EPS) is generally quoted using diluted shares outstanding. See also **diluted shares outstanding**.

**basis points:** One basis point is equal to one one-hundredth of one percent. For example 0.05 percent is equal to five basis points or 0.0005 and 1.0 percent is equal to 100 basis points or 0.01. Most debt securities are quoted in basis points over a same-dated U.S. Treasury security, LIBOR or the prime rate. See also **benchmark rate, credit spread, LIBOR.**

**basis step up:** A tax accounting concept. In asset purchases, Acquiror is allowed to record purchased assets in its tax books at their fair market value, which is generally (but not always) higher than the tax basis of those assets in Seller's tax books (therefore the term basis step up; there can be a basis step *down* if the fair market value of the asset acquired is *less than* the tax basis of that asset in Seller's tax books). In an acquisition of stock, a basis step up in Target's assets is not allowed, unless an exemption, such as a 338(h)(10) election, is granted. Since Seller's tax basis in the assets is carried over to Acquiror in an acquisition of stock, this is called a "carryover basis." A basis step up is desirable because it increases the asset's annual depreciation in the tax books, thereby resulting in a lower tax liability.

**benchmark rate:** Since U.S. Government Treasury bonds, notes, and bills are considered a proxy for "risk free" or "default free" securities, they are considered the benchmark rate for bonds in the U.S. Most debt securities are quoted and priced based on a credit spread (in basis points) over the benchmark rate for the same dated security (e.g., 100 basis points over the 10-year Treasury for a 10-year corporate bond). See also **basis points, credit spread.**

**best efforts deals:** Traditionally, investment banks underwrote security offerings for companies under a firm commitment agreement, which meant the investment banks purchased all of issuer's securities and then re-sold those securities to investors. Thus, the bank put its own capital at risk, owned the securities, and thereby assumed the execution risk (risk that the deal would not be completed). Firm commitment deals are also called underwritten deals and committed deals. Today, banks sell deals both on an underwritten basis and on a "best efforts" basis. Best efforts basis means that the bank will put forth its best effort to raise the desired funds on the proposed terms, but as an agent for the issuer, not as an owner of the securities. However, if the desired amount of capital cannot be raised on the proposed terms, the bank is not obligated to provide the total offering amount to the company, thereby transferring the execution risk to the issuer. Club deals are also becoming increasingly popular. A club deal occurs when a small group of the company's relationship banks underwrites the transaction together, as a club. See also **syndicate group, underwritten deals.**

**bid/offer spread:** The bid price is the price an investor is willing to pay for (i.e., bid for) a security. The offer price is the price a seller wants for a security (i.e., the price at which Seller offers the security for sale). The bid/offer spread is the difference between the offer price at which Seller would like to sell and the bid price at which Buyer would like to buy. It is sometimes referred to as the "bid/ask" spread to reflect the price that Seller asks for the security.

**blank check preferred stock:** Authorization for a certain amount of preferred stock, usually found in a company's governing documents (i.e., its bylaws or corporate charter). Blank check preferred stock is generally considered a corporate defense tool since it provides a board of directors the authority to issue up to a predetermined amount of preferred stock on an accelerated time frame, which might be useful in the event of a hostile overture.

**block trade:** A negotiated sale of a large block of equity or debt to one or a few buyers. Also referred to as an overnight transaction.

**bonds:** Debt that is sold directly to investors. Bonds pay periodic interest payments (usually semiannually) during the life of the bond or at maturity (as is the case for a zero coupon bond). The interest rate, or coupon rate, is usually fixed over the life of the bond (for this reason, bonds are also called fixed-income securities). Bond pricing is directly correlated with prevailing interest rates and the issuer's credit risk. Principal repayment is generally due at maturity but some bonds have sinking funds which provide amortization features. See also **amortizing debt, sinking fund.**

**bookrunner:** An investment bank that manages the offering process for the sale of a security. There can be joint bookrunners if more than one bank is managing the securities offering for the company selling the securities.

**book value:** The carrying value of an asset, liability or equity on the GAAP accounting books. The carrying value of an item on the tax accounting books is called the tax basis. Book value and tax basis refer to the same concept -- the carrying value of an asset or liability on the company's balance sheet, but book value is a GAAP accounting term and tax basis is a tax accounting term.

**book value of equity**: The GAAP accounting value of shareholders' equity. See also **Generally Accepted Accounting Principles.**

**borrower:** A borrower usually refers to an entity (e.g., individual, corporation, government, agency) which borrows money from a bank under a loan agreement. This is in contrast to an issuer, which usually refers to an entity that issues securities (e.g., bonds) directly to investors under an indenture. See also **issuer**.

**breakeven to EPS:** For any transaction (i.e., M&A or financing), the point at which there is neither accretion nor dilution to earnings per share as a result of the transaction. See also **accretion/dilution analysis**.

**breakup analysis:** See **sum of the parts analysis.**

**breakup fee:** A fee that must be paid by one party to the other party if a transaction falls apart between signing of the agreement and closing of the transaction due to one party breaching the contract and/or walking away from the deal. Breakup fees are usually two to four percent of the equity value of a transaction, but are subject to negotiation. See also **interloper**.

**bridge financing:** A type of interim financing often used to close an M&A transaction when cash is the acquisition consideration. Bridge financing is usually replaced by more permanent "take-out" financing soon after the M&A transaction has closed. Bridge financing provides companies the ability to fund an acquisition quickly and the flexibility to then replace the bridge financing with permanent financing at a lower cost and/or on more attractive terms and conditions once the exigency of the transaction has passed. Bridge financing is generally more expensive for borrowers than permanent financing, which is why borrowers want to replace any bridge financing with permanent financing as soon as practicable. A hung bridge occurs if the company cannot "take out the bridge" due to a change in company conditions, market conditions and/or investor appetite. In the case of a hung bridge, the issuer has no choice but to retain the higher-cost bridge financing until circumstances change.

**bullet payment:** Payment structure for debt in which the principal is due at maturity. This is in contrast to amortizing debt, in which the principal is repaid over the life of the debt. Most bonds have a bullet payment feature whereas most loans have an amortizing feature. See also **amortizing debt.**

**business purpose doctrine:** One of many IRS requirements for a transaction to qualify as a tax-free reorganization. The doctrine requires that a transaction be motivated by at least one valid business purpose. See also **continuity of business enterprise doctrine, continuity of shareholder interest doctrine.**

**buy-side process:** The process undertaken by Acquiror when acquiring an asset, business or company from Seller. See also **sell-side process.**

## C

**calendar year:** January 1 to December 31, which may be different from the company's fiscal year, which can be any 12-month period chosen by the company. See also **fiscal year.**

**call option:** Provides an issuer of debt or preferred securities the right to redeem the outstanding securities at a predetermined price and beginning on a predetermined date. If exercised, the most common reason is that the company can refinance the securities at a lower cost. Many debt and preferred securities have "non-call" periods during which the security cannot be called. Call option also describes an equity derivative which enables the holder to purchase an equity security at a predetermined price known as the strike price. See also **put option.**

**capital expenditures (capex):** Money spent on long-lived capital assets or investments, as opposed to money spent on expenses which flow directly through the income statement. Capital assets are placed on the balance sheet and depreciated (for tangible assets) or amortized (for intangible assets) to reflect their multi-year lives. A distinction is sometimes made between maintenance capex (expenditures on general upkeep of an asset) and investment capex (expenditures to improve an asset).

**capital gain/loss:** The difference between the selling price of a capital asset and the capital asset's tax basis (for tax purposes) or book value (for GAAP purposes) after accounting for recaptured depreciation, if any.

**capital gains tax:** Tax due on any capital gain. If the asset were sold at a loss (selling price is less than asset's tax basis), Seller would have a capital loss, which provides a tax benefit. See **income tax.**

**capital loss carryback:** When current capital losses are used to offset capital gains which occurred in the past. Carrybacks are subject to IRS limitations. Also referred to as tax loss carrybacks.

**capital loss carryforward:** When current capital losses are carried forward to offset capital gains triggered at some point in the future. Carryforwards are subject to IRS limitations. Also referred to as tax loss carryforwards.

**capital structure:** The debt and equity obligations of a company. Also referred to as capitalization. Components can include long-term debt, short-term debt, high-yield debt, preferred stock, and common stock.

**carry:** Participation of the financial sponsor in the profits of an investment. Carry, which is shortened from "carried interest," is usually 20 percent of the profits of the transaction after certain specified costs have been subtracted, such as after limited partners (the investors) are paid any preferred return owed, after subtraction of the management fee, and after expenses are subtracted.

**carry-over tax basis:** When Acquiror records in its tax accounting records assets purchased from Seller at Seller's tax basis. Thus Seller's historical tax basis in the assets is "carried over" to become Acquiror's tax basis in those assets.

**cash flow:** Amount of cash received or paid over time. This is separate from accounting profit or loss but can be reconciled to accounting profit or loss via the cash flow statement.

**cash flow accretion/dilution analysis:** A financial impact analysis that compares the cash flow per share of Acquiror pre-transaction to the cash flow per share of Acquiror post transaction. See also **accretion/dilution analysis.**

**cash flow from financing:** One of the three parts of the cash flow statement. Cash flow from financing represents the total cash flow payments and receipts related to financing activities, including the issuance and repayment of debt, the issuance and repurchase of equity, and the payment of dividends.

**cash flow from investing:** One of the three parts of the cash flow statement. Cash flow from investing represents the total cash payments and receipts related to non-financing assets and liabilities, such as capital expenditures or the sale of a capital asset or business.

**cash flow from operations:** One of the three parts of the cash flow statement. Cash flow from operations represents the total cash payments and receipts related to the day-to-day operations of a company.

**cash flow statement:** Financial statement that reconciles the income statement and the balance sheet at the end of a period to determine the actual cash flow generated by a company. Also referred to as the sources and uses statement. See also **balance sheet, income statement.**

**change of control provision:** A clause in a legal contract that allows a change to or termination of (depending on the language) the contract if one party to the contract enters into a change of control transaction. See also **change of control transaction.**

**change of control transaction:** Any transaction in which the previous owners are no longer "in control" of the company after the transaction is completed, meaning they have sold the majority and/or controlling interest in the company to another company or set of shareholders.

**Chinese Wall:** See **ethical wall**.

**classified board:** A corporate defense mechanism in which the board of directors is divided into more than one class (usually three classes, each with a three-year term) with one class of directors up for re-election at each annual meeting. With a classified board, the entire slate of directors cannot be voted off in one annual meeting. As a result, any proxy contest to dismantle a poison pill will require at least two years (2/3 of directors). If it exists, this provision is found in a company's bylaws or corporate charter. Companies choose whether or not to have a classified board. Also referred to as a **staggered board.**

**closing balance sheet:** The balance sheet at the end of the reporting period. For purposes of financial statement analysis, one needs an opening balance sheet (to see the status of all accounts at the beginning of the reporting period) and a closing balance sheet (to see the status of all accounts at the end of the reporting period).

**closing conditions:** Requirements written into a legal contract that must be met by a party before the transaction can close. There are usually closing conditions which apply to Acquiror and closing conditions which apply to Target.

**collars:** A contract or derivative which caps or limits the high or low value of a security, respectively. Collars are used in M&A transactions to bracket or bound the amount of fluctuation in an exchange ratio when stock is part of the acquisition currency.

**commercial paper (CP):** Short-term public debt with maturities between two and 270 days which is issued through brokers or directly to investors. Commercial paper is issued only by investment- grade companies and is often used by a company to fund working capital needs. It is usually one of the least expensive forms of capital due to its short duration and therefore low risk. At maturity, most CP is simply rolled over (extended) rather than redeemed. Issuers are required to maintain a traditional line of credit as an alternative if CP is unavailable for any reason. This line of credit is called a "CP backstop."

**common equity:** Capital that represents an ownership stake in the corporation and has a perpetual life. Common equity is lower in liquidation preference than preferred equity. See also **equity, preferred equity**.

**comparable companies:** Companies within the same peer or industry group and/or companies with similar operating or business profiles.

**comparable company analysis**: A multiples-based valuation method used to determine a company's valuation range based on current trading levels of the company's peers. Also referred to as trading comps analysis. Comparable company analysis is a relative valuation method (as opposed to an intrinsic valuation method) in that it derives a value for Company X based on how Company X's peers are trading. Comparable company analysis does not include a control premium. See also **control premium.**

**comparable transaction analysis:** A multiples-based valuation method used to determine a company's valuation range based on prices paid and, specifically, multiples paid in comparable M&A transactions. Also referred to as precedent transaction analysis. Comparable transaction analysis is a relative valuation method (as opposed to an intrinsic valuation method) in that it derives or implies a value for Company X based on transactions involving Company X's peers. Comparable transaction analysis includes a control premium. See also **control premium.**

**compounding:** The mathematical act of bringing one or more present values forward to a future value using future value formulas. The concept of earning interest on interest is also called compounding interest. Discounting is the mathematical action of bringing one or more future values back to a present value using present-value formulas. Both discounting and compounding recognize the time value of money. See also **discounting**.

**compound annual growth rate (CAGR):** The implied annualized growth rate based on a beginning and ending number. CAGR is a theoretical concept since it assumes the same year-on-year growth during the entire period. The formula to calculate CAGR is:

[ (Last number / beginning number) $^{1/n}$ ] $-$ 1   where n = number of compounding periods in the sample set

**compound interest:** The process of earning interest each period on the principal as well as the accumulated interest. See also **compounding, simple interest.**

**confidentiality agreement (CA):** A legal agreement that prevents the recipient of confidential information from disclosing that confidential information except under defined circumstances, such as to other members of the deal team to assist in the due diligence process. Also referred to as a **non-disclosure agreement (NDA).**

**consideration:** Within an M&A context, the form of payment used in an acquisition (e.g., stock, cash, and/or notes). Also referred to as **acquisition currency.** In a legal contract, consideration is anything of value which is exchanged for a good or service.

**consolidated tax return:** Currently, the IRS allows corporations that own greater than 80 percent of the voting stock of another corporation to file a consolidated tax return (i.e., one tax return for the two corporations as opposed to two separate tax returns).

**consolidation method:** A method of accounting that is used if an investor corporation is deemed to have control over the investee corporation. The investee is treated as a subsidiary of the investor and the investee's financial statements are consolidated into (included in) the investor's financial statements. See also **cost method, equity method.**

**contingencies:** Components of a merger or acquisition agreement which must affirmatively take place for the transaction to close. Also referred to as closing conditions.

**continuity of business enterprise doctrine:** One of many IRS requirements for a transaction to qualify as a tax-free reorganization. The doctrine requires that, following the reorganization, Acquiror continues a significant line of Target's business or uses a significant portion of Target's assets. See also **business purpose doctrine, continuity of shareholder interest doctrine.**

**continuity of shareholder interest doctrine:** One of many IRS requirements for a transaction to qualify as a tax-free reorganization. The doctrine requires that a material part of the consideration received by Target shareholders consist of stock of Acquiror (i.e., that Target shareholders continue to have an ownership interest in Acquiror by virtue of their receipt of Acquiror stock). See also **business purpose doctrine, continuity of business enterprise doctrine.**

**contractual subordination:** Results when debt is subordinated based on features written into the bank loan agreement or bond indenture (the contract between lender and borrower or between investor and issuer, respectively) which in substance or form names it as "junior" or "subordinated" debt. Subordinated debt is lower in liquidation preference than senior debt, meaning it does not get repaid until all senior debt is repaid. Contractual subordination is a common cause of credit rating notching. See also **structural subordination.**

**contribution analysis:** M&A analysis often used in a merger of equals (MOE). Premise is that the fair exchange ratio should be determined based on contributions of each party to various common operating metrics such as sales, EBITDA, net income, assets, and equity value.

**control premium:** Price paid over current trading levels by Acquiror in order to obtain voting control of a company (generally greater than 50 percent), as opposed to the price for a minority share, the ownership of which does not carry with it the ability to control the company.

**convertible securities:** Debt or preferred stock that can be converted into a set amount of common stock at some point in the future based on specified triggering events.

**corporate defense:** The act of helping a potential Target do what it legally can in order to remain independent in the face of a hostile overture from a corporate raider. See also **raider.**

**corporate development group:** see **strategic planning group.**

**corporate income tax:** Tax levied on a corporation's taxable income as determined on its tax accounting records (not the tax liability determined on its GAAP accounting records). See also **Generally Accepted Accounting Principles.**

**corporate level tax:** Tax owed and paid by a corporation. See also **double taxation, shareholder level tax.**

**corporate mergers:** The combination of two independent corporations in which one of the corporations survives as a legal entity. Mergers are governed by state corporation law. See also **statutory mergers.**

**cost method:** A GAAP accounting method to account for investments in other companies when the investor corporation does not exert significant control over the investee corporation and when the fair value of the investee's security is not readily available (e.g., if investee corporation is private). See also **consolidation method, equity method, Generally Accepted Accounting Principles.**

**cost of capital:** The return required by providers of capital, weighted to reflect the differing costs of debt and equity and the differing amounts of each in a company's capital structure. See also **weighted average cost of capital (WACC).**

**cost synergies:** Cost efficiencies created through improved operating practices and the elimination of redundant functions. See also **revenue synergies, synergies.**

**counter-parties:** Two parties that enter into a contract.

**coupon rate:** The interest rate on a bond. Most bond coupons are paid semiannually, but the coupon rate is quoted annually, usually based on a par value of $1,000 per bond. Thus a bond with an 8 percent coupon rate would pay $80 in annual interest, payable in two semiannual installments of $40.

**coverage bankers:** Investment bankers who focus their efforts on building relationships with clients (and are able to discuss numerous products and services with them) and winning business for the investment bank. Also referred to as **relationship bankers**. Coverage bankers often specialize in an industry (though sometimes in a geographic region) and are different from product bankers, who specialize in the execution of a particular type of financial product (such as M&A, equity capital markets or leveraged finance). See also **product bankers.**

**coverage ratio:** A type of credit ratio which is used to measure cash flow available to service interest obligations. Therefore, a higher coverage ratio is better since it indicates a larger safety margin. Common coverage ratios are EBITDA / interest expense and EBIT / interest expense. See also **EBIT, EDITDA, leverage ratio.**

**credit analysis:** Any of a number of analyses to determine the bankruptcy risk, debt capacity, financial risk, and business risk of a company. A number of factors are considered when performing credit analysis, including credit and financial ratios, the management team, the industry in which the company operates, and legal contracts or regulations in place which govern the receipt of cash flows that can be used to service debt. A common mistake is to assume that credit analysis is entirely dependent on credit ratios. Credit analysis is dependent on a wide range of factors; many are quantitative but some are qualitative.

**credit derivative:** An option that pays the investor if a company defaults on its debt obligations. Also referred to as **credit default swap (or CDS).**

**credit impact analysis:** Analysis that considers the impact of a transaction on an Acquiror's balance sheet and credit ratios.

**credit rating:** An opinion provided by a third party regarding the credit risk of a company, which opinion is denominated by a letter or combination of letters and numbers. Moody's, Standard & Poor's (S&P) and Fitch are the three largest rating agencies. Dominion Bond Rating Service of Canada was recognized as a rating agency by the SEC in 2003. The proper name for a rating agency is a NRSRO (Nationally Recognized Statistical Rating Organization). The designation of an NRSRO is provided by the SEC through a no-action letter. See also **no-action letter.**

**credit ratios:** Financial calculations used to help assess a company's credit risk.

**credit risk:** The likelihood that a company will default or fail to pay its debt obligations. See also **credit analysis.**

**credit spread:** Measure of the additional return above the risk-free rate which a debt investor or lender demands for investing in a debt security or loan. Credit spreads are typically quoted based on a given maturity and in basis points over an index, such as LIBOR or the benchmark Treasury rate for the same maturity, which are considered proxies for the risk-free rate. For example, if Company X issues 10-year bonds yielding 7 percent and the current 10-year U.S. Treasury bond yields 5 percent, then investors would say that this company's 10-year bond has a credit spread of 200 basis points (or 2 percent) over the same-dated U.S. Treasury bond. See also **basis points, credit analysis, credit risk.**

**cross acceleration rights:** See **acceleration clause.**

**crossover issuers:** High-yield issuers that are close to investment grade status and therefore can attract both investment grade and non-investment grade (or high-yield) investors. In general, debt investors invest in either investment grade debt or high-yield debt. See also **high-yield debt, investment grade debt.**

**crown jewel defense:** The sale by Target of critical assets, the loss of which is designed to make Target less attractive to a potential Acquiror.

**cumulative dividend:** A common feature of preferred securities in which the preferred dividend must be paid in full prior to the payment of any common stock dividend, regardless of the reason why the dividend was not paid (and therefore accumulated).

**cumulative voting:** A shareholder's ability to cast all of his or her votes cumulatively for one director as opposed to one vote per director. A provision preventing cumulative voting is a common corporate defense mechanism. If it exists, this provision is found in a company's bylaws or corporate charter. Companies choose whether or not to have cumulative voting.

**current assets:** Assets that are expected to be converted to cash within one year. Examples include accounts receivable and inventory. See also **long-term assets**.

**current liabilities:** Liabilities that are due to a third party in cash within one year. Examples include accounts payable, short-term debt and taxes payable. See also **long-term liabilities**.

## D

**DD&A:** Depreciation, depletion and amortization. See also **depreciation, depletion, amortization.**

**dead hand provision:** An optional feature in a poison pill. Provides that only directors who were in place prior to a proxy fight, or consent solicitation, are allowed to redeem the shareholder rights plan. Thus new directors, even if they won a seat on the board, would be unable to redeem the poison pill unless they were approved by the continuing directors. As such, this provision is also called a continuing director provision. See also **no hand provision, poison pill, shareholder rights plan**.

**deal protection:** Mechanisms written into an agreement to protect a transaction from attack by making it difficult and/or unattractive for a third party to break up a transaction. Examples include no shop / no talk provisions and breakup fees.

**debt:** Capital that is borrowed and must be repaid by the borrower. Usually (but not always) the borrower must pay periodic interest on the borrowed funds. Debt investors have claims to their invested capital only (including any interest and potentially underlying assets if the debt is secured). Debt investors are not owners of the company. Debt is higher in liquidation preference than equity. See also **equity.**

**debt capacity analysis:** An analysis used to assess the impact of a prospective transaction on a company's balance sheet, credit risk, and credit ratios. It is often done by Acquiror regarding a potential M&A transaction but is also done for other contemplated corporate actions such as a recapitalization or refinancing.

**deferred tax asset:** A balance sheet account that is created when taxes payable in the GAAP financial statements are less than taxes payable in the tax financial statement, or when a tax benefit is expected in the future, has been recognized in the GAAP books, but has not yet been recognized in the tax books. Also referred to as a deferred tax benefit.

**deferred tax liability:** A balance sheet account that is created when taxes payable in the GAAP financial statements are greater than taxes payable in the tax financial statements, or when a tax liability is expected in the future, has been recognized in the GAAP books, but has not yet been recognized in the tax books.

**depreciation:** The portion of a tangible asset's acquisition cost that is charged as an expense on the income statement against a period's revenues. Examples of tangible assets include factories and equipment. Intangible assets are amortized, not depreciated. Land is not depreciated for accounting purposes. See also **amortization, depletion.**

**depletion:** Similar to depreciation, but for assets that are depleted such as oil and gas reserves and other natural resources. See also **amortization, depreciation.**

**derivative:** A financial contract whose value is determined by an underlying asset, item or commodity such as an interest rate, the value of a stock, the cost of oil per barrel, or a credit rating.

**diluted shares outstanding:** The number of a company's shares outstanding, adjusted for any stock options and/or potentially dilutive securities such as the equity component of convertible debt or convertible preferred stock. Diluted shares outstanding may be equal to basic shares outstanding (if the company has no options or potentially dilutive securities) but it will never be less than basic shares outstanding.

**discounted cash flow analysis (DCF):** A valuation method that determines the value of a project, investment, or company based on the cash flows generated by the project, investment, or company discounted by the company's weighted average cost of capital. Measures the value of a firm to both debt and equity holders. See also **weighted average cost of capital**.

**discounted equity value analysis (DEV):** A valuation method that determines the value to the equity holders based on the cash flows generated by the company or asset which flow only to equity holders, discounted by the equity holders' cost of capital.

**discounting:** The mathematical act of bringing one or more future values backward to a present value number through division. Compounding is the mathematical act of bringing one or more present values forward to a future value through multiplication. See also **compounding**.

**discount rate:** The rate of return (r) used as the divisor in present value calculations and which represents the risk associated with a particular investment, asset, or business.

**divestiture:** The sale, separation, or disposition of an asset, division, or subsidiary by a parent company.

**dividend per share (DPS):** The dollar amount of dividends paid out to each share, usually quoted quarterly or annually. The indicated annual dividend is the latest quarterly dividend per share multiplied by four. Not all companies pay dividends. Smaller and/or cash flow negative companies tend not to pay dividends while larger, cash flow positive companies tend to pay dividends.

**dividend accretion/dilution analysis:** Financial impact analysis used to measure the effect of a transaction on the dividend per share. See also **accretion/dilution.**

**dividend yield:** The annual dividend received per share of stock divided by the current stock price. Dividend yield and share price appreciation are the two components of total return. See also **total return**.

**division:** A functional unit of a company that is not organized as a separate legal entity. The difference between a division and a subsidiary, for example, is that a subsidiary is itself a corporation, often majority owned by a parent corporation.

**double taxation:** Occurs when both corporate level tax and shareholder level tax are triggered. For example, corporate dividends are subject to double taxation: the first level of tax occurs when the corporation must pay taxes on its pre-tax earnings (corporate level tax) prior to calculating net income, and the second level of tax occurs when the shareholder must pay tax on the dividends received (shareholder level tax).

**DRD rules:** Dividends received deduction rules. The DRD is an IRS deduction which allows eligible U.S. corporations that receive dividends from other U.S. corporations to deduct some percentage of the dividends received from their federal taxable income (i.e., the deducted dividends are tax-free).

**dual path:** Occurs when a company pursues multiple strategic paths simultaneously. A company on a dual path prepares to execute two (or more) strategic options and, depending on market conditions, can decide between the options just prior to execution.

**due diligence:** The process of investigating and analyzing a company's assets or business.

**duration of an investment:** Length of time an investment is outstanding.

**E**

**earnings before interest and taxes (EBIT):** Line item on an income statement which represents earnings prior to the payment of interest expense and taxes.

**earnings before interest, taxes and DD&A (EBITDA):** Earnings prior to the payment of interest expense, taxes, depreciation, depletion, and amortization.

**earnings before tax (EBT)**: Earnings prior to the payment of taxes; also referred to as pretax profit, pretax operating income, and pretax earnings.

**earnings per share (EPS):** net income divided by diluted shares outstanding.

**earnings to common**: Net income after the payment of dividends. Earnings to common are the earnings which accrue to the common equity account (shareholders' equity) on the balance sheet.

**engagement agreement:** A legal agreement signed by a company when it hires or engages an outside advisor to do work on its behalf. The engagement agreement outlines the terms of the engagement. In the context of an investment banking engagement agreement, advisors can arrange an hourly or monthly retainer fee in addition to a "success fee" payable upon the successful culmination of a transaction. The success fee for an investment bank is usually tied to the size of the transaction. If the transaction does not close, the success fee is not paid. In an engagement agreement, it is common to request that the bank be reimbursed for reasonable out-of-pocket expenses.

**enterprise value:** Represents the value of both the equity (common equity and preferred equity) and the net debt of a company, based on the current market value of common equity. Also referred to as **firm value**. See also **equity value.**

**entry multiple:** The valuation multiple (e.g., enterprise value to EBITDA, price to earnings) paid when an investor buys a company. See also **exit multiple.**

**EPS accretion/dilution analysis:** Financial impact analysis used to compare the earnings per share for a company before and after a transaction. See also **accretion/dilution.**

**equity:** Equity is capital provided by investors to a company in exchange for an ownership stake in the company. In liquidation, equity holders get paid last, after all other providers of capital. An individual unit of equity is called a stock or a share. See also **debt**, **common equity, preferred equity.**

**equity method:** A method of accounting for investments that is used if the investor corporation has significant influence over the investee corporation's operating and financial policies but does not control the investee. See also **available for sale method, consolidation method.**

**equity value:** Represents the aggregate value of shareholders' equity based on the current market stock price. Also referred to as **market value**. See also **enterprise value.**

**ethical wall:** An internal firewall created within an investment bank between those groups with access to confidential client information and those without access to confidential information. Also referred to as a **Chinese Wall**.

**exchange offer:** An offer by Acquiror to purchase shares directly from the shareholders of Target in exchange for Acquiror stock or a mix of cash and Acquiror stock. The difference between an exchange offer (payment in all stock or stock and cash) and a tender offer (payment in cash) is the consideration offered by Acquiror to Target shareholders. See also **tender offer.**

**exchange offer prospectus:** The combination of the exchange offer and prospectus documents provided to Target shareholders in an exchange offer.

**exchange ratio:** The number of Acquiror shares offered for one share of Target in a stock-for-stock exchange. Calculated as offer price per share for Target (not Target's share price in the market since that does not include the control premium) divided by Acquiror share price.

**execution risk:** The risk that a transaction will not close.

**exercise price:** The price at which an option can be exercised. See also **in the money, out of the money, strike price.**

**exit multiple:** The valuation multiple (e.g., enterprise value to EBITDA, price to earnings) when an investor sells a company. See also **entry multiple.**

**F**

**fair market value (FMV):** The current value of an asset or security. See also **asset write up, asset write down.**

**fair price provision:** Requirement that all shareholders receive equivalent consideration in a tender offer. Developed as a counter-measure to two-tier bids. If it exists, this provision is found in a company's bylaws or corporate charter. Companies choose whether or not to have a fair price provision. In addition, many states have enacted fair price laws which apply to all companies incorporated in those states, whether or not the companies themselves have adopted a fair price provision.

**fairness opinion:** An opinion provided by an investment bank to a client that states that a proposed transaction is "fair from a financial point of view." The investment bank would perform a number of financial analyses and consider the specific characteristics of the transaction to determine whether the transaction were fair from a financial point of view. A fairness opinion is not tantamount to saying that the proposed price is the best available price or even a good price. The fairness opinion is generally delivered to a company's board of directors at the time the board of directors votes to approve or disapprove a proposed transaction.

**Financial Accounting Standards Board (FASB):** Independent body of accounting professionals responsible for Generally Accepted Accounting Principles (GAAP). Considered by the SEC and others as the authoritative body on GAAP. See also **Generally Accepted Accounting Principles.**

**financial buyers:** Private equity and venture capital firms. See also **financial sponsors**.

**financial covenants:** Requirements included in legal agreements (including bank loan agreements, bond indentures, and merger agreements). Examples of financial covenants in a bond indenture include requirements to maintain certain credit ratios or limits on capital expenditures. Financial covenants are designed to protect the lender/investor by alerting them to adverse changes in the borrower's financial profile.

**financial restructuring:** Making material changes to a company's capital structure as a means of enhancing shareholder value. Examples of financial restructuring transactions include the payment of a special dividend and a recapitalization, among other things.

**financial sponsors:** Private equity and venture capital firms that raise money for an investment fund from outside investors and invest the fund's money by acquiring businesses. See also **financial buyers.**

**firm value:** Represents the value of both the equity (common equity and preferred equity) and the net debt of a company, based on the current market value of common equity. Also referred to as **enterprise value**. See also **equity value.**

**fiscal year:** The annual period for a company's financial reporting. A company can choose its own fiscal year. For example, a company could have a fiscal year of June 1 to May 31, or December 1 to November 30. Many companies choose a fiscal year based on the calendar year (January 1 to December 31). See also **calendar year.**

**fixed exchange ratio:** An exchange ratio that does not change between the signing and closing of a transaction, regardless of whether there is movement in Acquiror's share price. This is in contrast to a floating exchange ratio. See also **exchange ratio.**

**flip-in exchange plan:** A shareholder rights plan (poison pill) in which shareholder rights are exchanged by Target for new shares, which are then distributed to Target's non-Raider shareholders without any action required on their part. See also **poison pill.**

**flip-over plan:** A shareholder rights plan (poison pill) that allows Target shareholders to buy Acquiror shares at a discount (usually 50 percent). See also **poison pill.**

**floating exchange ratio:** An exchange ratio that moves up or down between the signing and closing of a transaction, depending on Acquiror's share price. This is in contrast to a fixed exchange ratio. See also **exchange ratio.**

**flowback:** Issue that arises in cross-border M&A transactions. Occurs when Acquiror purchases a foreign company using stock as the acquisition currency, issuing Acquiror shares to Target shareholders in another country. The foreign shareholders might decide to sell Acquiror shares since they do not want to or cannot own shares of a foreign entity, thereby putting downward pressure on Acquiror's stock price as the shares issued to foreign Target shareholders flow back to Acquiror's home market. See also **acquisition currency, flowback analysis**.

**flowback analysis:** An analysis used to assess how many Acquiror shares will "flow back" into the home country as investors in Target, who have received Acquiror shares, sell them (because they cannot or do not want to own foreign shares), leading to post-transaction downward pressure on Acquiror's stock in its home market.

**follow-on offering:** An equity offering done by a company after its initial public offering. This is distinguished from a secondary offering, which is a sale of securities in which the seller is not the issuing company but rather existing shareholders (often large investors).

**football field:** A summary page created by investment bankers that graphically depicts the various valuation ranges calculated for an asset or company using different valuation methodologies.

**forward EPS:** Earnings per share for the current year or future years. FY1 (forward year 1) is often used to designate EPS for the current year, FY2 for the EPS next year, and FY3 for the EPS in two fiscal years. See also **trailing EPS.**

**free cash flow:** Cash flow generated by all assets (both tangible and intangible) used by the company in the provision of goods or services, adjusted for the cost of acquiring and maintaining those assets (e.g., capital expenditures). Free cash flow does not include the cash inflows or outflows related to financing the business and therefore are said to be unlevered or independent of the capital structure. Free cash flows during a projection period are the cash flows that are used in a discounted cash flow analysis. See also **discounted cash flow analysis.**

**fully marketed transaction:** When marketing a securities offering, the company meets with multiple investors to discuss the upcoming securities offering. A fully marketed transaction takes longer than an accelerated marketing transaction and is designed to drum up the maximum amount of interest in the transaction. See also **accelerated marketing transaction**.

**future value:** Nominal amount to be received in the future.

# G

**GAAP books:** Financial accounting records prepared according to GAAP rules and regulations. This is in contrast to tax books, which are accounting records prepared according to the rules and regulations of the IRS and other taxing authorities. See also **Generally Accepted Accounting Principles.**

**Generally Accepted Accounting Principles (GAAP):** A set of financial reporting guidelines. The Financial Accounting Standards Board (FASB) is considered by the Securities and Exchange Commission (SEC) and the American Institute of Certified Public Accountants (AICPA) to be the authoritative governing body of GAAP. Public companies listed on a U.S. stock exchange must file their GAAP financial statements with the SEC, where they become public record.

**golden parachute:** Severance package for senior executives payable upon termination.

**goodwill:** In purchase accounting, the value paid for the equity of Target less the net identifiable assets of Target. Goodwill is an intangible and unidentifiable asset and represents the portion of consideration paid in an acquisition that is not allocated to an identifiable asset or liability. Net identifiable assets is equal to the fair market value of Target's assets (excluding goodwill) less liabilities. Goodwill is no longer amortized but must be tested periodically for impairment (at least annually).

**greenfield:** To grow or develop a business internally. It is the opposite of (and generally the alternative to) purchasing an existing entity or business in order to enter a new geographic or product market.

**gross spread:** The fee an issuer pays an investment bank to underwrite a securities offering.

**growth rate accretion/dilution analysis:** An analysis used to compare the EPS growth rate of a company before and after a contemplated transaction. See also **accretion/dilution analysis.**

**guarantor:** An entity (a company or individual) that provides credit support to a borrower.

# H

**Hart-Scott-Rodino Act (HSR Act):** In the U.S., a company seeking to acquire or merge with another company must file advance notice of its intentions with the Federal Trade Commission (FTC) and Assistant Attorney General at least 30 days before closing of the transaction in order to determine if the transaction conforms to antitrust laws. Similar antitrust or competition requirements exist in other regions, especially in European and Asian countries.

**hedging:** The act of minimizing risk -- any type of risk -- by entering into a financial contract with a third party who will assume some or all of the risk for a fee.

**hell-or-high-water clause:** In a legal contract, provides that both companies must use their best efforts ("come hell or high water") to obtain all regulatory approvals required for the transaction to close. This provision, if the parties to a contract choose to include it, can require extraordinary measures on the part of either or both companies, depending on the specific circumstances of the transaction.

**high-yield debt:** Debt that has a credit rating of BB+ (or equivalent) or below. Investment grade debt is debt that has a credit rating of BBB- (or equivalent) or higher. Given the credit risk associated with the lower credit rating, high-yield debt is considered to be riskier than investment grade debt and therefore must provide investors with a higher return to compensate for this higher risk. High-yield debt is also referred to as junk debt and non-investment grade debt. See also **crossover issuer, investment grade debt.**

**historical stock price analysis:** Analysis of the prices at which a stock has traded in the past.

**hold level:** In a syndicated transaction, the percentage level each member of a syndicate group commits to holding or owning; the rest of each syndicate member's allocation can be sold off to reduce the syndicate member's exposure to the transaction in question.

# I

**impairment test (for goodwill):** Goodwill is periodically measured for impairment. If the impairment test concludes that (a) the fair market value of goodwill is less than the book value (value on the balance sheet) and (b) the lower fair market value is permanent, a company must write down the carrying value of the goodwill by the amount of the impairment. Goodwill impairment flows through the income statement as a charge and ultimately into shareholders' equity. A goodwill impairment charge is a non-cash event. See also **asset write down, goodwill.**

**income statement:** A financial statement that measures a company's profitability during a period of time (e.g., quarterly, annually). See also **balance sheet, cash flow statement**.

**income tax:** Tax due on ordinary income. See also **capital gains tax.**

**indemnification:** Provides that a party will be reimbursed for losses incurred in connection with certain events. Indemnification is protection, often in the form of financial compensation, against loss or damage.

**initial public offering (IPO):** The first public sale of a company's common equity. An IPO can be either a primary offering of shares (the sale of shares owned by the company, with sale proceeds going to the company) or a secondary offering of shares (the sale of shares owned by investors and/or insiders, with sale proceeds going to the sellers and not the company). See also **primary offering, secondary offering.**

**inside basis:** The tax basis that a corporation has in its assets. See also **outside basis.**

**intercompany transactions:** When preparing financial statements, GAAP requires companies to eliminate inter-entity transactions such as transactions between the parent corporation and subsidiary corporation. For example, the payment of a dividend from subsidiary to parent is an intercompany transaction. Most intercompany transactions are eliminated in consolidation. See also **Generally Accepted Accounting Principles**.

**interim operations:** A key section of a merger or acquisition agreement that states that, during the period from signing of the agreement to closing of the transaction, Target must continue to operate its business as it normally would.

**interloper:** A third party who attempts to break up a transaction. If there is a breakup fee provision in the deal which interloper attempts to break up, the cost of that breakup fee is usually passed through to the interloper. See also **corporate defense.**

**interloper analysis:** An analysis used to determine if any other companies and/or financial sponsors might have an interest in Target and/or the transaction being contemplated. Interloper analysis must take into account the financial effect of any breakup fee.

**internal rate of return (IRR):** For a stream of cash flows, the specific discount rate which yields a net present value of zero. IRR must be calculated iteratively, usually by a financial calculator or financial software. See also **weighted average cost of capital.**

**in the money:** When the exercise price of an option or the conversion price of a convertible security is less than the current price, indicating that the option or convertible security has immediate value if the option were exercised. See also **out of the money.**

**investment:** The purchase of any asset (physical investment) or security (paper investment) for valuable consideration (cash or stock) in exchange for a claim or right to the asset or a stream of cash payments from the asset and/or security in the future.

**investment grade debt:** Debt that has a credit rating of BBB- (or equivalent) or above. High- yield debt is debt that has a credit rating of BB+ (or equivalent) or below. Given the credit risk associated with the lower credit rating, high-yield debt is considered to be riskier than investment grade debt and therefore issuers must provide investors with a higher return for high- yield debt than for investment grade debt. Investment grade debt is also referred to as high-grade debt. See also **crossover issuer, high-yield debt.**

**issuer:** An issuer usually refers to an entity issuing securities (e.g., bonds, stock) directly to investors. A borrower usually refers to an entity borrowing money from a bank. Thus in a security issuance the company seeking the money is the issuer and the providers of the money are the investors who purchase the securities. This is similar to, but with different terminology from, a bank loan in which the company seeking the money is the borrower and the provider of the money is the lender.

# J

**joint venture:** When two or more companies contribute assets, businesses, and/or cash to a partnership. Most joint ventures are owned 50/50 by the owner companies. In addition, most joint ventures have an independent management team and board of directors, with shared representation by both owner companies.

# L

**league tables:** Investment banking rankings based on selected criteria, such as: volume of equity offerings, volume of M&A deals, and volume of syndicated loans. League tables exist for nearly every product offered by an investment bank and are used as a form of marketing by the banks to show their strength in a respective product area relative to other providers of that product (other banks).

**leveraged buyout (LBO):** A transaction in which a financial sponsor (usually a private equity fund or a leveraged buyout fund) acquires Target using private equity and debt. In leveraged buyouts, the purchase price is usually financed with 60 to 75 percent debt and 25 to 40 percent equity. Once a leveraged buyout has taken place, Target is a private company owned by the financial sponsor.

**leveraged buyout analysis:** A valuation method whereby the value for a company is determined based on (a) how much debt can be used to acquire Target and (b) the equity returns required by the financial sponsor.

**leverage ratio:** A type of credit ratio which is used to measure the absolute debt a company has outstanding at any given point in time. Common leverage ratios include the ratio of debt to total capital (sometimes called the capitalization ratio) and debt to equity. Total capital is all of the debt, preferred equity and common equity issued and outstanding by a company. See also **coverage ratio.**

**leveraged loan market:** Syndicated loan market for non-investment grade credits. The syndicated loan market competes directly with the bond market as an alternative source of debt capital for companies. Most leveraged loans are fully secured with full financial covenants, befitting their higher risk as non-investment grade credits.

**liability management:** The act of managing a company's debt mix to minimize the overall risk and cost of debt for a company. The goal of liability management is to minimize the company's weighted average cost of capital and thereby increase the company's return on equity and return on capital. See also **treasury group.**

**LIBOR:** London Interbank Offer Rate. The interest rate at which banks borrow money from one another in the London Interbank Market. Floating interest rates on bank loans in the U.S. are often tied to LIBOR.

**liquidation preference:** The order in which capital providers are repaid with the proceeds of a liquidation of assets. Also referred to as **priority of claim**.

**liquidation value:** The cash value received from selling off assets in a bankruptcy or liquidation scenario. This is different from the book value of assets, which is the accounting value based on historical cost. Liquidation value is sometimes referred to as the "fire sale" price.

**liquidity:** The nominal amount outstanding of any particular issue of a security not held by insiders. In general, investors prefer liquid issues compared to non-liquid issues because it is easier to buy and sell in a larger, more fluid market without altering the price of the security. In a separate use of the same term, liquidity also refers to the amount of cash a company has on hand.

**liquidity ratio:** Financial ratio used to determine if a company is able to service its short-term cash requirements.

**long-form merger:** Traditional merger path in which disclosures are sent to shareholders and shareholders must vote affirmatively in favor of the transaction in order for the transaction to close. See also **short-form merger**.

**long-term assets:** Assets that have lives longer than one year. Long-term assets can either be tangible such as a factory or intangible such as a patent or goodwill. See also **short-term assets**.

**long-term debt (LTD):** Debt that is due in more than one year. See also **short-term debt**.

**long-term liabilities:** Liabilities that have lives longer than one year.

**LTM:** Last twelve months. Sometimes referred to as latest twelve months.

**LTM EPS:** Earnings per share for the last twelve months.

# M

**management's discussion and analysis (MD&A):** Section of the financial statements in which management describes key issues and changes related to the business and the financial performance during a specified period. Financial statements should always be read in conjunction with the MD&A.

**marked to market:** Accounting method in which the carrying value of certain items on the balance sheet are adjusted up or down to reflect their current market value.

**market value:** Represents the aggregate value of shareholders' equity based on the current stock price. Also referred to as **equity value**. See also **enterprise value.**

**material adverse change (MAC):** Any event which materially changes the form and/or economic substance of a transaction for one, or both, of the parties. Most legal agreements have a MAC clause that allows the parties to walk away from a transaction if a MAC occurs. See also **no material adverse change condition.**

**maturity:** The amount of time (generally quoted in days for short-term debt and years for long-term debt) during which debt is outstanding, or until the security principal is due. Common equity (stock) does not have a maturity because it is perpetual, but preferred stock may have a maturity.

**medium-term notes (MTNs):** Bonds sold in tranches according to maturity (e.g., 2 years, 5 years, etc.). The difference between an MTN and a bond is that the tranches of an MTN program can be sold over time, as opposed to a bond issue which is generally sold in its entirety at one time. MTNs allow a company to access the fixed income market for small amounts based on market demand by prearranging their SEC documentation (a so-called shelf registration). Financial institutions are common issuers in the MTN market. See also **tranches**.

**merger:** The legal combination of two corporations as governed by state corporation laws. See also **corporate merger, statutory merger**.

**merger agreement:** The legal contract which represents the agreement between Acquiror and Target in a merger.

**merger of equals (MOE):** The combination of two companies of roughly equal size and value. In a merger of equals, there is no traditional Acquiror or Target. Both companies share in the management of the new company going forward.

**merger prospectus/proxy:** For public companies in the U.S., information and disclosure statement issued to Target shareholders by Target management prior to the shareholder vote to approve or disapprove a merger. A merger prospectus is used if Acquiror is offering some or all stock in exchange for Target's stock. A merger proxy is used if the transaction consideration is all cash.

**minority interest:** The portion of a consolidated subsidiary corporation that the parent corporation does not own. See also **consolidation method.**

**multiple compression:** A decrease in a valuation multiple.

**multiple expansion:** An increase in a valuation multiple.

**N**

**NASD:** National Association of Securities Dealers. A private-sector regulator of the U.S. securities industry. The SEC is a public-sector regulator of the U.S. securities industry.

**NASDAQ:** National Association of Securities Dealers Automatic Quotation system, an alternative stock exchange to the New York Stock Exchange and other traditional exchanges.

**natural historical exchange ratio analysis:** An analysis that looks at the implied market-based exchange ratio over time based on closing stock prices of Target and Acquiror. Often used when analyzing a merger of equals.

**negative covenants:** Covenants in a legal agreement that limit or otherwise put restrictions on which actions a party can take or enumerate actions which a party cannot take. See also **affirmative covenants.**

**net assets:** Assets minus liabilities. Net assets are also referred to as net asset value. Identifiable net assets are assets minus liabilities but excluding goodwill.

**net debt:** Short-term debt plus long-term debt plus minority interest (if any) plus preferred stock less cash and cash equivalents. Net debt is added to market value to arrive at enterprise value. See also **enterprise value, equity value.**

**net operating losses (NOLs):** Operating losses of a company. Can be used to offset future income tax (operating profits) or can be applied to previous years' income tax, subject to IRS or other limitations. Can also be used to offset future capital gain or can be applied to previous years' capital gain, subject to limitations. NOLs can offset operating profits or capital gains while capital losses can only be used to offset capital gains. See also **capital loss.**

**net present value:** The future cash flows of an investment discounted to a present value less the value paid for the investment at time zero. The discount rate that yields a net present value of zero is called the internal rate of return (IRR). Thus IRR is the discount rate which is calculated to cause the present values of the cash flows to equal the investment at time zero (present value of cash flows + initial investment (usually negative) = 0). See also **discount rate, internal rate of return.**

**no action by written consent provision:** With a no action by written consent provision, a written vote (i.e., action by written consent) is insufficient to take shareholder action. Requires that a physical shareholder meeting take place before shareholder action can be taken. If it exists, this provision is found in a company's bylaws or corporate charter. Companies choose whether or not to allow action by written consent.

**no-action letter:** A letter response from the SEC indicating that no civil or criminal action will be taken against an individual (broadly defined, which includes corporations) engaging in a particular activity. Companies request a no-action letter from the SEC when the law is unclear or vague regarding something the company plans to do. It allows the SEC the ability to review an action prior to the action taking place.

**no hand (non-redemption) provision:** Provides that no director can redeem a poison pill once the continuing directors are no longer in the majority. See also **dead hand provision, poison pill, shareholder rights plan**.

**no material adverse change condition:** Condition in a legal contract that no material adverse change in Target's business or assets has occurred between the signing of the Agreement and the closing which would cause a material decrease in Target's value. If such change has occurred, various remedies generally are available to Acquiror. See also **material adverse change.**

**non-compete provisions:** A provision in a legal contract that prevents Seller from creating a business to compete with the business just sold. Often required following a merger or acquisition. Also may apply when a senior executive or other person deemed important to a business leaves the business.

**non-disclosure agreement (NDA):** See **confidentiality agreement.**

**non-recurring items:** Income statement charges that are one-time occurrences and are not part of the company's regular course of business. Non-recurring items are usually excluded during financial analysis, which generally seeks to show the business performance on a regularized basis.

**non-solicitation provision:** A provision in a legal contract that prevents Acquiror from soliciting employees of Target for a specified period of time after a transaction closes, subject to certain exceptions. Often required following a merger or acquisition.

**no shop / no talk restrictions:** A provision in a merger or acquisition agreement that prevents Target, subject to Target board of directors' fiduciary duties, from negotiating a transaction with a third party. The provision protects Acquiror since Target could take Acquiror's bid and use it to "shop" for another, higher offer in the absence of these restrictions.

**notching:** Credit rating differentials for the same issuer. For example, if a company has a subsidiary with a credit rating of BBB+ from S&P and the parent company itself has a credit rating of BBB, this is referred to as notching.

# O

**offer to purchase:** The document provided to Target shareholders in a tender offer.

**one-line consolidation:** In GAAP, consolidation of Acquiror's investment in Target as well as its proportionate share of Target's earnings and losses into one line on the income statement and balance sheet. Used for investments classified using the equity method. See also **equity method, Generally Accepted Accounting Principles.**

**on the block:** A company or set of assets that is for sale is said to be "on the block," which is short for on the auction block.

**opening balance sheet:** The balance sheet at the beginning of the reporting period. For purposes of financial statement analysis, one needs an opening balance sheet (to see the status of all accounts at the beginning of the reporting period) and a closing balance sheet (to see the status of all accounts at the end of the reporting period). See also **balance sheet, closing balance sheet.**

**operating ratio:** Any of a series of ratios that show how profitable a company is and/or how efficiently a company is managed.

**opportunity cost:** Cost of foregoing an investment.

**option:** A security that allows the owner to buy (call option) or sell (put option) a share of common stock at some predetermined price in the future.

**out of the money:** When the exercise price of an option or the conversion price of a convertible security is greater than the current price, indicating that the option or convertible security has no immediate value if the option were exercised. See also **in the money.**

**outside basis:** The tax basis that a shareholder of a corporation has in the stock of the corporation. See also **inside basis.**

**P**

**personal income tax:** Tax levied on individuals, specifically on household income, dividend income, and income from unincorporated businesses such as sole proprietorships or partnerships.

**PIPE:** Private investment in public equity. Type of investment made by some private equity firms in public companies. This is not a "going private" transaction since the company remains publicly held.

**poison pill:** Provides existing shareholders with a "right" or "rights" to purchase or receive new shares in the company, thereby dramatically diluting the would-be Raider's voting and economic interest in Target. See also **shareholder rights plan.**

**power to fill vacancies provision:** Usually requires that any vacancy in the board of directors may only be filled by a majority vote of continuing directors. If it exists, this provision is found in a company's bylaws or corporate charter. Companies choose whether or not to have a power to fill vacancies provision.

**PP&E:** Plant, property and equipment. PP&E is usually quoted both on a gross basis (which is before accounting for accumulated depreciation) and on a net basis (which is after accounting for accumulated depreciation). See also **depreciation, depletion, amortization.**

**precedent transaction analysis:** See **comparable transaction analysis.**

**preferred equity:** equity with a preferential dividend to any common equity dividend and is ahead of common equity in liquidation preference. See also **common equity, equity.**

**preferred securities:** Similar to preferred equity in form, but structured in a way that can allow a company to deduct the dividend payments for tax purposes, as if they were interest payments on debt.

**premiums paid analysis:** An analysis that compares the premium under consideration to the premiums paid in previous and comparable transactions. See also **comparable transaction analysis.**

**present value:** The value of an investment stated in today's money.

**price to book ratio:** Represents the market value of equity as a multiple of the book value of equity. The price to book ratio formula is: market value of equity / book value of equity.

**price to earnings (P/E):** Represents the price of a share relative to its earnings (EPS) in a given period. P/E is usually calculated based on EPS for the last twelve months as well as the projected EPS for the next one, two, or three fiscal years. The price to earnings formula is: stock price / earnings per share (quoted annually)

**primary offering:** An offering of new shares to the public by a company (with sale proceeds going to the company), as opposed to a secondary offering of existing shares (sale of shares by investors and/or executives, with sale proceeds going to the sellers and not the company). See also **IPO, secondary offering.**

**priority of claim:** The order in which capital providers are repaid with the liquidation value of the assets. See also **liquidation preference.**

**private equity firm:** A private fund that acquires existing businesses using equity raised through private investors and debt. Also referred to as a financial sponsor or leveraged buyout firm. See also **financial sponsor.**

**private placement:** The direct sale of securities to a limited group of investors, subject to certain limitations. Private placements (which can be debt or equity securities) are not registered with the SEC.

**pro forma:** Pro forma financials are financial statements after giving effect to a proposed transaction (can be a strategic or a financing transaction). Thus pro forma financials for an acquisition would show the financial statements for Acquiror as if the acquisition had taken place.

**product bankers:** Bankers who specialize in the execution of a particular type of financial product (such as M&A, equity capital markets, or leveraged finance). Product bankers are different from relationship bankers, who cover clients in a specified industry or region and do not specialize in a particular financial product but rather are able to discuss numerous products and services. See also **coverage bankers.**

**proxy contest:** A method to gain control of a public company's board of directors. Shareholders use proxies to vote on a new slate of directors. If a company has a classified board or staggered board, it might take two years or more to take over a company using a proxy contest.

**purchase and sale agreement:** Legal agreement used for the sale of an asset or division of a company. A stock purchase agreement is used in the sale of a corporation. See also **stock purchase agreement.**

**purchase price:** For a publicly traded company, this is usually quoted as a price per share or an exchange ratio if the transaction is a stock-for-stock exchange. For a private company, a division, or subsidiary, the purchase price is usually an aggregate price.

**purchase price adjustment:** In a merger or acquisition agreement, a purchase price adjustment is used to capture changes in value between signing and closing of the transaction.

**purchase accounting:** The accounting method used to account for business combinations of unrelated entities in which Acquiror has control over Target.

**pure play:** Publicly held companies with one major business line. Diversified or conglomerate companies, on the other hand, have more than one major business line.

**put option:** In a bond context, allows an investor the right to force the issuer to repurchase the securities, generally at par (or face value). In an equity context, enables the buyer of the put option to force a sale of the security to the seller of the put at a specified price (the exercise price). See also **call option.**

# R

**raider:** An individual or company who seeks out companies with undervalued assets and then tries to take over Target by initiating a hostile takeover bid. See also **corporate defense, poison pill.**

**recapitalization:** A major change to a company's capital structure. Can be any major change but often refers to the issuance of a significant level of new debt, which is used either to repurchase equity or to pay a special dividend to equity holders.

**refinancing:** A change to a company's capital structure, including common actions such as renewing a line of credit with another line of credit (which may or may not have a different interest rate). Refinancing does not affect the asset side of the balance sheet, only the liability and shareholders' equity side. See also **recapitalization.**

**regulatory analysis:** An analysis used to determine what regulatory approvals, if any, would be required for a transaction to close.

**relationship bankers:** Bankers who focus their efforts on building relationships with clients (and are able to discuss numerous products and services with them). See also **coverage bankers.**

**relative valuation analysis:** An analysis that requires performing standalone valuation analysis of both Acquiror and Target -- using traditional methods such as discounted cash flow analysis, comparable company analysis and comparable transaction analysis -- and then calculating the implied exchange ratios based on the standalone valuation levels. This can be used in any stock-for-stock transaction but is most commonly used in mergers of equals.

**relative stock price performance analysis:** A technical analysis that assesses the performance of Target's stock compared to the stock of Acquiror.

**removal of directors "for cause" provision:** Prohibits the removal of directors other than "for cause" or other than by a supermajority vote. If it exists, this provision is found in a company's bylaws or corporate charter. Companies choose whether or not to have a removal for cause provision.

**reporting period:** Period in which a company's financial performance is measured, such as quarterly, semiannually, or annually.

**representations and warranties:** In a legal contract, statements by Acquiror and Target about various elements of their respective businesses. Also referred to as reps and warranties.

**restrictive covenants:** Restrictions on a party from taking certain actions. See also **affirmative covenants, negative covenants.**

**restructuring:** A major change to the structural organization of a company. A spin-off is an example of a restructuring transaction.

**return on equity (ROE):** Represents the earnings power of the shareholders' equity and is calculated by dividing earnings in a given year by the shareholders' equity as of that year.

**revenue synergies:** Generating greater revenues through the merger of two companies, for example if Acquiror is able to sell its products through Target's distribution network, thereby generating additional sales. See also **cost synergies, synergies.**

**reverse split:** A stock split which occurs in reverse, in which a company decides to exchange one new share for two (1-for-2), three (1-for-3), four (1-for-4) or more old shares (or whatever ratio the company determines) such that the owner of two, three, four or more old shares, respectively, becomes the owner of one new share. This usually occurs when the stock price has dropped sharply and the company wishes to increase the price per share by simply reducing the number of shares outstanding by exchanging new, higher-valued shares in place of old shares at some predetermined ratio. Reverse splits do not affect the overall market value of equity but increase share price, earnings per share, dividends per share, and all other per-share metrics by the exchange ratio chosen (e.g., multiply all metrics by two for a 1-for-2 split, by three for a 1-for-3 split, etc.). See also **stock split.**

**revolving line of credit (revolver):** A set credit limit given to a company by a bank, or a syndicate of banks, whereby the borrower can draw from it up to the credit limit, repay it and re-borrow from it without having to renegotiate terms with the bank. Most revolvers have a term of 364 days, although some are written as "evergreen facilities" which automatically renew every year for a period of three to seven years.

**risk arbitrage:** Investors who try to profit from simultaneously buying and short-selling stocks of companies in merger or other stock-based transactions.

**risk vs. reward:** A basic concept in corporate finance. An investor will lend money in exchange for a return on that money in the future. That return must compensate the investor for the risks involved with the investment. Also referred to as the risk/reward tradeoff.

# S

**Sarbanes-Oxley Act of 2002 (SOX):** Created the Public Company Accounting Oversight Board (PCAOB). Also requires that any accounting firm that audits an SEC-registered company must be registered with the PCAOB. Other requirements of the Act include greater auditor independence, certifications from a company's CEO and CFO regarding financial reports, stricter regulations of equity analysts, and greater accountability for corporations in the event of corporate fraud and criminal action, among other things. A detailed summary of Sarbanes-Oxley can be found in most comprehensive GAAP accounting books.

**Securities and Exchange Commission (SEC):** U.S. federal agency that regulates securities with the intent of protecting public investors.

**SEC Rule 13D:** A Securities and Exchange Commission rule requiring that an investor beneficially owning more than five percent of a publicly traded company must disclose, on a periodic basis in a public filing, the number of shares it owns and its intentions.

**secondary offering:** A secondary offering refers to the public offering of equity owned by selling shareholders, in which the sale proceeds go to the selling shareholders and not the company. See also **IPO, primary offering.**

**secured lending:** Holders of secured or asset-backed debt have claim to the underlying collateral (assets) in the event of default. Secured lending is a common cause of credit rating notching. See also **asset-based lending, credit rating, notching.**

**security:** A paper investment sold directly to an investor, which represents an interest in or claim to something. Stocks and bonds are types of securities.

**sell-side process:** The process undertaken by Seller when selling an asset, business or company.

**senior long-term debt:** Debt generally used to fund capital expenditures or other long-term needs. Senior long-term debt is higher in liquidation preference than subordinated debt and is generally payable in more than one year. See also **liquidation preference.**

**senior secured loan:** A bank term loan that is secured by assets of the company or other collateral. See also **asset-based lending, secured lending.**

**senior unsecured loan:** A bank term loan that is not secured by assets of the company or other collateral.

**Series 7:** An NYSE-developed and NASD-administered test required in order to sell securities to the public.

**shareholder level tax:** Tax liability owed by a shareholder of a corporation. Double taxation is the term that describes transactions that incur both corporate level and shareholder level tax. See also **corporate level tax, double taxation.**

**shareholder rights plan:** Provides existing, non-Raider shareholders with conversion rights for additional shares upon the occurrence of a triggering event, usually the purchase of a threshold ownership level by a Raider. See also **poison pill.**

**shareholders' equity:** See **equity.**

**shares traded analysis:** A technical analysis that combines share price performance with the volume of shares traded at each price point

**short-form merger:** Used after a tender offer or exchange offer to purchase any additional shares that were not tendered. A short-form merger does not require shareholder approval but must comply with the law of the state in which Target is incorporated. See also **long-form merger.**

**short-term debt (STD):** Debt used to fund working capital or seasonal financing, and which is generally due within one year. See also **long-term debt**.

**short-term liabilities:** see **current liabilities**.

**short-term loan:** Similar to a revolving line of credit except that instead of having an open line that can be drawn, repaid, and redrawn, the entire loan amount is provided to the borrower at the beginning of the term and is due within a specified period, often one year. See also **revolving line of credit.**

**simple interest:** Process of earning interest each period only on the principal. See also **compound interest**.

**sinking fund:** Fund managed by a trustee whereby the issuer of bonds makes periodic payments to the fund which represents the repayment of some of the outstanding debt. Allows for debt with a bullet payment effectively to have amortization features. See also **amortizing debt.**

**source document:** Any document used to determine assumptions when performing financial analysis. Examples include financial statements, loan agreements, company bylaws and articles of incorporation.

**special dividend:** Dividend paid to shareholders which is not part of a company's ongoing dividend program. See also **recapitalization**.

**special meeting:** A shareholders' meeting called outside of the regularly scheduled annual meeting.

**special meeting provision:** Provides that only certain parties (often directors, chairman, and/or CEO) can call a special meeting of shareholders. If it exists, this provision is found in a company's bylaws or corporate charter. Companies choose whether or not to have a special meeting provision.

**speculative grade liquidity ratings (SGLs):** A ratings grid that is meant to rate a company's liquidity only. See also **liquidity.**

**spin-off:** A public market separation technique in which shares of a subsidiary corporation are distributed to shareholders of parent corporation on a pro rata basis. In a spin-off, the parent corporation distributes control of the subsidiary to existing parent shareholders. After the spin-off, subsidiary is a publicly traded company that is no longer affiliated with parent, although it is still owned by the same shareholders as parent. See also **split-off.**

**split-off:** Similar to a spin-off, however, subsidiary stock is exchanged for parent stock based on a specified exchange ratio. Therefore, in a split-off, parent shareholders choose between owning parent stock or subsidiary stock, whereas in a spin-off, all parent shareholders receive subsidiary stock on a pro rata basis. See also **spin-off.**

**staggered board:** A board of directors that is divided into more than one class (usually three classes, each with a three-year term). If it exists, this provision is found in a company's bylaws or corporate charter. Companies choose whether or not to have a staggered board. See also **classified board.**

**stalking horse:** In an M&A transaction, the colloquial term used to refer to the bidder with the highest price. A stalking horse's bid is often used to try to encourage higher prices among other bidders in the process. See also **no shop / no talk restrictions**.

**statutory mergers:** Mergers are effected by operation of statute or state law, therefore mergers are sometimes referred to as statutory mergers. See also **corporate merger, merger**.

**stock purchase agreement:** Legal agreement used for the sale of the stock of a company. A purchase and sale agreement is used for the sale of an asset or division of a company. See also **purchase and sale agreement.**

**stock split:** Occurs when a company decides to exchange two (2-for-1), three (3-for-1), four (4-for-1) or more new shares (or whatever ratio it determines) for one old share such that the owner of one old share becomes the owner of two, three, four, or more new shares, respectively. This usually occurs when the stock price has risen sharply and the company wishes to decrease the price per share by simply increasing the number of shares outstanding by exchanging new, lower-valued shares in place of old shares at some pre-determined ratio. Stock splits do not affect the overall market value of equity but reduce share price, earnings per share, dividends per share, and all other per share metrics by the exchange ratio chosen (e.g., divide all metrics by two for a 2-for-1 split, by three for a 3-for-1 split, etc.). See also **reverse split.**

**strategic buyers:** Companies which buy other companies primarily for strategic reasons, as opposed to financial buyers, which buy other companies primarily for prospective financial gain.

**strategic planning group:** Group within a company which handles the strategic and/or financial planning, including preparing forward-looking financial statements and projections, and analyzing potential strategic transactions. Also referred to as the corporate development group. A Director of Strategic Planning usually heads the strategic planning group and reports directly to the CFO.

**strategic transaction:** Any action that helps implement a company's strategic plan.

**strike price:** The price at which an option can be exercised. See also **exercise price, in the money, out of the money.**

**structural subordination:** Results when the legal structure of an issuer of debt protects certain debt holders. The most common example is debt issued at a holding company level which is usually subordinate to debt issued at the operating level. Structural subordination is a common cause of credit rating notching. See also **contractual subordination.**

**subordinated debt:** Debt that is subordinated to senior debt in terms of liquidation preference. Due to this greater risk, holders of subordinated debt require a higher rate of return than holders of senior debt. See also **liquidation preference, senior debt**.

**subsequent offer period:** In an exchange offer or tender offer, the time period following the expiration of the initial offer period. During the subsequent offer period, an Acquiror is allowed to purchase the shares tendered up until that time and also to extend the offering period for an additional period from three to twenty days.

**subsidiary:** A corporation that is wholly owned or majority-owned by a parent corporation. See also **division.**

**sum of the parts analysis:** A valuation methodology which considers the value of the component pieces of a company, not the whole. Used to value conglomerates or diversified companies. Also referred to as breakup analysis.

**supermajority provision:** Requirement that a supermajority of outstanding shares must approve certain types of transactions, including change of control transactions. If it exists, this provision is found in a company's bylaws or corporate charter. Companies choose whether or not to have a supermajority provision.

**swap:** An option in which one counterparty assumes exposure to some event (such as exposure to interest rates or foreign exchange rates) in exchange for a fee.

**syndicate group:** A group of banks or lenders who together provide a loan or line of credit to a borrower. In addition to banks, other participants in syndicate groups include prime funds, insurance companies and, more recently, hedge funds.

**synergies:** A catch-all term to describe any manner of increasing earnings and/or cash flow associated with a merger or acquisition, either through increased revenues (revenue synergies) or decreased costs (cost synergies). See also **cost synergies, revenue synergies.**

**synergies analysis:** An analysis to assess the cost and revenue structure of Target to estimate potential synergies.

**T**

**taxable event:** Any action that triggers a potential tax liability.

**tax basis:** The depreciated value of an asset or liability on the tax balance sheet.

**tax books:** Tax accounting records prepared according to the rules and regulations of the IRS and other taxing authorities. Due to differences in rules and regulations between GAAP and tax accounting, a company's tax books are often different from a company's GAAP books. See also **Generally Accepted Accounting Principles**.

**tax credits:** Credits provided by a taxing authority that serve as an offset to the actual tax owed. Tax credits are similar to net operating losses in that they serve to reduce taxes, but tax credits reduce the actual tax liability while net operating losses only reduce taxable income (upon which tax liability is calculated) by the amount of the net operating losses. For example, in a 40 percent tax bracket, $1 in NOLs would reduce taxes payable by $0.40 while $1 in tax credits would reduce taxes payable by $1. Thus tax credits are comparatively more valuable than net operating losses.

**tax-deductible expenses:** Expenses that a company can subtract from its revenues prior to calculating its taxable income.

**tax-free reorganizations:** Transactions that qualify as tax-deferred under the reorganization provisions of the Internal Revenue Code (IRC). See also **business purpose doctrine, continuity of business enterprise doctrine, continuity of shareholder interest doctrine.**

**tax leakage:** In a transaction, the value lost to taxes.

**tax shield:** The reduction in income taxes provided by a tax-deductible expense.

**tender offer:** An offer by Acquiror to purchase shares directly from the shareholders of Target for cash. An exchange offer is an offer by Acquiror to purchase shares directly from the shareholders of Target in exchange for Acquiror stock or a combination of Acquiror stock and cash. The difference between a tender offer (payment in cash) and an exchange offer (payment in stock or stock and cash) is the consideration offered by Acquiror to Target shareholders. See also **exchange offer.**

**terminal value:** In a discounted cash flow analysis, terminal value represents the value of the business for the time period after the projection period and into perpetuity.

**termination provisions:** In a legal contract, rights of each party to cancel the agreement based on certain prescribed events or circumstances. Also referred to as "outs."

**time value of money:** A basic corporate finance concept. The value of $1 today is worth more than the value of $1 tomorrow because that $1 today can be invested to yield more than $1 tomorrow.

**total debt:** Represents the aggregate amount of debt that a company has outstanding at any given point in time. See also **debt, enterprise value, net debt.**

**total return:** The combination of stock price growth and dividends returned to a shareholder. See also **dividend yield.**

**total return accretion/dilution analysis:** An analysis used to measure the effect of a transaction on Acquiror's (or Target's) total return profile.

**tracking stock:** A separate class of stock designed to "track" the financial and operating results of a Subsidiary corporation within a larger company. With tracking stock, the parent corporation continues to retain governance, control, and consolidation accounting. Tracking stock is also referred to as letter stock since the first tracking stocks were issued by General Motors and were named for the businesses they represented (e.g., "GM-H" for the Hughes subsidiary, "GM-E" for the EDS subsidiary, etc.).

**trailing EPS:** Earnings per share for the last twelve months. See also **forward EPS.**

**tranches:** Sub-groups of debt issuance.

**treasury group:** A group within a corporation that handles functions related to financial and cash management. See also **liability management.**

**treasury shares:** Shares that have been repurchased by a company in the open market. They are considered issued but not outstanding and therefore are not eligible to vote or to receive dividends.

**treasury stock method:** Method used to calculate fully diluted shares outstanding for options and dilutive securities. Assumes that in-the-money options are exercised and that the company uses the proceeds from the sale of that stock (or security) to repurchase shares in the open market, thereby offsetting the dilutive effect of the exercise of the options or, in the case of convertible bonds, the dilutive effect of the conversion of the securities. See also **options, convertible securities**.

**trust preferred equity**: A form of capital that is lower in liquidation preference than subordinated debt, but higher than common equity. Holders receive a dividend, which is usually cumulative, based on a predetermined rate of return. This dividend is often tax deductible, as if it were an interest payment on debt. See also **debt, equity.**

## U

**underwritten deals:** Traditionally, banks fully underwrote security offerings for companies, which meant the investment banks purchased all of the issuer's securities and then re-sold those securities to investors. The bank put its own capital at risk and also assumed the execution risk, which is the risk that the deal would not be completed (and the bank would be left holding a significant percentage of the securities which it was unable to re-sell). Underwritten deals are also called committed deals. Today, banks sell deals both on an underwritten basis and on a best efforts basis. See also **best efforts deals.**

**unwinding:** Exiting from a contractually obligated transaction such as a joint-venture (JV).

# V

**value creation analysis:** An analysis used to estimate the expected valuation of the merged entity relative to Acquiror's valuation on a standalone basis and used to determine how much value would be created as a result of the proposed transaction.

**venture capital firms:** Private funds that invest in new businesses and new technologies, many of which are not yet cash flow positive. These firms tend to invest much earlier in a company's life cycle than private equity firms.

# W

**warrants:** Options to purchase equity that are issued with debt securities to increase the marketability of the debt securities by providing an element of equity participation. Also known as a sweetener or an equity kicker.

**weighted average cost of capital (WACC):** The discount rate used in a discounted cash flow analysis. Represents the return required by a company's debt and equity investors, weighted to reflect the proportion of the total capital contributed by each. See also **discounted cash flow analysis**.

**white knight:** A friendly partner who negotiates a deal with Target's management on mutually agreeable terms, thereby helping Target avoid a hostile takeover.

**working capital:** Current assets less current liabilities. The calculation of working capital usually excludes cash and short-term debt since they are considered financing related items.

# Y

**yield:** For a bond, yield represents the rate of return based on the bond's interest rate (coupon) and the price at which the investor bought the bond. Mathematically, yield is the discount rate or rate of return required by the debt investor.

**yield curve:** Graph depicting the rate of return for bonds of varying maturities. Although a yield curve can be drawn for any issuer, it generally refers to the yield curve for U.S. Treasury bonds.

# Recruiting Terminology

**analyst year:** One complete year for an analyst in investment banking. Analysts are generally hired for a two-year program, which normally begins and ends around July. Reviews and compensation discussions take place at the end of an analyst year.

**CV:** Curriculum vitae or resume.

**deal team:** A group of people working on a transaction together.

**decision committee:** A committee comprised of recruiting staff and senior bankers from various product and industry groups who review hiring recommendations, then decide which candidates will receive an offer.

**drop dead date:** The date by which a recruit needs to accept or decline an offer from a firm; the offer will expire after this date if the recruit does not accept or negotiate an extension.

**exploding offer:** An offer with a drop dead date made by a firm to a recruit. See also **drop dead date.**

**face time:** The act of staying around the office longer to appear busier than one actually is.

**fire drills:** Intense bursts of frenzied work to fulfill a client's or senior banker's urgent request.

**informational interview:** Informal meetings in which a prospective candidate comes to a professional's office to talk about the industry generally and the firm specifically.

**jumped:** When an analyst, associate or vice president is promoted ahead of his or her start class and moved into the next start class. See also **start class**.

**junior bankers:** Typically, analysts and associates. Senior bankers are vice presidents and managing directors.

**lateral hire:** A person who is hired as a mid-level analyst, associate, vice president or managing director. Lateral hires are usually hired from other investment banks but can be hired from law firms, consulting firms, accounting firms, or industry.

**line manager:** The senior banker responsible for staffing analysts and associates in a group. Also referred to as a **staffer.**

**on-line banker:** A banker whose primary responsibilities are to transact client business compared to those who work in internal or administrative groups.

**per diem:** Per day allowances for expenses during business trips.

**perks:** Non-monetary or non-compensation related benefits.

**pitch book:** A client presentation that is not related to a transaction on which the bank is already engaged to work on behalf of the company. Pitch books are used to try to generate new business with clients.

**quant jock:** One who is technically gifted and/or particularly good with numbers. Short for "quantitative jockey."

**recruiting season:** In North American and Europe, the period between August and February of each year, during which analysts and associates are recruited to work for a firm.

**red-eye flight:** A flight that leaves the departure city late at night and arrives in the arrival city the following morning.

**resume drop:** A place on campus where resumes are submitted; today, most are done electronically.

**resume drop date:** The deadline to submit one's resume or CV to a particular firm.

**resume hole:** A gap in the time sequence of a resume.

**school teams:** A group of bankers and members of the recruiting staff who are responsible for: (1) attending on-campus presentations for a school; (2) screening resumes; (3) conducting first-round interviews; and (4) communicating with recruits during both the recruiting process and the sell process.

**screening resumes:** The process of reading resumes and identifying recruits to interview.

**sell day:** The day a recruit returns to a firm to meet more people and for those people to "sell" the recruit on working for their firm.

**sell process:** The period after a firm has extended an offer to a recruit but before the recruit has accepted or declined the offer.

**start class:** The analyst or associate class that begins together as a group in a formal training program.

**super Saturday:** Second-round interviews held at an investment bank's headquarters, which usually take place on a Saturday morning.

**target schools:** Schools at which a bank will actively recruit students for analyst or associate positions.

**war for talent:** Competition among banks, other high-end service firms, and major corporations to hire and retain the most qualified candidates at all levels.

# Corporate Finance Review

## Present Value and Future Value

Numerical examples of basic corporate finance principles are included in this Appendix D.

PV or $CF_o$ = initial amount (cash flow at Time $_o$ or "today")
FV or $CF_n$ = future amount (cash flow in the future at Time $_n$ or "tomorrow")
$r$ = discount rate for discounting and interest rate for compounding
$g$ = annual growth rate
$n$ = number of periods over which the amount is being discounted or compounded
$m$ = number of payments per period

The present value formula is the inverse of the future value formula.

$$PV = \frac{CF_n}{(1 + r/m)^{nm}} \qquad FV = CF_o \times [(1 + r/m)^{nm}]$$

Present value = future cash flow ($CF_n$) **discounted** to a present value (value *today*)
Future value = present cash flow ($CF_o$) **compounded** to a future value (value *tomorrow*)

---

### ᴏ̃ᴏ Discount rate vs. interest rate?

Discount rate is different from interest rate since an interest rate is the stated amount you will *earn* on an investment (such as when you put your money in a bank account or when you buy a bond with a stated interest rate or coupon rate). The discount rate, on the other hand, is a measure of the opportunity cost of capital, meaning the return you would earn on similarly risky investments (and therefore the return you require for the investment). The interest rate is *not necessarily* indicative of the risk of the cash flows (meaning the interest rate is not necessarily equal to the discount rate). If the investment is priced properly, then it will pay a level of interest commensurate with its risk. However, the market is not always efficient in the short term and therefore you cannot be sure that the security will be priced perfectly. Therefore be careful in assuming that the interest rate and the discount rate are identical because any market inefficiency will cause them to be different.

*Present Value Example 1:* You will receive royalties of $500 per year for five years for music you have written. How much is this royalty worth today if the discount rate for the royalties is 8 percent?

**Table D.1 – Present Value Example 1**

| Year | 0 | 1 | 2 | 3 | 4 | 5 |
|---|---|---|---|---|---|---|
| Cash flows (CF$_n$) | | $500 | $500 | $500 | $500 | $500 |
| Discount rate (r) | | 8.0% | 8.0% | 8.0% | 8.0% | 8.0% |
| Present value formula | | $=\frac{\$500}{(1.08)^1}$ | $=\frac{\$500}{(1.08)^2}$ | $=\frac{\$500}{(1.08)^3}$ | $=\frac{\$500}{(1.08)^4}$ | $=\frac{\$500}{(1.08)^5}$ |
| Present value | | $462.96 | $428.67 | $396.92 | $367.51 | $340.29 |
| Total present values | $1,996.36 | | | | | |

*Present Value Example 2:* You will borrow money from the bank. You will repay the bank $100 per year for three years and $150 per year for the next two years. How much will the bank lend you today if its discount rate for you is 5 percent?

**Table D.2 – Present Value Example 2**

| Year | 0 | 1 | 2 | 3 | 4 | 5 |
|---|---|---|---|---|---|---|
| Cash flows (CF$_n$) | | $100 | $100 | $100 | $150 | $150 |
| Discount rate (r) | | 5.0% | 5.0% | 5.0% | 5.0% | 5.0% |
| Present value formula | | $=\frac{\$100}{(1.05)^1}$ | $=\frac{\$100}{(1.05)^2}$ | $=\frac{\$100}{(1.05)^3}$ | $=\frac{\$150}{(1.05)^4}$ | $=\frac{\$150}{(1.05)^5}$ |
| Present value | | $95.24 | $90.70 | $86.38 | $123.41 | $117.53 |
| Total present values | $513.26 | | | | | |

*Present Value Example 3:* Assume you have won $100,000 in a lottery. You can elect to receive $100,000 in a lump sum payment at the end of five years or you can elect to receive the $100,000 in equal annual installments of $20,000 for five years beginning in year one. Your discount rate is 10 percent. In the first scenario, you calculate the present value by using the present value formula on the Year 5 cash flow.

## Table D.3 – Present Value Example 3

| Year | 0 | 1 | 2 | 3 | 4 | 5 |
|---|---|---|---|---|---|---|
| Nominal cash flows (CF$_n$) | | | | | | $100,000 |
| Discount rate (r) | | | | | | 10.0% |
| Present value formula | | | | | | = $100,000 / (1.10)^5 |
| Present value | | | | | | $62,092 |
| Total present values | $62,092 | | | | | |

For the second scenario, you simply add the present values of the cash flow streams from each year to calculate the present value of the investment. For each year, you would use the same present value calculation applied above.

| Year | 0 | 1 | 2 | 3 | 4 | 5 |
|---|---|---|---|---|---|---|
| Cash flows (CF$_n$) | | $20,000 | $20,000 | $20,000 | $20,000 | $20,000 |
| Discount rate (r) | | 10% | 10% | 10% | 10% | 10% |
| Present value formula | | $= \dfrac{\$20,000}{(1.10)^1}$ | $= \dfrac{\$20,000}{(1.10)^2}$ | $= \dfrac{\$20,000}{(1.10)^3}$ | $= \dfrac{\$20,000}{(1.10)^4}$ | $= \dfrac{\$20,000}{(1.10)^5}$ |
| Present value | | $18,182 | $16,529 | $15,026 | $13,660 | $12,418 |
| Total present values | $75,816 | | | | | |

Since the value of receiving cash today is greater than the value of receiving cash tomorrow, the present value of receiving the $100,000 spread out over five years in equal installments is worth more ($75,816) than the value of receiving the $100,000 in one lump sum five years from now ($62,092).

***Future Value Example:*** You invest $1,000 in a certificate of deposit, or CD (an investment whereby you contribute funds up front in exchange for the principal plus interest at maturity), at a rate of 6 percent. What will you receive from the bank in five years?

## Table D.4 – Future Value Example 1

| Year | 0 | 1 | 2 | 3 | 4 | 5 |
|---|---|---|---|---|---|---|
| Cash flows (CF$_0$) | ($1,000) | | | | | |
| Compound rate (r) | | | | | | 6.0% |
| Future value formula | | | | | | = $1,000 × (1.06)^5 |
| Future value at Time 5 | | | | | | $1,338 |

## Net Present Value

There are times when an investor will pay an amount that is greater than the present value of the future cash flows and there are times when an investor will pay an amount that is less than the present value. The **net present value** or **NPV** of an investment is equal to the value initially paid for the investment (stated as a negative cash flow number because the money is paid out or invested at the outset) plus the present value of the investment's future cash flows.

$$\text{NPV} = CF_0 + PV_{\text{future cash flows}} \text{ where } CF_0 \text{ is generally a negative number}$$

If the net present value is equal to zero, then the investor is "earning his cost of capital." In other words, the investor will earn a return on his initial cash flow (i.e., his investment) that is equal to the discount rate he applied in calculating the present value of the investment. Said another way, the investor's discount rate is equal to the interest rate that his money is earning.

Let's consider a simple bond. Assume that DebtCo is issuing or selling $100 million of bonds with a five year maturity and paying interest of 8 percent. Interest will be paid annually. This means that DebtCo will sell bonds (which are essentially interest-paying IOUs) and each year for five years DebtCo will pay investors 8 percent on their investment (or $8 million per year during the life of the bond). At the end of the fifth year, DebtCo will pay its last interest payment and return the principal to the investors. How much would this investment be worth to an investor considering buying $10,000 of these bonds at par (at the face value of the bonds)? The investor's discount rate is 8 percent.

### Table D.5 – NPV Example 1

| Year | | 0 | 1 | 2 | 3 | 4 | 5 |
|---|---|---|---|---|---|---|---|
| Interest rate | | | 8.0% | 8.0% | 8.0% | 8.0% | 8.0% |
| Interest received | | | $800 | $800 | $800 | $800 | $800 |
| Principal received | | | | | | | $10,000 |
| Cash flows ($CF_n$) | | | $800 | $800 | $800 | $800 | $10,800 |
| Discount rate (r) | | | 8.0% | 8.0% | 8.0% | 8.0% | 8.0% |
| Present value formula | | | $=\dfrac{\$800}{(1.08)^1}$ | $=\dfrac{\$800}{(1.08)^2}$ | $=\dfrac{\$800}{(1.08)^3}$ | $=\dfrac{\$800}{(1.08)^4}$ | $=\dfrac{\$10,800}{(1.08)^5}$ |
| Present value at Time$_0$ | | | $740.74 | $685.87 | $635.07 | $588.02 | $7,350.30 |
| Total present value (PV) | $10,000 | | | | | | |
| Cost of investment ($CF_0$) | ($10,000) | | | | | | |
| NPV ($CF_0$ + PV) | $0 | | | | | | |

Notice that the discount rate is equal to the coupon or interest paid on the bond. In this situation, the present value (or investment value) of the cash flows is equal to the original investment amount. Why is that? Because, if you can earn your "cost of capital," then the present value of an investment is equal to the amount paid for the investment. This is an example of a situation in which the NPV is zero. The amount paid was $10,000 and the present value of the cash flows earned was $10,000 because the interest earned was 8 percent and the investor's discount rate was 8 percent. The investor's discount rate is 8 percent because there are similarly risky investments available in the market that are currently paying 8 percent – not because the bond is paying a coupon of 8 percent interest.

What would happen if, instead of 8 percent, the cost of capital, or discount rate, were 5 percent but the investor still paid $10,000 for the investment? Let's see how the net present value of the investment would change.

### Table D.6 - NPV Example 2

| Year | | 0 | 1 | 2 | 3 | 4 | 5 |
|---|---|---|---|---|---|---|---|
| Coupon or interest rate | | 8.0% | 8.0% | 8.0% | 8.0% | 8.0% |
| Interest received | | $800 | $800 | $800 | $800 | $800 |
| Principal received | | | | | | | $10,000 |
| Nominal cash flows ($CF_n$) | | $800 | $800 | $800 | $800 | $10,800 |
| Discount rate (r) | | 5.0% | 5.0% | 5.0% | 5.0% | 5.0% |
| Present value formula | | $=\dfrac{\$800}{(1.05)^1}$ | $=\dfrac{\$800}{(1.05)^2}$ | $=\dfrac{\$800}{(1.05)^3}$ | $=\dfrac{\$800}{(1.05)^4}$ | $=\dfrac{\$10,800}{(1.05)^5}$ |
| Present value at Time$_0$ | | $761.90 | $725.62 | $691.07 | $658.16 | $8,462.08 |
| Total present value (PV) | $11,298.84 | | | | | | |
| Cost of investment ($CF_0$) | ($10,000) | | | | | | |
| NPV ($CF_0$ + PV) | $1,298.84 | | | | | | |

A positive NPV, as in this example, means that you bought an investment or asset at a price that was less than the present value of its future cash flows. That is good since it means that you earned a *return* on your capital which is greater than the *cost* of your capital (the opportunity cost or your discount rate for the asset). An NPV-negative transaction, on the other hand, is not good since it means that you do not even earn enough to cover your cost of capital.

> ## ˆOˆOˆ Not earning the cost of capital
>
> People in the financial community will often say something "is not earning its cost of capital ..." They are referring to this concept of NPV-positive versus NPV-negative transactions. If an investment is NPV-positive, then it is earning a return greater than its discount rate. If an investment is NPV-negative, however, it is earning a return that is less than its discount rate. Such a transaction is "not earning its cost of capital" and, therefore it costs more to put money in this investment than what the investor will earn on it.

## Internal Rate of Return

Now that we have described NPV, we can introduce the **internal rate of return** or **IRR.** IRR is simply a specialized discount rate, namely the discount rate that yields a net present value of zero.

For example, if an investment will pay $10,000 in five years and the investor paid $8,000 for it at time zero ($t_0$), then the internal rate of return IRR is equal to 4.6 percent.

| | | | |
|---|---|---|---|
| 0 | = | Amount paid at Time 0 | The sum of the present values of cash flows. Where all of the cash flows are discounted using the *same* discount rate. This discount rate is called the IRR |

$$0 = (\$8,000) + \frac{\$10,000}{(1.046)^5}$$

Since an IRR is simply a discount rate that yields a certain NPV (0), calculating an IRR involves trying many iterations until you arrive at the correct discount rate. As such, it is easier to use a financial calculator or spreadsheet software to perform the iterations required. The important point is that the IRR is simply a specified discount rate in which the present value of the investment is equal to the amount paid for the investment. Said differently, the IRR is the discount rate when the NPV is equal to zero.

IRR is often used by investors to measure their return based on varying purchase prices. In our example above, if the investor paid $5,000 instead of $8,000, the IRR would be 14.9 percent (as compared to a return of 4.6 percent if the investor were to pay $8,000 for it). Investors will compare the projected IRR with their opportunity cost of capital and some will choose to invest if the IRR on a project is greater than their cost of capital – which is the same as determining whether the NPV is greater than zero.

## Multiple Payments in a Compounding Period

If you are paid interest semiannually, you will earn slightly more at the end of the year than if are only paid interest once a year. With interest paid semiannually, the interest earned in the first half of the year will itself earn interest for the remaining six months of the year.

Let's consider a simple example of an investment of $1,000 that pays 6 percent annually and compare that to an investment that pays 6 percent semiannually.

### *Annual Interest Payments Example:*

Interest = principal × 6% interest for one year
= $1,000 × 0.06
= $60.00

### *Semiannual Interest Payments Example*

Interest = (principal × 3% interest for first 6 months) + (principal × 3% interest for second 6 months) + (interest from first 6 months × 3% interest for second 6 months)
= ($1,000 × 0.03 = $30) + ($1,000 × 0.03 = $30) + ($30 × 0.03)
= $60.90

Thus over the course of one year, an account earning interest semiannually with the interest rates set forth above would earn $0.90 more in the year than the same account earning interest annually. In terms of applying the present value formula to account for compounding interest within periods, let's consider the following example.

Assume you will loan $1,000 today to a local café. The café owner will pay 6 percent interest annually. However, the interest payments will be paid four times a year (in other words, the interest will be compounded quarterly). How much money will you receive after five years?

Recall the future value formula is:

$$FV = CF \times [(1 + \tfrac{r}{m})^{nm}], \text{ where m is the number of payments in the period}$$

$$CF = \$1,000$$

$$r = 6\% \text{ or } 0.06$$

$$n = 5 \text{ periods of one year each}$$

$$m = 4 \text{ (assumes that interest is paid four times per year)}$$

$$FV = \$1,000 \times [(1+(0.06 / 4)]^{(5) \times (4)}$$

$$= \$1,000 \times (1.015)^{20}$$

$$= \$1,000 \times (1.347)$$

$$= \$1,346.85$$

Compare this to the same investment for which interest is compounded only once per year:

$$FV = \$1,000 \times [(1+(0.06 / 1)]^{(5) \times (1)}$$

$$= \$1,000 \times (1.06)^{5}$$

$$= \$1,000 \times (1.338)$$

$$= \$1,338.23$$

Notice how the present value is greater when the interest is compounded quarterly ($1,346.85) than when the interest is only compounded annually ($1,338.23).

## Annuities and Perpetuities

Calculating the present values of multiple years' cash flows can become tedious, especially if you are not using a financial calculator or computing software. Fortunately, there exist a few shortcuts that can be applied in certain situations. Annuities and perpetuities are seen in a number of investment scenarios. Understanding how to apply these formulas will lead to greater efficiency in your work.

An **annuity** is a financial instrument whereby the investor will pay something today in exchange for *equal payments* paid periodically in the future for a predetermined period of time. The financial instrument will have no value at the end of the period (future value will be zero). The payments in the future will include an implied interest rate such that at the end of the period the investor will have received the initial investment plus the corresponding interest. The present value of the annuity is the amount the investor will pay today in exchange for the future payments. An example of an annuity is a mortgage. With a mortgage, the bank lends money to the homeowner and the homeowner makes equal periodic payments to the bank.

A **perpetuity** is an annuity without a term (or, said differently, with a *perpetual* term). An example of a perpetuity is a royalty with no expiration date.

The formulas to calculate the present value of a perpetuity and an annuity are as follows:

*Perpetuity (perpetual or infinite term; CF is the same in each period)*

$$PV = \frac{CF}{r}$$

*Growing perpetuity (perpetual or infinite term; CF grows at a growth rate "g")*

$$PV = \frac{CF}{r - g}$$

*Annuity (fixed term)*

$$PV = \frac{CF}{r} - \frac{CF}{(r \times (1+r)^n)}$$

Compare the two formulas and notice that [CF/r] is the first part of the annuity equation and that from [CF/r] you subtract the quantity [CF / (r × (1+r)$^n$)]. Consider if $n$ (the number of periods) were 1,000, or 10,000 or even 1,000,000. Play with the numbers in your calculator and you will notice that as $n$ gets larger, the second value (in the annuity calculation) becomes smaller and smaller, heading toward zero (the denominator moves toward infinity so the quotient moves toward zero). Therefore, if you are calculating the present value of a perpetuity (which technically means that you will receive the cash flows *forever*), you can see why you would not need to calculate the second part of the annuity calculation. Rather, you can assume that the value of this second part of the equation moves towards zero as $n$ gets larger (i.e., toward infinity). Therefore, the value of the perpetuity is simply equal to [CF/r] since there is no need to write [CF/r] - 0.

***Annuity Example:*** If the bank were to offer a thirty year mortgage for which the annual mortgage payment were $36,000 and the annual interest rate 7 percent, what would be the present value of the annuity, or the amount of cash the bank would provide today in exchange for the $36,000 annual payments for 30 years?

CF   =   $36,000

r   =   7% or 0.07

n   =   30

*Solution:*

PV   =   ($36,000 / 0.07) - [$36,000 / (0.07 × (1.07)$^{30}$)]

     =   $514,285.71 – ($36,000 / 0.533)

     =   $514,285.71 – ($67,560.23)

     =   $446,725.48

The $446,725.48 represents the present value of the annuity or the mortgage amount, which is the amount of cash the bank would give you today in exchange for thirty annual payments to the bank of $36,000 each. If you simply multiplied $36,000 per year by 30 years you would get $1,080,000. Notice how the present value of $446,725.48 is significantly less than $1,080,000. This is because the present value to the bank of those payments spread out over 30 years is only $446,725.48. Said another way, in exchange for $446,725.48 today, you must pay your bank $1,080,000 over 30 years.

**Perpetuity Example:** Assume your father receives $60 each year forever from the royalties of a song he wrote many years ago, and that royalty will transfer to his heirs (therefore the royalty is perpetual). Assume a 5 percent discount rate. What is this royalty worth on a present value basis today?

CF   =   $60

r   =   5% or 0.5

n   =   Perpetual

*Solution:*

PV   =   $60 / 0.05

     =   $1,200

If the amount received each year were to grow by a certain percentage (the "growth rate"), then the present value of a perpetuity formula would change as follows to become the present value of a growing perpetuity.

$$PV = \frac{CF}{(r\text{-}g)}$$

*where g is the annual growth rate.*

In our previous example, assume the royalty of $60 per year were to grow by 2 percent per year, then the calculation would change as follows:

PV    =    $60 / (0.05-0.02)

       =    $60 / 0.03

       =    $2,000

## Valuing a Bond

A bond is a financial instrument whereby the investor pays an amount today in exchange for (1) a stream of interest payments (or **coupon payments**) during the life of the bond and (2) the repayment of the **face value** (or **principal**) of the bond at the end of the period. A bond is a form of debt for a company since the bondholders or investors only have claim to the value of the bond and do not have an ownership claim to the company (as an equity holder or a shareholder would). Now that you have learned the formula for an annuity and a perpetuity, you can calculate the present value of a bond using shortcuts.

You can think of a bond as two separate financial instruments. First, you receive a fixed stream of interest payments over a set period of time (this is an annuity). Second, you receive the face value, or the principal amount, at the end of the period (for this you would use a present value calculation). The present value of a bond is simply the sum of these two values: (1) the present value of the interest payments during the term of the bond plus (2) the present value of the principal payment at maturity.

For example, consider an investment in a bond that has a face value of $10,000, a semiannual coupon of 6 percent and a ten year term. Let's assume that your discount rate is 5 percent (because there are other investments of similar risk that will allow you to earn 5 percent). How much is this bond worth to you today? Let's first divide it into two parts, valuing the interest payments or the annuity portion first.

| | | |
|---|---|---|
| $CF_{annual}$ | = | $600 (or $10,000 principal amount × the coupon rate of 6%) |
| $CF_{semiannual}$ | = | $300 |
| $r_{annual}$ | = | 5% or 0.05 |
| $r_{semiannual}$ | = | 2.5% or 0.025 |
| n | = | 20 periods of six months each |

Recall that the formula for an annuity is:

$$PV = \frac{CF}{r} - \frac{CF}{(r \times (1+r)^n)}$$

*Value of the interest payments (the annuity):*

| | | |
|---|---|---|
| PV | = | ($300 / 0.025) - [$300 / (0.025 × (1.025)^{20})] |
| | = | $12,000 − ($300 / 0.0410) |
| | = | $12,000 − ($7,323.25) |
| | = | $4,676.75 |

*Now let's value the principal paid at the end of 10 years:*

| | | |
|---|---|---|
| CF | = | $10,000 |
| $r_{annual}$ | = | 5% |
| n | = | 10 years |
| m | = | 2 (since interest compounds semiannually) |

*Recall that the formula for present value is:*

$$PV = \frac{CF}{(1 + {}^r/_m)^{nm}}$$

*Value of the principal paid at the end of 10 years is:*

| | | |
|---|---|---|
| PV | = | $10,000 / [(1+(0.05 / 2)]^{(10) \times (2)} |
| | = | $10,000 / (1.025)^{20} |
| | = | $10,000 / 1.639 |
| | = | $6,102.71 |

*Now add the two portions together to get the value of the bond today:*

| | | |
|---|---|---|
| PV of annuity | = | $4,676.75 |
| PV of principal | = | $6,102.71 |
| Total PV of bond | = | $10,779.46 |

$10,779.46 represents the combined present values of two sets of cash flow streams: the coupon payments of 6 percent per year as well as the repayment of principal at the end of ten years. Since you would receive both of these two cash flow streams, you should be willing to pay $10,779.46 for this bond if your discount rate were 5 percent. Note that the discount rate is *less than* the coupon or interest rate, and so the investment is worth *more than* the face value of $10,000.

Said differently, since the discount rate of 5% is *less than* the interest rate of 6%, the net present value of this investment (that is, the value after accounting for the $10,000 face value of the bond) is greater than zero.

Net present value = value associated cash flows - cost of purchasing the asset

$$\$10,779.46 - \$10,000 = \$779.46$$

NPV = $779.46 when r = 5%

With a calculator try this same exercise when r = 6% and you will find that NPV = 0. Going back to the earlier discussion on IRR, the IRR of this particular bond is 6%. Since the discount rate of 6% is *equal to* the interest rate of 6%, the net present value = 0.

NPV = 0 when r = 6%

Now try this same exercise when r = 7% and you will find the NPV - $710.62. Since the discount rate of 7% is *greater than* the interest rate of 6%, the net present value of this investment is less than 0.

NPV = - $710.62 when r = 7%

# Suggested Reading and Other Resources

## Bibliography and Suggested Reading

Anders, George. *Merchants of Debt: KKR and the Mortgaging of American Business.* New York: Beard Books, 2002.

Argenti, Paul A., ed. *The Portable MBA Desk Reference: An Essential Business Companion.* New York: John Wiley and Sons, 1994.

Bandler, James. *How to Use Financial Statements: A Guide to Understanding the Numbers.* New York: McGraw-Hill, 1994.

Benninga, Simon Z. *Financial Modeling.* Cambridge, MA: MIT Press, 1997.

Benninga, Simon Z., and Oded H. Sarig. *Corporate Finance: A Valuation Approach.* New York: McGraw-Hill, 1997.

Brealey, Richard A., and Stewart C. Myers. *Principles of Corporate Finance.* 5th ed. New York: McGraw-Hill, 1996.

Carey, Omer L., and Musa M. H. Essayyad. *The Esssentials of Financial Management.* Piscataway, NJ: Research and Education Association, 1990.

Comiskey, Eugene E., and Charles W. Mulford. *Guide to Financial Reporting and Analysis.* New York: John Wiley and Sons, 2000.

Crerend, William J. *Fundamentals of Hedge Fund Investing: A Professional Investor's Guide.* New York: McGraw-Hill, 1998.

Damodaran, Aswath. *Investment Valuation: Tools and Techniques for Determining the Value of Any Asset.* 2nd ed. New York: John Wiley and Sons, 2002.

Downes, John, and Jordan Elliot Goodman. *Dictionary of Finance and Investment Terms.* 4th ed. Hauppauge, NY: Barron's, 1995.

Elton, Edwin J., and Martin J. Gruber. *Modern Portfolio Theory and Investment Analysis.* 5th ed. New York: John Wiley and Sons, 1995.

Epstein, Barry J., Ralph Nach, Ervin L. Black, and Patrick R. Delaney. *Wiley GAAP 2005: Interpretation and Application of Generally Accepted Accounting Principles.* Hoboken, NJ: John Wiley and Sons, 2004.

Fabozzi, Frank, and Franco Modigliani. *Capital Markets: Institutions and Instruments.* 2nd ed. Upper Saddle River, NJ: Prentice Hall, 1996.

Fridson, Martin. *Financial Statement Analysis: A Practitioner's Guide.* 3rd ed. New York: John Wiley and Sons, 2002.

Ginsburg, Martin D., and Jack S. Levin. *Mergers, Acquisitions, and Buyouts: A Transactional Analysis of the Governing Tax, Legal, and Accounting Considerations.* 3 vols. New York: Aspen Law and Business, 1997.

Henderson, Schuyler K., and John A. M. Price. *Currency and Interest Rate Swaps.* London: Butterworths, 1984.

Horngren, Charles T., Gary L. Sundem, and John A. Elliott. *Introduction to Financial Accounting.* 6th ed. Saddle River, NJ: Prentice Hall, 1996.

Hull, John C. *Options, Futures, and Other Derivatives.* 3rd ed. Upper Saddle River, NJ: Prentice Hall, 1997.

Ji, Lin and Fiona Wang. *Leveraged Buyouts: Inception, Evolution, and Future Trends.* Perspectives, Vol. 3, No. 6. Rockville, MD: Overseas Young Chinese Forum, 2002.

Koller, Tim, Marc Goedhart and David Wessels. *Valuation: Measuring and Managing the Value of Companies.* 4th ed. New York: John Wiley and Sons, 2005.

Lander, Guy P. *What is Sarbanes-Oxley?* New York: McGraw-Hill, 2004.

Morris, James E. *Accounting for M&A, Equity, and Credit Analysts.* New York: McGraw-Hill, 2004.

Palepu, Krishna G., Victor L. Bernard, and Paul M. Healy. *Business Analysis and Valuation: Using Financial Statements.* Cincinnati: South-Western Publishing, 1963.

Reed, Stanley Foster, and Alexandra Reed Lajoux. *The Art of M&A: A Merger Acquisition Buyout Guide.* 3rd ed. New York: McGraw-Hill, 1999.

Rickertsen, Rick, and Robert E. Gunther. *Buyout: The Insider's Guide to Buying Your Own Company.* New York: Amacom, 2001.

Slifer, Stephen D., and W. Stansbury Carnes. *By the Numbers: A Survival Guide to Economic Indicators.* Cincinnati: International Financial Press, 1995.

Stickney, Clyde P., Roman L. Weil, and Sidney Davidson. *Financial Accounting: An Introduction to Concepts, Methods, and Uses.* 6th ed. San Diego, CA: Harcourt Trade Publishers, 1991.

Tjia, John S. *Building Financial Models: A Guide to Creating and Interpreting Financial Statements.* New York: McGraw-Hill, 2004.

Tracy, John A. *How to Read a Financial Report: Wringing Vital Signs Out of the Numbers.* 6th ed. New York: John Wiley and Sons, 2004.

Wasserstein, Bruce. *Big Deal: 2000 and Beyond.* New York: Warner Books, 2000.

Weaver, Samuel C., and J. Fred Weston. *Finance and Accounting for Nonfinancial Managers.* New York: McGraw-Hill, 2001.

Wert, James E., and Glenn V. Henderson, Jr. *Financing Business Firms.* 6th ed. Homewood, IL: Richard D. Irwin, 1979.

White, Gerald I., Ashwinpaul C. Sondhi, and Dov Fried. *The Analysis and Use of Financial Statements.* 2nd ed. New York: John Wiley and Sons, 1998.

Williams, Jan R., and Joseph V. Carcello. *2005 Miller GAAP Guide Level A: Restatement and Analysis of Current FASB Standards.* New York: Aspen Law and Business, 2004.

## Other Resources

### Securities and Exchange Commission
Search for SEC filings of public companies and review U.S. securities laws
www.sec.gov

### Financial Accounting Standards Board
Review GAAP standards – current and proposed
www.fasb.org

### American Institute of Public Accountants
Learn about the AICPA and its role in the U.S. securities industry
www.aicpa.org

### The Robert Toigo Foundation
Sponsor of diversity programs, internships, and scholarships in the financial services industry
www.toigofoundation.org

### Sponsors for Educational Opportunity
Sponsor of diversity programs, internships, and scholarships in the financial services industry
www.seo-ny.org

### TMG & Associates
Training seminars in financial modeling
www.tmga.com

### Deal Maven
Online training in financial modeling
www.dealmaven.com

# INDEX

# Other Circinus Business Press Books

**SCOOP**BOOKS

### The Practitioner's Guide to Investment Banking, Mergers and Acquisitions, Corporate Finance

Jerilyn J. Castillo and Peter J. McAniff

704 pages; 6" × 9"; hardcover
ISBN: 978-0-9761548-0-8
List price: U.S.$95.00

**THE PRACTITIONER'S GUIDE** provides a thorough grounding in mergers and acquisitions and corporate finance for those who want to know more about the world of investment banking. A practical handbook, **THE PRACTITIONER'S GUIDE** presents comprehensive explanations of the analytical processes used to evaluate and structure mergers, acquisitions, divestitures, and capital raising transactions. Finance professionals, corporate attorneys, accountants, corporate development teams and MBAs will find **THE PRACTITIONER'S GUIDE** essential as a resource and desktop companion.

**Highlights include:**

- Dedicated chapters for each of the major valuation methods used in M&A, including comparable company analysis, comparable transaction analysis, discounted cash flow analysis, leveraged buyout analysis and breakup analysis

- A multi-step description of how to perform accretion/dilution analysis and other merger consequences analyses

- Specific sections dedicated to tactical concepts in M&A, including the benefits and challenges of using stock versus cash as an acquisition currency, the pros and cons of various methods of selling a company, fiduciary obligations of the board of directors, fixed versus floating exchange ratios, deal structuring, and mergers of equals, to name a few

- Insights into important aspects of deal mechanics such as preparation for due diligence, players' roles, and key components of a merger agreement described in layman's terms

- A complete chapter on assessing credit risk, including descriptions of credit ratings, the rating agencies and how banks make lending decisions

- A comprehensive introduction to the sources of capital available to a company, including plain vanilla debt and equity as well as more complex forms of capital such as leveraged loans, trust preferred securities and convertible debt

- Clear descriptions of the various tax issues that arise in transactions, including deferred taxes, inside and outside basis, capital gains tax, and tax deferred transaction structures

- A review of major defense techniques used to counter a hostile bid, including numerical examples of how a "poison pill" works in practice

- Corporate Finance Basics and Financial Statement Basics, written for the practitioner by practicing finance professionals - these sections focus on what you need to know to do the job as opposed to the academic perspective often taken in traditional business and university textbooks

"This book is a valuable "must have" for MBA students interested in entering (or recent hires who have entered) the world of investment banking."
**Bill Cockrum,** FINANCE PROFESSOR, ANDERSON SCHOOL AT UCLA, FORMER VICE CHAIRMAN OF A.G. BECKER & CO.

"Jerilyn and Peter have spent many years in investment banking and are highly competent practitioners. Also, this book has been reviewed, edited, and improved by senior bankers, attorneys, and specialists at some thirty major investment banks, law firms, private equity firms, and corporations. The collective experience of these seasoned professionals has been distilled and included in this practitioner's guide."
**Jimmy Elliott,** JPMORGAN, GROUP HEAD OF NORTH AMERICAN M&A, FROM THE FOREWORD

"An absolute must-read for anyone considering a career in investment banking. It's everything I wish I had been told when I was making the decision to go into banking."
**Matthew Rho,** VICE PRESIDENT, SV INVESTMENT PARTNERS

**To order, visit us at www.scoopbooks.com**

circinus business press

# About the Authors

Peter McAniff has worked in the mergers and acquisitions groups at JPMorgan, Lehman Brothers and Banc America Securities. Jerilyn Castillo has worked in the mergers and acquisitions and global power and energy groups at JPMorgan. Their 18 years of combined investment banking experience spans corporate mergers, sales of companies and assets, acquisitions, restructurings, and capital raising transactions for multinational companies in the energy, utilities, industrials, consumer products, and food and beverage sectors. In addition to their work on behalf of corporate clients, both Jerilyn and Peter have spent a significant amount of time recruiting as well as developing and leading training and mentoring programs. They have reviewed thousands of resumes, interviewed hundreds of aspiring bankers, and have trained numerous investment banking analysts and associates as well as strategic planning professionals and corporate executives. Jerilyn is a graduate of UC Berkeley's Haas School of Business. Peter holds an MBA from the Anderson School at UCLA and a JD from the UCLA School of Law.

Jerilyn and Peter believe strongly that success in any endeavor is a function of hard work and access to the proper tools. They wrote *The Practitioner's Guide to Investment Banking, Mergers and Acquisitions, Corporate Finance* and *The Recruiting Guide to Investment Banking* to help those who work hard but who have not necessarily had access to the proper tools. If these books helped you in any way or if you have comments as to how to improve future editions, the authors would enjoy hearing from you.

You can contact them at *jerilyn@scoopbooks.com* and *peter@scoopbooks.com*.

circinus business press

www.scoopbooks.com